The RTE Book

Town House, Dublin
in association with RTE

Contents

NUALA Ó FAOLÁIN
ON
RTE's SECRET WEAPON

When people think about Irish broadcasting they think, first of all, of its stars. The individuals who present radio programmes seem to colour the different parts of the day, and parts of every night and of the weekend are similarly given their flavour by the personalities of the TV presenters. Most casual talk about RTE is about these men and women. 'I love so-and-so,' people say. 'I think so-and-so's programme is great.'

What they don't notice is that, often, it isn't the star that makes the programme; it's the unknown ordinary person, who is either ringing in or in the audience, or doing or saying something that the presenter is using. I don't think that there can be another broadcasting service in the world that can rely, with such confidence, on non-professionals. The articulate and original way in which Irish people quite naturally express themselves is the great secret weapon of RTE.

Think of the *Late Late Show* audience. Often the warmest, funniest moments of the entire evening come from them. Remember the old lady dancing with Gay at the end of the show about Dublin? Think of the letters he gets that transform his radio show. Think of *Liveline* and the extraordinary candour of the people who ring in to Marian. They ring Gerry Ryan too, and they queue up to do quizzes for Ronan Collins, and they send endless messages to each other on all the record programmes. The Irish audience is not the passive recipient of whatever the broadcasters choose to do to them. It is a partner—arguing, laughing, contributing.

Sometimes whole programmes are made about these 'ordinary' people. You would never see that in other countries, where only the famous and the rich are seen as having a right to celebrity. There, you have to be criminal or eccentric to attract the attention of the cameras. On RTE recently there was a programme about a group of women who used to work in the same business when they were girls. They arranged to meet every ten years or so, just to see how life was going for each other. Last year, the camera was at their reunion, and so a most truthful and touching little film called *The Varian Girls* was made.

RTE wouldn't make films like this but that the audience is willing to watch them. The audience doesn't demand celebrities all the time. It isn't bored by the everyday. British television made a series called *Mothers and Daughters* which was very interesting, but limited by the requirement that the people on it be famous already. You could make that series in Ireland, and make it with completely unknown people, and it would still be watched.

When I worked in RTE, I often made programmes with people who thought they had no qualifications at all for being on television. 'Who, me?' they would say, 'sure, I couldn't be on the television. I'd die.' But of course they didn't die, they were marvellous. I made a series called *Plain Tales* specifically to seek out the kind of quiet, obscure people who would never normally reach the screen. Each contributor just sat there and told the camera their life story. And, simple as this was, the programmes got a great audience. Just as many people watched them as would watch something far more glittering. This wouldn't happen but for the fact that community is still alive in Ireland. RTE is not just a distant establishment, and people are not distant from each other.

Irish people find ordinary people like themselves entertaining. This gives a unique vitality and realism to our home-produced programmes.

Long may it last!

Nuala Ó Faoláin is a columnist with The Irish Times

OUR KATIE

Deirdre Purcell on the hot lines of Katie Kahn-Carl, one of RTE's two foreign-news editors

It is called Katie's 'little hole in the wall'. It is in the RTE newsroom and from a little box within the tiny room, comes a constant stream of chatter and static. From time to time, Katie herself can be seen pressing a key and talking. It is really the Eurovision News studio and it is a vital part of RTE's news-gathering organisation.

'Our Katie' is Katie Kahn-Carl, one of RTE's two foreign-news editors, but all over Europe and beyond, she is known simply as Katie. There are a few 'Katies' within the Eurovision News exchange—doughty females, referred to by Dermot Mullane as The Inner Knitting Circle. In the manner of Madame Defarge, you understand. They are not shy, these Katies. 'There are about six of us and we're toughies,' says Our Katie, 'we're all very experienced. Some people are too shy to press the key to interrupt. I press whenever I want, I interrupt whenever I want. RTE is paying for the service, my business is to get what I want for RTE...'

Our Katie's business, as part of the 31-member Eurovision News exchange network, is to get as much foreign-news coverage for RTE's news bulletins as she can, as cheaply as possible. It is also her business to sell—and to sell hard—any item of Irish news of interest to Europe.

And through Europe she sells and buys throughout the world. 'Because the EBU (European Broadcasting Union) got so well organised, other parts of the

world formed groups too. Now all the groups are interlinked.' Eurovision, with programme and news headquarters in Geneva, is linked in turn with Intervision—a television organisation of countries behind the Iron Curtain—and Sin, the South American/Iberian News exchange. It has offices in New York and Washington, for intake and selling from and to the US networks. It links with Australia, Japan and the Far East through offices in Kuala Lumpur. 'North Africa is no problem, Morocco, Algeria, Egypt, Libya, Tunisia are all part of our exchange, Jordan, Israel, although not Lebanon or Syria. We exchange with them through the Arab Exchange. And when the

Gulf War was going on, we got stuff directly from Iran and Iraq.' Intervision is headquartered in Prague. 'They are always listening, but they cannot chip in. They can respond by telephone or telex. Before *glasnost*, we used only get wreath-laying or kissing of dignitaries, and they never admitted a disaster. Since *glasnost*, within hours we had Chernobyl and the Armenian earthquake.' The only dark spot, from which news pictures are not available world-wide almost instantly, is inland Africa.

'GOOD MORNING EVERYBODY'

The buying and selling is done through daily conferences three times a day, on radio links left permanently open (Katie's little box in her little room is the speaker for this network). Each of the 31

member-countries will plug in at the given time and will offer what it considers to be of interest to its fellow members, explaining what the story is and what the pictures will show. This is where the interrupting takes place. 'Being an old hand, I hate yesterday's news. When RAI (the Italian television network) comes in with "a nice little item" I jump in. I immediately query it: "Excuse me—RTE coming in—did I catch the date, is that *yesterday's* story?" You'd be amazed at how quickly that kills the interest!'

RTE's first conference is at 10 o'clock each morning, although there is an earlier one at 4.30 am for those members with breakfast television. Each member-country has its representative sitting in his or her little booth, listening to the 31-way conference. There is a chairperson of the day who can be sitting in a booth anywhere on the network. 'Good morning everybody' the chairperson begins, before outlining what he or she thinks will be the main stories of the day. The news is then brought in from New York, so that members may hear what the overnight stories are from the US networks. 'We talk about what New York expects for that day out of the White House, out of Congress, who the visiting dignitaries are; if there is a disaster, we'll get the disaster. Then we go on to who's offering what out of Europe. On any given day, there are usually no more than four or five people who have stories worth offering. You can sell an item by telexing in advance. It's like any marketplace, you can sell

Katie organises 'piggy-backs' on the satellite feeds of our richer cousins, BBC and ITN. Time on a satellite must be booked for at least ten minutes and in the case of the Gibraltar inquest, for instance, that would have cost RTE £1000 per day. So Katie rang her pals in the BBC—knowing that they would have a satellite feed—and organised that RTE could take two minutes nightly of the Beeb's ten, paying pro rata. 'In return, in case you think we're the poor relation always, when the BBC come here, we give them everything, facilities, editing. When we have elections, we give them a whole studio free. They have the run of the place when they are here, in return for what they do for us.' And she will tip them off if anything important is coming through.

Katie, who speaks fluent French, German and Italian as well as English, sets her alarm for three minutes to seven every morning. 'I hear the seven o'clock headlines on radio, so I know what kind of a day I'm going to have...' Everyone in news world-wide contributes to the kind of day Katie will håve. When Tom McSweeney went to cover the Ethiopian famine for RTE in 1984, he and his crew began filming within minutes of arriving at the airport at Addis Ababa. A man approached him on the tarmac: 'I'm Michael Buerk of the BBC, please give me your film, I'll bring it to Nairobi and satellite it back from there. The pictures will be on RTE tonight.' Tom was slightly dubious about handing over the vital footage. 'It's alright,' said Michael Buerk. 'Katie says it's ok...' The pictures were transmitted on RTE that night.

hard. I wouldn't offer anything that I didn't consider worthy. Northern Ireland is a tricky one. Technically it is in the BBC and ITN's catchment area, but very often it will be our crew that has the pictures. I've tremendously good relations with BBC and ITN so I certainly wouldn't want to cut across them.'

Any member-country that wishes to buy what is on offer must buy the whole package, usually about six items. And only if there are several members interested will the package be transmitted. It is not unusual for the transmissions, especially the early ones, to be cancelled for lack of interest.

The chief news agencies sell into this conference too. For Europe, they are Visnews and World Television News, and CBS to some extent. In the case, for instance, of the tragic death of Ireland's three UNIFIL soldiers in the Lebanon last Easter, Katie rang Visnews and World Television News in advance to make sure that they would have pictures from the Lebanon. Then, during one of the daily conferences, she said that in case there was no Eurovision interest in taking pictures on the news exchange, she would pay for a 'unilateral'. A 'unilateral' is where one organisation pays all production and satellite transmission costs for pictures of an event. Because Katie mentioned it, the other countries who have UNIFIL soldiers on peacekeeping duties, such as Norway and Finland, Sweden and Holland and France, immediately chipped in and said they were interested too. 'It is possible to spur interest by showing interest yourself.'

'The marvellous thing about being experienced and knowing all these people is you don't ring and say, "Excuse me, is that French Television, may I speak to so-and-so?" You ring and say "Hello Gerard, this is Katie. Remember that favour I did you? Well, I need a favour today!" You ring up and you sock it to them...'

MILES AND MILES OF MUSIC

Séamus Ennis (1919—1982)

Éamon de Buitléar pays tribute to his friend, the piper and broadcaster

In 1947 dramatic changes took place in Radio Éireann. A symphony orchestra, a light orchestra and a repertory company were formed in the one year. Many new positions were created, including that of outside broadcast officer. The three people appointed at that time were Seán Mac Réamoinn, Proinnsias Ó Conluain and Séamus Ennis. This was the beginning of Radio Éireann's mobile unit and the instructions to the three officers were 'to seek throughout the country, including the Gaeltacht, material for subsequent broadcast'. Séamus was the specialist whenever musical items were being collected and he spent a great deal of time working in County Clare where there had always been a very strong musical tradition. He also recorded the fiddle playing of the famous Pádraig Ó Cuív and Denis Murphy in Kerry.

In the early sixties Séamus Ennis took part in *Ballad Session*, his first TV series on RTE, with Seán Mac Réamoinn as presenter. He made many appearances in various programmes down through the years, including his own series for children, *Ask my Father*.

Séamus Ennis described his introduction to piping when I filmed him for a documentary I made on him for RTE in 1973: 'My father had cut me a pair of sticks as make-believe pipes and they tell me that I used be humming away merrily imitating my father's piping, which I am told was second to none in his time. I inherited my piping and my pipes from my father who used play for me in my cradle, and my mother played a little on the fiddle. His piping was the synthesis of all that was best in the piping of the old men who were brought to Dublin by the early Oireachtas Musical Festivals and he got his finishing tuition from the master piper, Nicholas Markey, a County Meath man. He was the curator of a men's lavatory on the North Circular Road, behind the Mater Hospital. He had a little office in this emporium, where he gave my father tuition.'

PEN, PAPER AND PUSHBIKE

It was dance music for the most part which James Ennis taught his son Séamus. The wonderful skill he was to develop in collecting pieces of music and his love of slow airs was to come a little later, through the influence of a very talented and colourful personality. 'At the sign of The 3 Candles, printers and publishers at Fleet Street, Dublin, I learned more and more about music and song from Colm Ó Lochlainn. He taught me how to write the tunes of the slow songs so well that when I'd hear a song sung I'd automatically visualise it on paper. This in turn qualified me for the post of folk music collector with the Irish Folklore Commission, now the Irish Folklore Department of University College, Dublin. Songs and stories now in the university's archives, I collected with pen and paper and a push bike, travelling north, south, east and west in all weathers, for it was during the war years. Seán Ó Súilleabháin was the archivist at that time and my place was in Seán's office, when at headquarters, transcribing and finalising for archives the material I brought back with me.'

A HIVE OF SONGS

Séamus paid regular visits to the Gaeltachts and his musical ear quickly enabled him to become an expert in all the local dialects. He seemed to adopt Conamara as his second home and the influence which that part of our western seaboard had on him was obvious whenever he spoke Irish. 'The greatest repository of songs and tunes in their background in fact and fable I found in a little pocket of north Conamara, on the south shore of Cuan na Beirtrí Buí, the bay of the yellow oyster bank, in a place known as Glínsce, 'clear water' in English. It was there that I met Colm Ó Caoidheáin and I wrote 212 items straight from his memory.'

Much of the music collected by Séamus came from Feenish Island near Carna. There he would borrow a boat and row out to meet Seáinín Choilmín Mac Donnacha and his family. Séamus described the island at that time as a proper hive of songs. In telling about his first visit to the place Séamus says: 'I asked this man on the island where was Seáinín Choilmín Mac Donnacha's house, and he said "that's it over there, the one with the two chimneys", and he walked along with me and came in the door with me and then welcomed me, disclosed his own identity that he was the man I was looking for! I know that these people enjoyed my visits too. I sang strange songs for them and it seemed they couldn't do enough for me when I played on my pipes for them.'

THE MAD IRISHMAN

The severe winter of 1946-47 saw Séamus Ennis collecting folklore and music in the Hebrides and in the highlands of Scotland. Swimming in the sea every day while staying on the islands during that harsh winter earned him the name 'the mad Irishman'. Later, much of that material which he had collected both in Scotland and here in Ireland was given a very wide listenership when Séamus took part in the long running and very successful BBC radio series, *As I Roved Out.* Séamus Ennis has set a standard too high for most of us even to try and attain. Apart from his unique style of piping, he had a very extensive knowledge of his native language, he could sing songs from all the Gaeltachts, including tunes in Scots-Gaelic, he was an excellent storyteller and a very professional collector of folklore.

Some years ago when a certain well-known piper was given the title 'King of the Pipers' on a record sleeve, somebody jokingly asked Séamus Ennis if he, the best piper in the country, had been demoted. His reply was 'No, not at all, they just forgot the Ard Rí (High King)!'

Miles and Miles of Music, a documentary by Éamon de Buitléar on Séamus Ennis, was commissioned by RTE in 1973.

Séamus Ennis and Colm Ó Caoidheáin, from whom he collected 212 items straight from his memory

ALICE TAYLOR LIVES HERE

RTE came to film the best-selling author of *To School Through the Fields* at her Cork home. With some nervousness she faced the crew...

Sitting in the train on the way home from Dublin on Sunday, 12 March, I thought back over the activities I had packed into the previous few days. On the Thursday my husband, Gabriel, and I had flown from a rain-drenched Cork Airport to a sunny London, to attend the Irish Book Fair, where I was to do a reading. Meeting the Irish emigrants had been a wonderful experience, made especially enjoyable by the fact that so many of them had read and loved *To School Through the Fields*. Before flying back to Dublin on Saturday, an early morning radio interview with Henry Kelly was slotted in. On Saturday night in Dublin the Irish Book Sellers held their annual dinner where I, as the guest speaker, had the delightful experience of meeting Maeve Binchy for the first time.

We arrived back in Cork on Sunday to find the sun shining and our son Gearóid, together with our ten-year-old daughter, Lena, who was dancing with excitement, waiting at the railway station. While driving home Gearóid filled us in on the usual family activities during our absence. I am one of those people who always feels that I am missing out on interesting happenings if I am away from home. Going in the door I felt the house putting its arms around me. I was happy to be home.

As we sat having tea in the kitchen, the rest of the family drifted in and Diarmuid, our youngest son, told me that there had been a phone call from an Ann McCabe

Alice Taylor: best-seller

in RTE about doing a programme called *I Live Here*. Ann McCabe was the producer. My first reaction was one of slight apprehension, almost as if someone had asked if they could come inside my head.

Seán, the artistic one of the family, was arranging the beautiful flowers presented to me in Dublin. Taking what was left over, I went upstairs to my attic room, or 'the garret' as we call it. While arranging the flowers in an old jug I thought about the idea of a television programme. What exactly was involved? How did I really feel about it? What on earth would they find to make a whole programme about? To me, my life at home was so ordinary that I could not visualise it making interesting viewing for a full hour. Speaking to Ann McCabe on the phone the following day I said just

that, to which she replied, 'That's exactly what we want, ordinary living.'

So it was decided that she would come to Innishannon and we would discuss it. I suppose we all have our preconceived ideas of what people in different walks of life should look like, but Ann McCabe was definitely not my preconceived idea of a TV producer. Maybe I was expecting a brisk, efficient, high-powered lady. Ann, however, was slim, curly haired and what my grandmother would term 'a slip of a girl' with a bubbling personality and laughing eyes. During our long chat up in my garret I knew that I would make *I Live Here*. She obviously enjoyed her work and I felt that working with her would be a pleasant experience. After talking for a few hours she said to me, 'If we had a camera here this evening, half the programme would be in the can.'

That weekend we walked around the woods and roads of Innishannon and she outlined what she had in mind and I filled her in on what was available. She made another trip south the following week to finalise the arrangements and I showed her the old school, a little restored cottage called 'Tig Noni' and the home farm. Ann met the entire family, including my mother, and everybody felt that RTE in the person of Ann McCabe was not going to put undue pressure on anybody.

The last two weeks in April were set aside for the filming. I felt that my Innishannon would look bet-

Alice Taylor and her daughter Lena: woods near their Innishannon, Co. Cork, home

ter later in the year when the woods would have donned their summer coats, but the big wheel that is RTE cannot be turned by the colour of the leaves. God smiled on us and filming commenced down at the old school of Dromanarigle on Tuesday, 18 April, in glorious sunshine. Where the previous week we had shivered with the cold, now we peeled off layers of winter woollies. It was a strange experience to see a TV crew at work in the overgrown grass around my old school and I was glad that they were recording a way of life that so many of us had experienced. The cameraman, Ken Fogarty, perched high at a precarious angle on top of a crumbling wall to get a good view of the old dry toilets. These relics of another day would cause modern mothers to recoil in horror. Three children who dressed up to recreate a scene from those days wondered how we could possibly have run barefoot across the fields. The crew work-

ed patiently and painstakingly with the children and Anna Ryan's application to detail smoothed the way forward. The soft-spoken sound man, Jim Wylde, moved around wordlessly, while the birds, as if knowing they were being recorded, sang their hearts out on top of every tree.

RTE producer: Ann McCabe

Getting down into the 'glaise' where we had once played on the way home from school was a hilarious experience. As sure-footed country children we had been like mountain goats. But for adults, getting filming equipment in under the overhanging trees, while underfoot was soft with mud, resulted in one of the crew sliding down the slippery slope in a very undignified position and the seat of his pants told the story for the rest of the day. When awkward scenes like this were completed, we all held our breath, lest gentle John Hall would announce quietly 'hair in the gate', which we soon learned meant a retake. The indoor scenes in 'Tig Noni' were far less arduous and here Dermot O'Grady in his easy methodical way angled lighting with infinite precision and the entire crew worked in silent harmony.

For these three filming days of the first week we were blessed with

(From left) RTE cameraman Ken Fogarty; producer Ann McCabe; RTE Guide photographer Eve Holmes

sunshine, though a slight haze prevented long-distance shots of my favourite hills. I discovered the importance of light and learned to wait patiently while the sun came from behind a cloud. The RTE crew were patient, meticulous people, who worked long hours with immense concentration. I decided at the end of the first week that the real stars of television are behind the camera, not in front of it.

The crew went back to Dublin on Friday, returning the following Monday, so that gave us all breathing space. However, I was booked to speak at two conferences that weekend, one on Friday and the other on Saturday and had a radio interview on Monday. But all went well and I had Sunday free to enjoy a long walk.

We were delighted when the sun shone again on Tuesday morning for the filming in beautiful Shippool Wood, which is my favourite corner of Innishannon. Ann directed operations with a delicate touch and Ken's creative eye discovered interesting angles. As well as the usual crew of six, that day we had two photographers,

Eve Holmes from the *RTE Guide* and John Rowe from the stills department in RTE. In between filming takes, they took photographs and I was glad that Shippool Wood was the background for these photographs. From the woods we went to the old historic graveyard and the tower in the village. Doves nest in the old tower and I had the bright idea that a flutter of wings up through the tower would make a nice shot. Unfortunately, at that particular time there were only a few doves in residence and instead of a flutter of wings, the cameraman was anointed by a well-aimed blessing.

During the filming period in the village, everybody was interested and helpful, and the greatest excitement was created when the crew moved in to take scenes in our supermarket. I wondered, as I watched people walk in the wrong direction and block the view of the camera, how order could be got out of this chaos. This I imagine is where the greatest skill and patience is required.

Another more daunting experience was when they moved into our kitchen where a rather make-shift meal was thrown

together on the table, around which the family gathered to project the image of an ordinary meal—which was rather difficult with the light, sound and camera beamed on us. The family was relieved when that was over but by now they knew the crew pretty well and a lot of good humoured slagging went on.

We finished up on Thursday with the signing of my new book of poems, *Close to the Earth*, in Easons of Cork. Some of my wonderful neighbours came in for this signing and it was a morning of laughter and fun. The people who came into Easons just to have their books signed could not figure out what on earth was going on. One woman, when I told her that it was RTE filming, just dropped her book and ran, saying 'Holy God, let me get out of here'.

Making the programme was an interesting experience, made enjoyable by the very pleasant crew. They were six professional people, each efficient at their own job and never infringing on each other's space. They worked in a relaxed, good-humoured fashion which drew all of us who worked with them into their mood.

WHO DOES WHAT IN TELEVISION?

Somebody Someone's Guide for the Bewildered
by Cian Ó hÉigeartaigh

First, a word about how programmes are put together and recorded.

A 'studio programme' is one which is mainly filmed in the television studio. It may be transmitted live, or recorded on videotape and transmitted later. If it is recorded, it may be edited before transmission. If it goes out live, obviously there can be no editing.

Studio programmes (whether live or recorded) are usually filmed using three electronic cameras. There will normally be one camera on the left of the studio, one somewhere in the middle and one on the right. They will move back and forward and use their lens controls to get closer or wider shots as necessary (the *Late Late Show* usually has four or five).

Each of these cameras relays a continuous image to a control room, somewhere above or beside the studio. In this room (a small, dark, enclosed space with a bank of monitors and a control desk) sit the **director**, the **vision mixer** and various others. Usually the director cannot see the studio. His/her only visual contact is through the images from the various cameras. The output of each camera is shown on a separate monitor, and the vision mixer selects the image to be transmitted or recorded by pressing buttons on the control desk. Usually there is a fairly rapid rotation between cameras.

The director carries overall responsibility for everything that happens in a programme—sound, picture, lighting, the lot—but his/her main job is to direct the movement of the cameras. The director has to ensure, first, that a transmittable picture is available at all times; second, that an alternative picture (the next shot) is ready when needed; and third, that the cameras are in a position to cover anything unexpected that may happen in the studio. The director may instruct the vision mixer to select a particular shot, although that usually is not necessary.

Events on the studio floor are controlled by the **floor manager**, who is in two-way contact with the director through an intercom system known as 'talkback'. The same system allows the director to talk to the camerapersons. Studio presenters usually cannot hear talkback (since the continuous flow of instructions to cameras would disrupt their concentration); they take their instructions via the floor manager.

The **sound supervisor** is responsible for placing microphones before the programme begins and for monitoring sound quality as it proceeds. The **lighting supervisor** places and adjusts the studio lights to give the desired effect (sometimes this is done manually, sometimes through a computer system).

The **designer** is responsible for the layout and appearance of the studio set—its size, shape, colouring, the materials used, the furniture, and any special items or props which may be needed. The **graphic designer** looks after any two-dimensional images used in the programme—slides, photographs, drawings, texts, and also the brief introductory sequence (with a signature tune) which tells the viewers that their favourite programme is about to begin.

Of course many programmes are filmed outside the studio, using either a film or a video camera. There is usually only one camera, and a simple action (such as a person entering a car and driving off) may be repeated several times so that it can be filmed from different angles. The various shots will be edited into a continuous sequence by the **film editor** or **video editor**, and the sound track will be mixed in a special studio by the **dubbing mixer**.

As with a studio programme, the director has overall responsibility for all aspects of the filming process. The director will tell the cameraperson what shots to take, and will direct the actions of the various participants.

Lighting is usually required and, just to confuse matters, the person who sets up the lights for a film item is described as the **electrician**. The placing of the lights (as

Who Does What in Television?
(cont. in from page 11)

distinct from their operation) is the responsibility of the cameraperson. In a complicated film operation (for example, a drama) there may be two kinds of cameraperson: the **lighting cameraperson**, who supervises the placing of the camera and lights, and the **camera operator**, who actually presses the button for camera.

Most programmes will also have a **producer**, who may or may not be the same person as the director. Broadly speaking the producer is responsible for organising a programme while the director is responsible for executing it in studio or on film. The producer's responsibilities include editorial judgments, selection of participants, and the administration of the budget.

In large-scale productions, there may be an **executive producer**. Generally speaking he or she is responsible for negotiating budgets and project outlines, and for ensuring delivery on target.

In programmes where several producers work together, the person in overall charge is usually described as the **series producer**—except in current affairs programmes, where the person in charge is called the **editor**, and his or her deputies may be called **executive producers**.

That just leaves the **production assistant**, who provides administrative support to producers and directors, and the **reporter** and **researcher** whose functions are fairly self-evident.

Still bewildered? Don't worry. The people who work there often can't make sense of it either.

GARDA PATROL 25 YEARS ON

Ann O'Donnell on the stars in blue

Garda Patrol is one of the oldest programmes on RTE television. (It's running almost as long as Gaybo!) Every week for the last twenty-five years—since 28 October 1964—an episode of *Garda Patrol* has been broadcast. In those twenty-five years, the basic programme format has not changed. The central characters have, however, changed many times. One of the earliest presenters of the programme was a young sergeant called Tom O'Reilly— Tom is now assistant garda commissioner in charge of the Dublin metropolitan area. Ted Nealon was one of the original scriptwriters. *Garda Patrol* has quite a history.

For the last four years Sergeant John O'Mahony has had responsibility for the programme, which he describes as a one-man show. The aims of the programme are to prevent and detect crime. Generally speaking, the programme concentrates on identifying stolen property and locating missing persons and it seeks information to help solve crime. It also gives advice to the public about how to avoid crime and protect themselves and their property. Over the years, the programme has been very effective in tracing missing persons. An item about a missing person is often repeated several times in a year to remind the public of the person's description. The gardaí are also very

Garda Tom O'Reilly, one of the earliest presenters of Garda Patrol, *is now an assistant garda commissioner*

happy with how successful the programme has been in finding owners for stolen goods and in getting information from the public which leads to solving crimes of robbery.

Sergeant O'Mahony has the task of deciding which crimes will be featured each week. Information on all crimes in the country comes in on teleprinter to the Crime Prevention Unit in Harcourt Square, Dublin, where Sergeant O'Mahony is based. He invariably selects for broadcast any very serious crimes which have recently occurred, in the hope that some information may be forthcoming from the public. He also selects crimes which there is a good chance of solving. Extremely valuable or unusual stolen items are suitable, as they will be easily recognised or remembered by the public. It would be very difficult for a thief to sell stolen goods which were featured on *Garda Patrol*; this must be one of the few situations when all publicity is not good publicity.

Sergeant O'Mahony works on his own and his week is centred around the transmission day of the programme. It provides him with 'a great opportunity to meet gardaí in different stations'. In the course of each week he visits many garda stations with a photographer, collecting data about crimes and taking photographs of stolen items and other material. He also has a number of colleagues in the Crime Prevention Unit with whom he can discuss the programme. The script is written the night before

the weekly transmission day, by an RTE journalist, using the material prepared by Sergeant O'Mahony. Sergeant O'Mahony arrives for the recording—armed with slides of the items/crimes to be featured—along with the garda presenter and the garda who is to do the voice-overs.

Approximately twelve to fourteen items are featured per programme. The programme is recorded and transmitted later the same day. The following day Sergeant O'Mahony resumes the process of collecting information for the next programme.

Garda Patrol is an extremely important public relations exercise for the gardaí. They are conscious of using the programme to project a good public image. Presenters are selected with this in mind. Sergeant O'Mahony is amazed at the level of response in the force when he advertises for the selection of a panel of garda presenters. He should not be surprised at this—wouldn't every young garda love to be a 'star' on the TV! It must certainly make a change from patrolling the streets in the freezing cold or endless drizzle.

Sergeant O'Mahony makes the initial selection of a group of possible presenters and RTE makes the final selection, based on screen and voice tests. At any one time there is always a panel of eight trained garda presenters who are used in rotation for the programme.

What qualities does he look for in candidates who apply to present the programme? He outlines a number of essentials including the requirement that candidates should have a relatively nondescript accent. 'I could not select a garda with a very strong accent which might not be easily understood all over the country.' He is also looking for presenters who project the kind of image the gardaí wish to convey to the public—clean cut, good-looking, well mannered, friendly, open. Basically, the kind of boy every mammy would be proud of. No, I'm not being sexist, as there is only one woman on the current panel of presenters and no doubt she would be every mammy's ideal daughter.

More power to the boys and girls in blue—why shouldn't they use the most effective and popular means of communication to help prevent and solve crime, and let us know that many of them are just like the rest of us—nice and normal and dying to be on the telly.

Let's hope that RTE will throw a party for them to celebrate twenty-five years of broadcasting—maybe Gay could do a special *Late Late Show...*

PAPER TALK

P P O'Reilly first addressed the nation in 1948. Since then, he has been heard regularly on *It Says in the Papers*

'But yesterday, the word of Caesar might have stood against the world.'

'Words, words, words'—**My Fair Lady**

Words are part of ourselves and for many years now it has been my lot to weave them into a script and commentary on the passing show. So let me look back to that Easter Monday in 1948, when I was first to address the nation. Equipment—microphone and bulky disc-cutting machine. Never saw it before, let the technician handle it! Target—people, sounds. Location—Westland Row, Bachelors' Walk, Fairyhouse.

The war, now over two years, leaving a comet's tail of shortages like coal and petrol. At last the wood and turf engines of CIE's railroad receive their fill of black diamonds. Puff, puff, the smoke comes in palpitating, rushing, soot-stained clouds; the clank of gears, the metallic strokes of the slow-turning wheels. We're off! The war at last is over. It is Easter, 1948.

On the Dublin quays, the buses line up, their bellies awash at last with all the petrol we need for Fairyhouse and beyond. The nation is on the move again, this Easter Monday. The ambulance-shaped recording car of Radio Éireann leaves the footpath in Henry Street and prowls in search of the news of the day, and knows where to look for it—by the rail tracks, where the buses are,

where the new CIE enquiry office is. It's go, go, go day. Last word to control inside the GPO: 'Record Michael O'Hehir on the National and hold the disc for us till we get back from our odyssey in the south city.' For the first time ever, RÉ News goes among the people to hear what they have to say. We still do, over forty years later, but this time we carry our recorders on our shoulders.

'Up the gum tree'

Millions of words later, the news is recorded on the spot, not by either of the two men of '48, but by a team big enough to man a centurion's cohort, most of the team remembering not '48. They were not yet born then.

In between, memories many for the grown-ups of those early

days. It helps to be able to remember. They call it experience. It helps you to note the hole in the evidence before you—or even the precipice that looms up when you wish it wouldn't.

To avoid the drop down the cliff is the first rule of those who would review the morning papers. If the papers get it wrong but you did not know that before you unleashed their story upon the listening audience, and if it is defamatory, hard luck. The legal officer could send for you. That you merely repeated what was in the papers is no excuse. Repeating the libel has you and RTE up the gum tree.

People in high places often do not know what they are talking about as any educated parrot would tell you. Yes, they have their advisers, who might be very well informed, but equally they might carry axes, which they wish to grind. The person in high place then becomes dependent on the fall of an axe. Hard luck! He might end up in the headlines, unhonoured and unsung.

Headlines are minefields. Avoid them if you wish to become a serious reviewer of newspapers. Sometimes the headline over a report might be quite wrong. Recently a headline on a front page indicated that a minister was about to do a specific thing. It was an attractive headline but the matter under it contained a complete denial that the minister was going to do anything of the sort. The sub-editor in the newspaper had not read the matter before he or

P P O'Reilly—'Headlines are minefields'

set by Niall Toner

1. What American city has become known as the country music capital of the world?

2. Which American state has given its name to a well-known form of traditional country music?

3. Who is known as the man in black?

4. Name the Irish guitarist (born in Dublin) who has played on Nashville sessions with Nanci Griffith, John Prine and Guy Clark.

5. What is the origin of the name 'Fleadh Cowboys'?

6. Who was nicknamed 'The Hillbilly Shakespeare'?

7. With which country music legend did Elvis Costello record in Nashville?

8. What British-born guitarist is one of the most sought after session players in country music?

9. Name the song recently composed and recorded in praise of Hank Williams by a well-known rock band based in Dublin.

10. *Drop kick me Jesus through the goalposts of life* was a major hit in the US for Bobby Bare. Name the Irish country band that had a hit with the same song in the seventies.

11. What was Willie Nelson's first hit record?

12. Name Steve Earle's current band.

(cont. page 123; answers page 158)

she invented the erroneous headline. Equally, an RTE sub-editor didn't read the matter either and had to change the story for the next bulletin.

So you see, a headline used by a reviewer of newspapers can be a torpedo. Also, many people think that you only look at the headlines if you mention that naughty word, so it's better to avoid it. When you hear me or somebody else saying 'the paper describes it as a shocking tragedy', then your comment should be 'of course it is'. What else would they say?

The RTE morning review of the papers consists of about seven hundred words, equivalent to one typical newspaper column. So there's little space for so much and wastage should be eliminated. Another unacceptable error is repetition like 'all the papers carry

the story of the earthquake in County Clare'. Well, of course they do. Give them some credit. Another cliché is: 'The fall of the government dominates the front pages.' Wouldn't it just!

The task of the paper reviewer is to seek out the good stories that the radio news hasn't got. It is the practice in the RTE newsroom to mention the best points of all the papers under review. These are the four Dublin papers, the *Cork Examiner* and the two Belfast papers. So you see, it's rather like seven rich men trying to get through the one eye of the needle. But we hear on the grapevine that our colleagues in the print media like to be mentioned and so indeed do the editors.

As for the writers at the radio end, we like talking to our friends. Friends, hopefully.

THE FASHION DESIGNER

Ann O'Donnell met him

Michael Mortell was born in Mallow, County Cork, in 1950. His ambition as a child was to be a sailor. 'There was nothing practical in my desire to be a sailor; it was all about fantasy and adventure, voyaging to the South Sea islands and all over the world.' He always loved the family holidays in Ballybunion and recalls one summer when a beautiful three-masted ship anchored in Ballybunion bay: 'It was like a vision, and totally reinforced my ambition to be a sailor.' Michael, who was only nine at the time, had to be restrained from swimming out to the ship.

By the time he reached his teens, Michael's ambition had changed. He was, like so many of those who grew up in the sixties, obsessed by music and was greatly attracted to the bohemian life style. He wanted to travel and be part of the art and music world. Always a dreamer, he tells how he dreamt incessantly about getting into the music world. Ironically he studied neither art nor music, explaining that 'it was not cool to learn the piano'. Now, like so many others, he regrets not having learned it. Michael taught himself the guitar; his first instrument was an Egmond semi-solid. He kept it up until his Leaving Cert, at which time his taste in music outpaced his capabilities on the guitar. He hung about the cafés with juke-boxes and emulated the Stones and the cool rocker-types who would occasionally come back to Mallow from London!

At this stage, fashion didn't feature anywhere in his dreams and fantasies. He was interested in the gear he wore himself and in changing styles and trends but only in relation to his own peers and heroes. He most certainly was not the type who drew dresses on copybooks.

By the time he did his Leaving Cert, his ambition was to go to art school. His parents were very much opposed to this idea. However, they struck a bargain, which he considered fair. They asked him to try accountancy and if he didn't like it he could then study art. He lasted two months in accountancy and then went to the School of Art in Cork. He was very happy there but was still not interested in fashions, except in his own hipsters and other personal fashion.

It is obvious that Michael always experienced his world in a very visual way. His memories of being a child and teenager are like very vivid pictures, and as he himself says, 'I loved music as a teenager, but I never knew the words of my favourite songs. I always dreamed while listening to them.'

His sister Patricia entered Michael for a scholarship in Hollings College in Manchester, where he spent two years studying clothing design and management. Michael didn't enjoy the course. There was a much greater emphasis on management than on design, but he did love living in Manchester and looks back on the two years as a very happy period of his life. He then spent six months working with Ib Jorgensen, observing his work. Ib was so good at pattern-outlining that Michael realised he would have to acquire skill at this task if he were to become a successful designer.

His next move was to Belfast, where he spent six months studying pattern-cutting. From there he went on to do a post-graduate course in St Martin's College in London. Half way through his year at St Martin's he realised that his 'ivory tower' phase had to come to an end. It was 1975 and the recession had hit London; Michael felt he had to stop being a student and 'get working'.

In 1978 he set up on his own in Dublin, and was successful from the beginning.

Michael disagrees with the commonly held view that designer clothes are over-priced; he points to the costs of travelling abroad to select fabrics and to the time involved in drawing up designs and getting fits right. He believes that the price of such clothes is fairly based on the manufacturing cost. He feels that the mark-up on designer clothes is greater in British department stores than it is in Irish ones.

Michael Mortell is a very private man. 'I keep up with fashion trends through travel, visual arts and magazines.' The designers he likes most are the very extrovert ones, such as Montana. He agrees that people are generally more fashion and design conscious now than before. 'TV is responsible for that, as it brings much more visual imagery and information into people's lives.' He is very complimentary about the *Head-to-Toe* programme on RTE television: 'Making a fashion programme in Ireland is a very difficult task as the fashion base is so small.' He is also full of praise for the *Late Late Show* fashion awards, which he won three times and judged

several times, and believes they have given a great boost to the fashion trade.

Michael is happy in his career but he finds his work very hard. He didn't expect this to be the case. Nor did he ever dream that he would be so successful. Being a 'success' for Michael is, however, a transitory notion, as the goal posts keep changing. He points out that if you look at a *Vogue* magazine from the sixties you will find all the fashions to be of a kind. 'Here in 1989, everything goes,' says Michael, 'current *Vogue* magazines contain literally hundreds of images and fashions'—making his job quite

difficult, as ideas burn up very quickly.

Michael Mortell is a modest and unusual man. He wishes he could stop admiring his fashion heroes and start admiring his own work. Even when he wins awards and accolades his first thought is not that he's great but that 'they're bound to find out'. It's refreshing to talk to a man who is so successful and who still feels insecure from time to time.

When asked if he had a special ambition, he answered, 'I would love to play second guitarist to Keith Richards on his next solo album.'

Some of the Michael Mortell autumn/winter '89 collection. Photographs by Sandra Lousada, September '89 Image.

The wardrobe department: (left to right) Barbara Jennings, Jane Ann McNeice, Marie O'Halloran, Karen Dodson, Frank Devereux, Tony Murphy, John Kennedy, Anne Quinn, Margaret Roche

THEY'LL HAVE US IN STITCHES

Deirdre Purcell addresses the wardrobe department

When Zig and Zag go to Paris, where do they get their French berets? Where did Fortycoats get such an extraordinary garment? When the 'host of stars' on *Sunday Night At The Olympia* need daisy outfits, who supplies them? And as for Boris, when he dresses up as a leprechaun on St Patrick's Day, to act as the *Nighthawks'* crier/bouncer for Shay, who makes the costume for him? Who dresses Seán Duignan and Eileen Dunne for *Six-One*? Or Biddy, or Miley, or Bosco, or Pajo? The answer to all these questions is, of course, the RTE wardrobe department, tucked away in a bright half-basement in the television building at Montrose, where men slave over steam irons and women labour on tailor's dummies...

There are only twelve people in all in this busiest of busy departments. 'We seem to go through various stages,' says Tony Murphy, the head of his department, who himself learned his tailoring craft on a factory floor. 'There was a time when we did no light entertainment and now we seem to be doing nothing but light entertainment. Now we have hardly any drama, except for *Glenroe* and the new urban drama *Fair City*...'

The people who work in wardrobe are usually recruited from the Grafton Academy, from the fashion industry generally, or from a theatre background. There is no shortage of applicants because in RTE, unlike in other television stations, a wardrobe assistant, once assigned to a production, is responsible for all aspects of the costuming. He or she will work very closely with the designer of the show, from the inception of the designs through the making, fitting and completion. Then the assistant will go on location when the programme is being shot. There is no compartmentalisation; no-one who solely cuts, or solely sews, or fits.

Even though to the outside, inexperienced eye, there appears to be a sameness about the costuming of *Glenroe*, it is by no means boring to work on for the wardrobe assistant. 'We have rails here, five or six of them, that are purely *Glenroe* stuff,' says Mr Murphy as he surveys his warehouse-like storeroom; rail after rail of costumes, jammed together; shelf after shelf of brown cardboard boxes, labelled 'men's spotted bow-ties', 'striped shirts' or 'pampooties'; compartment after compartment of hats, belts; heaps of shoes, boots, sequinned evening bags; pyjamas, suits, biblical robes, uniforms, beaded dresses, raggedy coats; glitter, hip pads, bustles, buckles; grizzly-bear costumes, Santa Claus outfits, fairy queen dresses, even Uncle Sam top hats.

The criteria for hiring people to work in the wardrobe department

DRESSING FOR TELEVISION

Take Mary O'Sullivan's advice and you won't go wrong

are flexible. Skill at the craft is a *sine qua non* of course, but 'I always think it takes all sorts in a department like this,' says Mr Murphy. 'There is no point in having a fabulous tailor or seamstress if they can't understand the temperaments of actors and directors—if they can't fit in to a production.' Commitment and enthusiasm are all-important.

Technology, too, changes the demands. There was a time, for instance, when no newscaster could wear the colour blue because of a technique known as chromakey. Chromakey was the projection of a picture behind the presenter and blue was its dominant colour. Should the presenter wear blue, the picture being projected would have been visible all over the blouse or skirt! And there was a time when cameras could not handle costumes of black or white. White is still problematic in some cases, but black is generally acceptable.

Some things have not changed, however. Television cameras 'read' what they see as a moving pattern, rather than transmit static pictures, and certain vivid reds seem to ooze away from the confines of the garment (or even women's lips!); men who insist on wearing houndstooth checks appear to have their garments crawling all over their bodies—and tiny, close stripes produce a 'strobing' effect, where the garment appears to shimmer on the wearer. These are the cases in which the wardrobe person's most valuable asset is brought into play, especially where stars are involved. That asset is 'tact'.

When I was first asked to present *Head to Toe*, the fashion programme, my imagination ran riot. I thought I'd have great fun putting together a wild and way-out wardrobe and that I would thrill and enthral viewers with a selection of outfits which I fondly thought would be the last word in fashion. How wrong I was!

Gradually I came to understand what looks best and what's to be avoided and so, for what it's worth, here's my guide to dressing well for television.

WATCH OUT!

1. If you're asked to appear on a TV programme, what you wear will depend greatly on the kind of programme it is, so try and watch at least one of the series before you appear. If that's not possible, it's wise to ask the producer or researcher whether or not they'd like you to dress up. Chat shows and game shows generally like their guests to be as glamorous as possible. If it's a serious discussion it's best to avoid the kind of outfit which distracts attention from the message you wish to get across. Remember, your best outfit is not necessarily the most suitable choice. It's an artificial situation and set design and lighting vary enormously from programme to programme, so tell the producer what you're planning to wear and even bring a choice in case you clash with another guest.

REDS BLEED

2. Certain colours are forbidden in studio, for example, white is not recommended as it's virtually impossible to get it right from a lighting point of view. Bright post-box red is frowned on as it has a tendency to bleed and, depending on the set, some other colours may not be suitable. Imagine my chagrin when I discovered that black, *the* fashion colour, was out for me as the set in which we worked was by its nature dark.

MATT'S BEST

3. Matt fabrics are best, that is, fabrics like wool, jersey, velvet. Shiny materials like satin, especially in pale shades, play havoc with lighting and drain the colour from your face.

SHARP SHAPES

4. Sharply defined shapes are most flattering. When I first

TEN BEST DRESSERS

by Geri Lawlor
of Jo-Maxi

'Manners maketh man' or so the Bard says! The French, perhaps arrogantly, would deign to differ, purporting that style makes the man, so much so indeed, that they claim 'Le style est l'homme'. Bearing this in mind, I set about the assignment of choosing the ten best-dressed people in RTE . . . no mean task, considering the place is replete with glamorous and elegantly clad bodies! However, sticking to the tenet of the French, I looked for those people who exhibited true style in their sense of dress those whose personalities are enhanced by their clothes, not swamped by them, those who are relaxed enough to *wear* clothes and do not allow clothes to wear them. Distinct, personal style that transcends mere fashion and sets apart the people I chose from the fashion slaves. Thus, without further ado, I offer you my selection:

Mairéad Ní Nuadháin (*Iris*)

Thelma Mansfield (*Live at 3*)

Bryan Dobson (*News room*)

Orla Guerin (*News room*)

Frances Duff (*Head-to-Toe*)

Ciana Campbell (*Health Programme*)

Ann-Marie Hourihane (*Nighthawks*)

Seán O Tuairisc (*Cursaí*)

Vincent Wall (*Newsroom*)

started presenting, I began to watch TV programmes purely to see what the presenters were wearing, and the one who impressed me most of all was Sue Lawley. She made the most of the good points. She has a very neat figure and always emphasises it with tailored suits—a short fitted jacket teamed with a straight skirt. She has excellent legs and knows it—she always keeps the skirt short and wears high heels. Fashion was dictating culottes, city shorts, palazzos, but Sue knew otherwise.

PADS POINT

5. Shoulder pads are supposed to have gone out, but not on TV they haven't. Soft shawl collars were big for '88/89 but they gave me a round-shouldered appearance unless I added pads. On the other hand, if you're sitting down and only going to be seen in mid-shot, pads shouldn't be too large, as they distort your shape.

INCHES ADDED

6. Always remember that TV adds inches, so if you have any doubts about how slimming an outfit is, the old maxim is best,'when in doubt, don't'.

MAKE SURE

7. Don't leave anything to chance. One of the most an-noying things about TV is that while the camera blurs a lot, it'll always emphasise the one thing you wanted to ignore. For example, my feet were rarely in shot but the one programme on which I tried to get away with black shoes and a brown suit, everyone noticed. So just in case, make sure tights, shoes and other accessories are just right.

FACE FACTS

8. Remember, you'll usually be seen from the waist upward, so it's best to add interest to the neckline—a bow tie, a shawl collar, some nice jewellery; any of these can be just right for drawing attention to your face and what you're saying.

BE COMFORTABLE

9. Above all, it's essential to be comfortable. In the course of the *Head to Toe* series, once or twice I took the chance and wore things which I knew looked well but which had certain pitfalls—for example, a fairly low-necked blouse—and I must say it wasn't worth it. Interviewing three people, while at the same time trying to ensure that the collar moved not a centimetre, did little for my guests' confidence and even less for my composure.

BE HAPPY

10. Once you've decided what to wear, forget about it and enjoy being a star. Television is fun.

This is a photograph of 'The Ladies in the Office' as they were in May 1988 (apologies to John and Gay!): (left to right) Mary Martin, Nuala O'Connor, Gail Seacamp, Lorelei Harris, John Caden, Fionnuala Hughes, Gay Byrne, Caroline Murphy, Eveline Rodin, Cathy Moore

'THE LADIES IN THE OFFICE'

Deirdre Purcell on Gay Byrne's engine room

It all started when Fergie got pregnant. The pregnancy had not been made public, but the ladies in the office knew well. They know everything, you see, and things they don't know, they know very well how to find out. Gay's series producer at the time, John Caden, knew very well that the ladies were always right and he wanted Gay to announce on the air that Fergie was pregnant. But he had to be cautious about it—it would not sound right, really, Gay announcing it right off his own bat, so to speak. So he told Gay to tell the nation that it was the ladies in the office who had confirmed that Fergie was pregnant. Of course the Irish people believed it straight away then and in that way the Irish people were ahead of everyone else in the world, and the ladies started getting mail addressed to them, personally, with little boxes of sweets and other little tokens of appreciation attached.

The ladies in the office, at the time of writing, were, in alphabetical order, Mary Aguiar, Máire Ní Chaidhain, Lorelei Harris, Mary Martin, Cathy Moore, Nuala O'Connor, Anne Walshe and Julie Walshe. The head lady was Julie Parsons and the man was Joe Duffy. There was also a Gay Byrne...

Gay is very appreciative too, deep down, but if you were to listen to him you would believe that those ladies give him a terrible time, not letting him get away with a single thing.

Well, why should they, they point out. They do *real* work, ringing up social welfare and P J Mara and Tony Gregory and all the rest of them, arguing for justice for the people of Ireland, and not letting anyone get away with easy

answers, and making sure everything is shipshape when Gay goes on air. It's not all fun and frills and furbelows and chatting to celebrities on the *Gay Byrne Show*, the ladies would like you to know—it's tough gritty work.

'Most of us are in here from about a quarter to eight in the morning and are still here after six in the evening,' says one of them, eyes glinting with fervour. 'And frequently, we work nights as well...'

They are tolerant about the appellation, on the whole: 'It is an extremely handy device for dealing with topics which a man might not feel easy with,' says one lady. But typically, not all of them agree: 'I wonder...' says another, 'it's the Irishman's way—if it's not his mammy, it's his wife getting at him or it's the ladies in his office...' 'Ah no,' says a third, 'the ladies in the office thing is used as a tool to help to get into a specific type of script or debate. If it's used in that way I think it's wonderful. You'd be missing something if you didn't have it.' A fourth would prefer Gay to call them The Women I Work With... You can see that the ladies are their own women...

You can have great gossipy bits in the *Gay Byrne Show* followed immediately by a serious interview. And they are all researched and produced by the ladies (at the time of writing, by the way, there was a lone man in the office too) who all contribute ideas and expertise: 'The meetings are not directed in any way, but are fairly democratic. Everybody has an input and puts

'The Ladies in the Office'
(contd from page 21)

THE RTE AUTHORITY

by Jim Culliton, Chairman, the RTE Authority

up their idea, which is then discussed by us all.'

They all have different areas of interest—'I like doing investigative stuff'; 'I like show-business and entertainment'; 'I'm interested in the environment and ecology'; 'I do a lot of stuff on books'—but all will do anything that comes up. 'It's a most wonderful training ground for any other programme.'

And they all write scripts for Gay to read. 'It's a skill one acquires,' says one. 'It's very difficult when you first come in, to write for speech, to get into how Gay speaks, and how Gay will say something.' (One got so good at this that when she was writing a letter to her sister in America she had to stop. 'Oh my God,' she said, 'I'm talking like Gay Byrne!')

The old-timers have seen the programme change dramatically over the years. They now use cellular telephones, 'more outside broadcasts, more phone calls, more link-ups, we've gone out much more. There's much more performance now'. The differentiation between producer and researcher, they say, is not as evident on this show as elsewhere: 'Everybody has to pitch in and be able to take on responsibility to finish what they have started.' Not everything works like clockwork, of course, and 'working on these kind of programmes does take a terrible toll if you do it for too long'.

When things go wrong for the ladies it can be nightmarish; one sums up the feelings of them all: 'It's an adventure playground!'

When the Broadcasting Authority Bill 1960 was being debated in Dáil Éireann, the minister, Michael Hilliard, in responding to comment on the appointment of Eamonn Andrews as chairman, described Eamonn as 'an exemplary young Irishman of good character and fine ability, who thought it his patriotic duty to place at the disposal of the government the knowledge and experience he undoubtedly had gained by virtue of his active association with television and in the presentation of programmes'. That concept, of having people with wide-ranging experience and particular cultural, social, sporting, trade union and business interests, which began with the first Authority in 1960, has continued ever since.

The first Authority, under the chairmanship of Eamonn Andrews, had two members of the old Comhairle Radio Éireann: Charles J Brennan, who had been its chairman, and Dr T W Moody, FTCD, then senior lecturer and professor of modern history at Trinity College, Dublin. It also had two members of the Broadcasting Advisory Committee: Commander George Crosbie and Edward B MacManus. The other members were Ernest Blythe of the Abbey Theatre, who was a former minister for finance; Fintan Kennedy, general secretary of the Irish Transport and General Workers' Union and a member of the National Executive of the Irish Congress of Trade Unions; Áine Ní Cheannain, teacher, Gaelic scholar and writer, and James

Fanning, founder of the Little Theatre Group in Birr and editor of the *Midland Tribune*.

The functions of the Authority were set out succinctly and somewhat prosaically in Section 16 of the Broadcasting Authority Act 1960, which said: 'the Authority shall establish and maintain a national television and sound broadcasting service and shall have all such powers which are necessary or incidental to that purpose.' It went on to detail the many functions of operating the broadcasting service which came under the overall control of the Authority through its director general and staff.

'Impressed by commitment'

During my term as chairman of the RTE authority, I have been impressed by the commitment of each member of the Authority to RTE and to the success of the broadcasting services, even though this commitment has meant a considerable input of time and effort. Generally, the public hears of the RTE Authority only when there is a real or alleged 'crisis', either involving broadcasters or the relationship with government or with the minister of the day.

In practice, the role of the Authority could be summed up under five headings:

● **To ensure that RTE complies with its obligations under the Broadcasting Authority Acts 1960-76**

The present RTE Authority:
(left to right, front) Mary Leland,
Máirín O'Byrne, Jim Culliton,
John Carroll, Carmel O'Reilly;
(left to right, back) John Sorohan,
Bobby Gahan, Vincent Finn, Liam
Ó Maollmhicil, Frank Flannery,
Dan McAuley, Tom Quinn, Pat
Kenny and W D Flackes.

- **To reflect the views and interests of the public at large and to see that programmes mirror those interests**
- **To support the director general and his executive in their efforts to improve programmes and increase home production**
- **To be responsible for the financial well-being of RTE**
- **To maintain a good working relationship with the minister for communications**

The Broadcasting Authority Acts clearly define the function of the RTE Authority and outline its responsibilities in reasonable detail. The Acts are, however, silent on the role which the Authority should adopt in fulfilling its function and discharging its responsibilities. The concept of the Authority acting as public trustees has been developed over time as its members sought to articulate their role.

In its public trustee role, it understands itself to be bound by the broadcasting legislation to serve the public good as the public perceives it. The primary duty of the Authority is, therefore, to adopt a perspective which neither politicians nor professional broadcasters can always be expected to share.

In doing this, the Authority requires the application of certain norms in programme-making—integrity, fair-mindedness, openness, excellence and competence. Its commitment to high standards must be absolute if it is to fulfil the responsibilities imposed on it by the Broadcasting Acts. The Authority has no function to crusade for or against particular ideologies or particular forces in society and neither is it its function to preach to the nation in any didactic sense. Rather, on matters of public interest, it aims to ensure that RTE programming stimulates the kind of interest that will lead to better understanding of the issues.

How well the present Authority has fulfilled these obligations and met the criteria outlined is in the final analysis a matter for you, the reader, to judge; but I believe that, using any basis of measurement, RTE has continued to develop, improve its services and meet those obligations. Indeed, if one applies objective criteria, RTE was never in better shape as a broadcasting organisation, as a contributor to Irish society and as a strong competitor to maintain its dominant position on the Irish broadcasting scene.

I feel that the Authority, management and staff, working together, can say with confidence that:

- **RTE is highly regarded by viewers and listeners**
- **our media are regarded as the main source of news and information**
- **home television production is at an all-time peak**
- **home-produced television programmes on RTE 1 and Network 2 dominate peak-time viewing**
- **the new schedules on Radio 1 and the relaunch of 2FM have created a total radio medium for Irish listeners**
- **RTE is profitable and has no debt other than long-term exchequer loans**
- **RTE provides first-class working conditions and job satisfaction for more than two thousand people in Dublin and in ten other centres throughout the country**

1989-90 will see many changes on the broadcasting scene in Ireland, as new national and local radio stations begin operating and as a commercial television station opens. RTE is ready for this competition and it will be the duty of the RTE Authority to support the executive and to see that viewers and listeners continue to receive the quality of programming and the standards of coverage and information that have been part of the RTE tradition for more than sixty years.

DARINA ALLEN
talks to Deirdre Purcell

For a while there, it became impossible to find a steel whisk anywhere in the country. On the telly, Ms Darina Allen held up her own whisk; she said it was her favourite, indispensable tool—she even went so far as to say she would bring it with her to a desert island—and out went half of Ireland in search of one like it.

No need to describe Ms Allen—the uncompromisingly straight hair caught with an Alice band, the formidable spectacles, the lean frame—Ms Allen is now recognised wherever she goes. Thanks to the television series *Simply Delicious* (shot with a single camera) the lady is a celebrity. Car-loads of people now drive into the gravelled courtyard of Kinoith, the lovely old house at the centre of the Ballymaloe Cookery School, to try to have a quick look at her. This she does *not* appreciate.

What she does love, however, is that people, Irish and foreign, are now flocking to her school: 'Ireland had such an appalling reputation. American people, in particular, make such an act of faith in coming to Ireland, they have to put up with cracks from their friends (What's an Irish seven-course meal? A six-pack and a potato!).'

Kinoith's inhabitants seem to be an ever-shifting mélange of family and friends. There are always people staying ('There's someone in my bed!' resounds in the kitchen—via a squawk box—from one of the Allen boys upstairs), there are always cups of tea and (homemade) biscuits and buns on the go; other people's cooking bubbles fragrantly on the big range. 'What's that?' says Darina, standing up in the middle of this interview. 'I've got to see what that is... ' She goes over to the cooker and lifts the lid off the saucepan. The smell intensifies hugely. 'Oh yes. It's Rory's...' Rory is her brother, a chef in the kitchen of Ballymaloe House Country House Hotel, two miles down the road. The concoction on the cooker is for a wedding. Satisfied, she replaces the lid and sits down again to talk about her mission.

Yes, mission. It is difficult adequately to convey the enthusiasm, the missionary zeal, with which she invests her teaching. The big glasses flash in the soft light of the conservatory off her kitchen as she tries to explain it: 'I absolutely love teaching, I really do love it. I never get fed up with cooking and I never get fed up with teaching people how to cook. You teach someone how to make a loaf of bread or a soup or a gravy , and it's actually something they're going to use, not like teaching them a theorem in maths—they give pleasure to their families and friends.' She is particularly excited about the professional courses she runs 'for people who are going to make their living out of cooking'—and with her scheme whereby she brings in international guest chefs to teach the best of their own specialisation: Madhur Jaffrey, Jane Grigson, Anthony Worrell-Thompson, owner of Ménage-à-Trois restaurant in London.

Over the last couple of years, the courses have been consistently and heavily over-subscribed, with long waiting lists for cancellations. And with the success of the TV series and its spin-off book of the same name, the level of enquiries shot to unprecedented levels. All those people wanting to learn to cook! No space to teach them! Darina's glasses glinted with determination. She looked around the outhouses around Kinoith. A-ha! A disused applehouse! A large space in front of it! And *voilà*! In September of this year the school doubled in size.

When first she decided, in consultation with her mother-in-law, the renowned and redoubtable Myrtle, to open her own school, she went to the bank for a loan. She was turned down. She surmises, with wicked glee, that it was because she was a woman, 'the usual story at that time—but he's very sorry now!'

Darina O'Connell was born in Cullohill, Co. Laois. The next time you are flying down the main road from Dublin to Cork and you have passed through Durrow—the lovely village with a castle and a village green—and then have shot through the next little village without noticing it, that will have been Cullohill...

Darina is the eldest of nine children. 'We had a small business there—but it was all the businesses in the village. Pub, undertaker, auctioneer, grocery, post office, petrol pump, manure, seeds—everything you can imagine. If you wanted nails, or a hat to go to a funeral, we supplied them—the lot. People didn't travel much in those days and we had to get things for them. In a small village like that you had to be all things to all men.' But the father of this enterprising family died when his eldest daughter was just fourteen, 'so Mother quickly got rid of a lot of the businesses within businesses which weren't making money.'

Darina was sent as a boarder to the Dominican College in Wicklow. She had always been interested in cooking, 'not in any calculated sort of way, it was just sort of unconscious. My mother was a very good cook—naturally so—always making bread and all of that, and since there were so many of us, there was always cooking going on in the house.' So when she left secondary school, she went on to the College of Catering in Cathal Brugha Street. 'It was a catering management course, but I realised very quickly that I wanted to do the cooking end of things.' But in 1969 there were very few options for a girl who wanted seriously to cook. 'There was the Russell in Dublin, Jammets—but they weren't too keen on taking girls into their kitchens. The principal of the school had just heard of this farmer's wife down in Cork who was famous for her cooking with fresh herbs and so on and who had just opened her house—Myrtle was the very first to do this country house restaurant business...'

Darina wrote to Myrtle Allen, who accepted her as an apprentice. (And as she stepped out of the car on her arrival, Myrtle's son, Tim, looked up from his croquet game on the lawn in front of Ballymaloe and fell in love. Darina and Tim now have four children, Isaac, Toby, Emily and Lydia.) Time passed and Myrtle got very busy with the restaurant side of the business. Darina dreamed of having her own school. She advertised locally and the result was 'Saturday morning classes in the kitchen of my own little house. I

had a group of Cork ladies who used to come out to me all dressed up. They were so nice. I never thought anyone would come to *me*. I had small children at the time. I am always very fond of those ladies who came to me on that first course...'

She had been thinking all along of opening a formal school, 'but it was very difficult with small children and so on...' Nevertheless, she bashed on and knocked on the doors of the famous cookery schools in England—the Cordon Bleu, Tante Marie's La Petite Cuisine—to see how they ran their businesses. 'I went to them all. And to tell you the truth, I didn't change my ideas about what I wanted after seeing them all. If anything, my ideas became even more fixed.' Apparently, in many professional cookery schools, the students cook in individual booths, separated by

dividers. The results of their labours are bunged in together and served in a canteen 'so they are not even sure that what they are eating has been cooked by themselves'. Darina's idea was to make cookery into an odyssey of personal discovery and fun. Students always eat what they themselves cook ('otherwise how would they know what it tastes like?').

The other major factor at the Ballymaloe Cookery School is the quality of the fresh ingredients— the school is surrounded by vegetable and herb gardens, with an acre of greenhouses. This can draw down some negative reaction: 'Students sometimes complain to me that they will never again be able to get such good fresh ingredients'—and that therefore, the dishes they cooked could never be replicated. 'Pooh!' is Ms Allen's attitude to such faintheartedness. 'The students must know what the dish *should* taste like. They must know what to aim for. I teach people that they absolutely must look for good raw ingredients. And they can do—if they are aware of it themselves. They must search—and not just pick up the first cauliflower in the basket of the first supermarket!' To help them on their way to a new and more fulfilling life, most students leave the school with plant-pots full of herbs, fingers itching to get going on the patios, kitchen gardens and even window-boxes.

The uniqueness of this school has a lot to do with the family, who themselves created the gorgeous gardens around it, initially hacking through a brambled wilderness with chainsaws—but mostly to do with Darina herself. 'It wasn't going to be just a cookery school. It was going to show students a sort of 'way of life'. A way of life which has nothing to do with being wealthy, which makes you think about just sticking the milk bottle or the pound of butter on the table... This was my romantic dream.'

THE MAKING OF A DOCUMENTARY

Cian Ó hÉigeartaigh writes about the making of his film *The Varian Girls* broadcast in the Tuesday documentary series

The word 'documentary' is often used loosely, but properly speaking it means a programme which is comprehensive, which explores a subject fully, and which expands or deepens the viewer's understanding. A documentary should be memorable.

Most documentaries begin as a gleam in somebody's eye. *The Varian Girls* owes its conception to a letter which Betty McMahon wrote to Gay Byrne's radio programme in the summer of 1988. She told him about a reunion planned by a group of friends, now in the autumn of their years, who had worked together in Varian's brush factory in Dublin during the far-off days of the Second World War.

It was in fact their fourth reunion in almost fifty years. It all began on 4 April 1944 when Betty typed the date on a postcard. 'Look!' she said, 'it's all fours! Now I wonder where we will be when it's all fives?' They agreed on the spot that they would all meet—ten of them—at the Gresham Hotel, just around the corner from Varian's in Talbot Street, on 5 May 1955. And so they did; and again on 6 June 1966, and on 7 July 1977. Now they were planning what must surely be the final reunion on Monday 8 August 1988 for the eight who still remained.

'Now that's a lovely, lovely story of love and friendship lasting through the years,' said Gay to his listeners. Indeed it was; and at least one listener decided that someone should make a television programme about those women.

The listener was Linda Bent, a production assistant with RTE. For the next few days she tried to get someone interested in filming Betty McMahon's story. I was one of the people she approached. Initially, I was sceptical. I knew from experience that filming with old people can present problems. They often tire easily and may be intimidated by the hustle and bustle of a television crew. But when Linda brought me to see Betty McMahon I began to change my mind. I could see that the warmth of Betty's personality, the variety and colour of her conversation, would come across strongly; and she obviously got on well with Linda and felt at ease with her. When she produced her photographs I was instantly converted. There were about a dozen of them, tiny box-Brownie snapshots, razor-sharp and of extraordinary quality. Girls on a sunlit hillside, posing in a row; girls with bikes at the end of a summer afternoon; girls making tea in a field somewhere; girls relaxing in the splendour of their youth—photographs full of innocence and tenderness and nostalgia.

So we went to see Clare Duignan, then head of features and documentaries for TV. Clare thought it was a wonderful idea, but there was a problem. The filming of documentaries is usually

planned some time in advance, and Clare had committed all her resources to a full series of Tuesday documentaries being filmed that summer. There was literally nothing left—no filming, no editing, no budget.

That was the bad news. The good news was that Clare told us to go ahead anyway. Somehow, she said, she would find a film crew for the day of the reunion itself. That would give us the essential core of the programme, and the rest could be picked up later.

'We need not have worried'

In the end, we got two full days' filming on 8 and 9 August, with one of RTE's best cameramen, Tom Curran. In a documentary, the choice of a cameraperson can mean life or death. In this case we had no choice, but we couldn't have done better. Tom is quiet,

unobtrusive, quick, energetic and absolutely reliable. I had only to explain what we were looking for and let him get on with it.

On the Monday morning we filmed Betty going to the hairdresser in Marino (I was hoping this would make an opening for the programme), and in the afternoon we recorded a long interview in her back garden. This was the moment of truth. The programme turned on Betty's story, and if for any reason the interview had not been a success, we would have been in trouble. But we need not have worried.

The reunion itself was on Monday evening, in a pleasant room on an upper floor of the Gresham Hotel. Seven of the eight remaining members of the group were there, including May who came from England, and Con who travelled round the world from New Zealand. We were anxious not to spoil the evening for the ladies

The Making of a Documentary
(cont. from page 27)

(cont. from page 27)

themselves, so we filmed only three short segments at the beginning, middle and end of the proceedings, although I think they hardly noticed we were there once they had begun to swap photographs and stories.

The next day we filmed four more interviews—all in the Gresham, to save time—and a lot of old photographs. There were plenty of these, but unfortunately none that showed the girls at their workplace in Varian's. Nor could we film the factory as it was in their day, because the firm moved to new premises near Kilmainham some years ago. The Irish Life Centre now stands where Betty and May and Peg and Con typed their letters and filled their ledgers.

So there were gaps in the material, but the interviews and the reunion itself had gone so well that I was sure it would make a good programme—provided I could find the right way to put it together. This is the hardest time for the director of a film. Your material is there, in a heap of metal boxes. You know that some of it is good, some perhaps less so. In your head is a concept, some ideas about beginnings and endings, high points, gaps to be bridged and so on. From these initial fragmentary ideas, you must develop a coherent structure that will allow the story to emerge clearly and effectively, with as much drama and colour and variety as possible.

The first step is to view all the material with the film editor.

VARIAN GIRLS 'WONDERFUL'

Extract from RTE telephone log, Tuesday 7 February 1989:

The Varian Girls
'Wonderful, wonderful viewing.'
'Told a very warm and moving story very well.'
'Fantastic programme, brilliantly done.'
'Charming and so natural. Compliments to the producer.'
'Superb piece of television. Enjoyed the archive material.'
'Compliments to everybody. Beautifully done.'
'Compliments on the programme. It was superb.'
'It was excellent. A pity you don't have more like that.'

There are always surprises at this stage. Interviews which seemed slow and halting during filming may turn out to have a compelling quality of reflection and honesty; interviews which seemed fluent and expressive may turn out to be garrulous and theatrical.

MAKING A COLD JUDGEMENT

Either way, you have to make a cold judgment on what you see, and there is an iron rule: if in doubt, leave it out.

With *The Varian Girls*, we began with the interviews. I listened to each one many times, marked off the bits that were most relevant and expressive, and spent several

sleepless nights almost till dawn trying to shape these bits into a coherent telling of the story.

After a week I was able to give our film editor, Arthur McGuinness, an outline on paper of the shape of the programme. He and his assistant, Pat Mulvey, assembled the bits of interview in the order indicated, leaving gaps where archive film would be added later. Then we began to work on this outline, dropping bits that didn't seem to fit, reversing the order here and there to improve the thrust of the narrative, cutting out repetitions and digressions. That took another week, and could have taken much longer if we had the time. Finally we added the archive sequences and the music.

The relationship between director and film editor is complex and vital. Initially, the director must be able to explain what he/she wants in broad outline; but when it comes to working out the details, a good editor (and Arthur is very good) will make the running most of the way, providing solutions to problems which the director may not even have foreseen. A suc-

QUIZTIME
CLASSICAL MUSIC

set by Fionn O'Leary

cessful film documentary is the result of a successful collaboration between editor and director.

Neither Arthur nor I was sure that *The Varian Girls* would work until the film was almost finished. Linda had found some good archive film, but we were still very short of illustrative material, and of necessity much of the film consisted of faces talking to the camera. That is usually thought to be bad television; but these were interesting faces, marked with a lifetime's experience, and what they said was full of humour and humanity and verve. Our trump card was a two-minute sequence drawn from Betty's old photographs, set to a haunting track of Judy Garland: 'Somewhere, over the rainbow, bluebirds fly . . . Birds fly over the rainbow, why, oh why can't I?' The music seemed to echo a sense of unrealised potential, of pinioned energy, in the young and carefree faces of the girls in the photographs.

It was a very strong sequence, and I was sure that anyone who stayed with the film to that point would stay to the end. But it came almost fifteen minutes into the film. Would the viewers wait that long?

In the event, they did. The viewing figures were good, with virtually no drop-off from beginning to end, and the audience reaction was excellent: so much so that I think it points to a gap in RTE's programme schedules. We make a lot of films about issues and subjects; we make very few about people and their lives. Perhaps there is food for thought there.

1. Name a song associated with a cable railway on Mt Vesuvius.

2. True or false: John McCormack defeated James Joyce for the first place in the 1903 Feis Cheoil?

3. What composer accorded himself the most fragrant of signatures?

4. What is the popular title for the principal theme of Bach's Cantata No. 208?

5. Who really composed Purcell's *Trumpet Concerto*, Haydn's *Serenade*, and Haydn's *Toy Symphony*?

6. *Arms and the Man*, the play by G B Shaw, is the basis of what operetta and by whom?

7. What Dublin-born composer demonstrated pianos for the firm of Clementi & Co?

8. Whose voice so cheered the melancholia of Spain's Philip V that he was offered 50,000 francs a year to remain in Madrid?

9. Of what piece of music did Brahms say: 'Unfortunately, not by Johannes Brahms'?

10. Who is generally considered to have first perfected the violin?

11. What are nakers?

12. What Irish composer survived an earthquake, a mutiny on a South Seas voyage and an explosion in a ship's engine room?

13. What Irish composer made his debut as Figaro in the *Barber of Seville* by Rossini?

14. What English composer wrote the music for what became the signature tune for the longest running record programme on the BBC?

15. Name the only Irish orchestra and conductor to have been included in the *Guinness Book of Records*.

16. Who is known as the father of the symphony?

17. What famous song did Martini the German write?

18. Who was the Swedish Nightingale?

19. Name the famous tenors who were born in Cork and Limerick respectively.

20. What are the instruments in a piano trio?

21. Who started Schubert's *Unfinished Symphony*?

22. Which is the higher note within the same octave—A flat or G sharp?

23. Mi-a-ou, and Kitty-Valse are movements from what suite?
(Answers on page 105)

CROKE PARK OR CHELTENHAM?

Tim O'Connor decides what sport will be broadcast on TV

Someone once said—I think it was me!—that television was the art of trying to please most of the people most of the time. So even when that goal is achieved, this broad-based, democratic philosophy still leaves a significant—and usually vociferous—minority sometimes merely dissatisfied but mostly hopping mad.

In any world list of no-win situations, television sports programming must figure at the top. Because for every guy who hates tennis there is a girl who hates horse racing; golfers stare in disbelief at greyhound-racing; motorsport looks just like traffic to athletes; and even more than ten years after the abolition of The Ban there are still GAA men who resent the airtime given to soccer and vice versa!

But they must all be accommodated in a television schedule. Because despite their singleness of purpose, their narrowness of interest, their canny, their cunning, their ranting and raving, they, all of them, constitute a valid majority: they are the public, the licence-payers, our audience.

RTE currently broadcasts 750 hours of sport on its two television channels each year. On average that's over two hours every day—two hours too many for the avowed sports-hater, not nearly enough for the armchair enthusiast.

Determining factors? The events that make up the sports output are determined by just two factors: public interest in them and their cost. The former is predictable but the latter, unfortunately, is not.

Although it may appear obvious, it does not seem to be generally understood that a sports event is usually a private property, capable of being owned and traded like any other commodity. Quite properly then, television companies are required to pay a fee to the owner if they wish to film or broadcast an event. And, as in any other market, the price is determined by the laws of supply and demand.

MONEY RULES!

So clearly, when instructed to provide 750 hours of sport, a programmer does not simply find 750 hours he'd like to buy, but 750 hours he can afford to buy.

This requires keeping a close eye on the sports' commodity market (for instance, in 1989 the new owners of Wimbledon's television rights were asking ten times the price RTE paid in 1988—they didn't get it!), as well as constantly trying to solve odd equations (how many English League games equal one Tyson fight?).

In the United States the battle for sports events between the major broadcasters became so intense that analysts now assert there were no winners. The underbidders sometimes panicked into an alternative shopping spree while the company that won the contract teetered on the brink of bankruptcy trying to service it. For instance, CBS (or Clobbered By Sport, as they're known within the industry) are committed to a schedule of payments totalling two billion dollars after topping the bidding in the auction for the new basketball and baseball contracts (each baseball game will cost them a staggering five million dollars!). And one of the underbidders, NBC, responded by buying the American rights to the Barcelona Olympics for a record 401 million dollars, despite the fact that they are still counting the cost of a disastrous Olympic experience in Seoul in 1988.

With the advent of new satellite channels, some of which are churning out twenty-four hours of sport per day, one might imagine that the appetite of even the most voracious fan would be satisfied. But all the indications suggest otherwise: speedway on ice hasn't really set the world alight, high-diving in Acapulco looks good, but..., while the transatlantic Race on a Breadboard doesn't quite measure up to...to...to anything! Certainly not to the championships we know from Augusta to Aintree, from Croke Park to Cheltenham, from Wembley to Wimbledon, and certainly not to the champions we love, from Roche and Kelly to Barry and Jacko.

These are the standards and the standard-bearers of yesterday: we

are told they are under threat by today's expediencies. But all romantics and every true sportsperson are confident that, in the end, sport will win out—and so

too will television as long as its practitioners continue their attempt to master the art of trying to please most of the people most of the time.

LÚIDÍN MAC LÚ LEIPREACHÁN

Is mar chlár raidió a cuireadh tús le *Lúidín Mac Lú Leipreachán* i mbliain 1961. An deis a bhí ann clár nua do pháistí a thionsnamh, thapaíos é chun scéal barrúil a insint dóibh agus ag an am gcéanna chun a gcluasa a chur i dtaithí na bpíob uilleann. Tá an-chion ar an bpíb inniu ach ní

mór cuimhneamh nach mbíodh ag éisteacht leis sna luathsheascaidí ach beagán díograiseoirí agus nach raibh ach fíorbheagán píobairí ann.

Go bunúsach baineann an scéal le Lúidín Mac Lú agus le Luichín, luichín bán a bhí ina dhlúthchara

aige. Cibé ponc ina mbíodh Luichín shaoradh Lúidín é le fonn draíochta ar an bpíb.

I ndubh agus i mbán (go monochrómach mar a deir siad inniu), gan amhras, a bhí *Lúidín* le feiceáil i mbliain 1969. Tionscnaíodh an tsraith ina hiomláine sa stiúideo ag bun mo ghairdínse. Thógadh sé tamall de laethanta na pictiúir bheoite a tharraingt agus a scannánú. Ba í Nóra, céile mo dhearthár, a dhéanadh an chuid sin den obair. Pat Hayes a thaifead na fuaimeanna éagsúla, ina measc ceol píbe Phaddy Moloney. Sheinnfeadh na Chieftains ar ball cóiriúcháin a bheadh bunaithe ar chuid de na píosaí ceoil sin. Fúmsa a fágadh guthanna na nainmhithe agus fuaimeanna éagsúla eile. Tháinig *Lúidín* amach mar scannán daite sa deireadh i mbliain 1971 agus b'é an chéad chartún Gaeilge é, a ndearnadh an obair cheart bheochana air, dár chraol RTE.

Éamon de Buitléar

JO-MAXI   JO-MAXI   JO-MAXI   JO-MAXI

When I was told I'd got the job as presenter on *Jo-Maxi* I was ecstatic, I just couldn't wait. All that fun, all that glamour! I could just see my name on the credits. What I didn't see was all the hard work! They had warned us at the interview but I was pretty starry-eyed then. You see, we're employed as presenter/reporters, which means that aside from presenting—which is pretty taxing—we do a lot of our own research, reporting, and all of our own script-writing. And on a five-night-a-week show, that's a lot of work!

However, although the work has been tough, the crack has been mighty and everyone's delighted with *Jo-Maxi*'s first season, though I must admit that the whole production team and the four presenters are probably eligible at this stage to take up residence at the BBC—that's the Bothered and Bewildered Club!

I suppose the most fascinating aspect of the presenter's job has got to be its versatility. And I reckon young people's program-

Geri Lawlor

ming is the most versatile area of all. *Jo-Maxi* covers a broad spectrum so that it can appeal to a huge age group with a huge interest span. What that means is that we get to do lots of interesting, amazing and, more often than not, crazy things! Fashion's been the area I've dealt with most over the season and I've been able to see and do things connected with fashion that I've never had the opportunity to do before—and it's been brilliant, really exciting. Besides, in what other job could I talk to the nation

from the arms of 100 per cent prime American beefcake footballers? Or jump out of a helicopter and then get 'rescued' by the Air Corps? Or interview Carol Decker one day and Michael D Higgins the next? It's all in a week's work!

This season has been great and I think I'll be approaching the next one a little bit more realistically, with the benefit of experience—forget the 'glamour' and the 'celebrity' bit—I'll be concentrating on the hard work! Anyway, my friends keep my feet on the ground. I'm renounced for being a chatterbox since my schooldays. I was rabbiting on one evening in my friend's house, and Bera, my friend's mum, came into the room, put her fingers in her ears, threw her eyes up to heaven and with a look of twisted agony that would rival anything the Spanish Inquisition could achieve, she cried, 'God almighty, don't tell me we're going to have to put up with that in our living rooms every night, are we?' Somebody give me a break, I can't be that bad!

Antoinette Dawson

A ntoinette Dawson is the one with the long curly hair who for years has wanted to shave it all off but hasn't got the guts.

Antoinette was born in Limerick and moved to Dublin when she was ten. She went to St Raphaela's Secondary School in Kilmacud: 'School was fine, but it was such a small school that if anything happened they knew exactly who did it, not that we did anything truly bad—the worst, I think, was putting cling-film over the toilets. And for some strange reason that I still can't figure out, they made me a prefect in sixth year. When I left school I wanted to be a fashion designer, which meant three years studying, but I also wanted money.' The money won out in the end and Antoinette got a job in a fashion company and studied fashion design at night.

Before working on *Jo-Maxi*, Antoinette organised two Dublin

Street Carnivals, which she says was great fun. She also ran the Dublin Contemporary Dance Theatre for a couple of years and before that she worked in the Arts Council. But of all of these jobs her favourite has got to be *Jo-Maxi*: 'It's just great fun; you get to do things you've always wanted to do—like falling off motorbikes, going to boarding schools, behind the scenes at the circus—the lot! I get bored very easily, and with most jobs this is a problem, but you'd never get bored working on *Jo-Maxi*. Fun, fun, fun!'

The things that interest young people

When I was a young teenager, two events which were to shape my life occurred in the same year:

JO-MAXI JO-MAXI JO-MAXI JO-MAXI

'When they asked me to write about the past year and a half of *Jo-Maxi*, my mind drew a blank. So the only option left open to me was to cheat, and so I did (shame on me!). I sat a little friend of mine down and got him to ask the questions, reversing the roles from what happens on *Jo-Maxi*. He sat a stiff exam for me and proved to be a tough marker too. Here's what happened.

Norman Kavanagh (aged 14) interviews Cliona Ní Bhuachalla

Paper 1—Subject: Likes

Q. What's the best thing about presenting *Jo-Maxi*? (Answer only what's asked and stick to the point.)

A. Meeting all the guests, usually about five a day, chatting to them before the show and finding out what they like or dislike about *Jo-Maxi*. They can be brutally honest! At this stage we know an amazing network of previous guests, their friends, friends of friends.

Cliona Ní Bhuachalla

Marks: (5 out of 10) Good opening but strayed from the point towards the end.

Paper 2—Subject: Viewers

Q. What is the biggest concern of the young people of Ireland?

A. Young people of Ireland, I luv them. Ha! Sorry. I suppose pocket money, or the lack of it, as many of the reviewers mention the price of plays, cinemas, concerts, etc. They seem to gobble up babysitting and pocket money all at once. Mind you, young people have very strong opinions on a lot of things and as our Max-blast slot showed, they aren't afraid to voice them. Yep, I luv them!

Marks: (2 out of 10) Your answer showed a silly attitude that would want to improve or I'm not doing this anymore. Also, how much are you paying me, if you're so concerned about our pocket money?

Paper 3—Subject: Scariness

Q. What was the scariest thing that happened on *Jo-Maxi*?

A. Getting marooned on Oyster Island in Rosses Point with the crew and four friends. Overall the treasure hunts are a bit of crack, apart from all that running. Mind you, I'm nearly fit, which is more than I can say for Joe, the cameraman!

Marks: (4 out of 10) You're messing again Cliona, this is a serious interview!

Paper 4—Subject: Mishaps

Q. Tell me about some booboos.

A. Well, I kept calling Tom from *Something Happens* Tony, which he didn't like. Geri presented flowers to the wrong person one day and Ray couldn't figure out how they curled the Radiccho lettuce until the chef put him straight that it grows that way. Silly guy! Antoinette pays me not to tell on her—and I need the money! So for now I can't remember Anto doing any booboos.

Marks: (7 out of 10) Getting better, stuck to the point but still could try harder. Overall you've passed, but more revision would help—so it's head down into the annual for the Christmas holidays. And I expect a free copy for me or I'm never watching the programme again.

A) spots and B) my first date. B would have been fine except that it was influenced by A. What can you do when you arrive at the front of the cinema all excited in the coolest of cool new clothes, wrapped from forehead to chin in a Dr Who multicoloured knitted scarf? I don't think Niall recognised me—he thought that his mates had hatched some dirty trick on him and it was one of them (whose voice hadn't broken yet) all dressed up—so he walked off! Life is very tough as a teenager.

I never saw Niall again (I was too embarrassed to say hello to him) but myself and the spots had a wonderful relationship which lasted three years.

They were the most active three years of my life. I tried every anti-spot cream, liquid, lotion and potion that ever existed. I cut out and sent away for mixtures and magic formulas that weren't even available in Ireland.

But I learned a lot in those three years and I'm now going to pass on this knowledge to you... NOTHING WORKS when you have spots and the peanut butter sticks to the roof of your mouth.

I've got a question though... How come none of the guests we have on *Jo-Maxi* arrive dressed in a scarf? Has something new been invented? Why didn't somebody tell me?

I think I'll check out how people are getting on with their first date!

JO-MAXI JO-MAXI JO-MAXI JO-MAXI

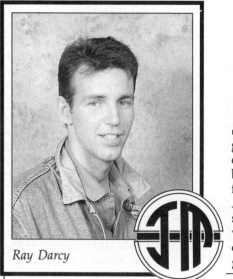

Ray Darcy

A risk that paid off . . .
by Ann O'Donnell

All through last winter and spring, five evenings a week, four young people, previously unknown, presented *Jo-Maxi*—a programme for young people. None of the four had ever worked in TV before, so it was a daunting task for them and a big risk for RTE. According to Declan Eames, the series producer for *Jo-Maxi*, RTE wanted something new and exciting in a young people's programme and they felt there could

be excellent talent around the country which had previously been untapped. So they conducted a talent trawl by advertising on radio, television and in the *RTE Guide*, looking for young people interested in a career in TV. All of the applicants were asked to submit a video about themselves and their skills. There were 350 applicants, fifteen of whom were shortlisted for interview and screen test. RTE invited two teenagers, Darren and Victor, to be members of the interview panel and to be involved in the final selection. By incredible coincidence, the four people chosen by RTE were (and still are) the same four chosen by Darren and Victor: Geri Lalor, Cliona Ní Bhuachalla, Ray Darcy and Antoinette Dawson. The four were selected primarily on ability, rather than age, although obviously middle-aged talent was not under consideration. The presenters range in age from twenty-three to twenty-nine and the average age of the production team is twenty-eight to twenty-nine years. The four were given two weeks' training and a one week dry-run in studio. Interestingly, the overwhelming bulk of talent among the 350 applicants was female. (So women, young women and girls—go for it—there are possibly hundreds of potential Olivia O'Learys out there!)

RTE's big risk paid off and the programme received a very favourable response from young people. The presenters, whom Declan describes as 'four aces', made an incredible impact, and by the end of the first year the audience had tripled. The level of interest among young people was especially apparent from the huge response they had to invitations to participate in challenges, discussions and competitions. The ball skills challenges received a particularly outstanding response. 'Lots of kids are willing to do book, film and concert reviews, live on the programme,' says Declan.

I remember I was the first Mod in Kildare. I got my grey three-button suit from a local shop—I'd say it was there since the war. My shirt was Bri-Nylon and it wasn't even comfortable, but it looked the part. My shoes were Winstanleys' best, and to top it all off I went to Dublin for my long green parka—no self-respecting Mod would have been seen without one. Oh yeah, I nearly forgot the music—The Jam, The Who, Secret Affair and all the Two Tone bands. That was 1979, or was it 1977? Here we are in 1989; Mods are still around but so too are B-Boys, Cure Heads, Heavy Metallers and Skaters, to mention just the best known.

Peter is a self-confessed B-Boy. His leather boot sneakers are laced up with thick multi-coloured laces, but they're not tied! A yuppie would be proud of Peter's designer track suit. His head was shaved but his hair is growing back—at least as far as I can see it is. His coveted DMC hat covers most of his head. Back in '83 he was fairly good at the auld body popping. He has every streetwave dance compilation ever brought out and he says Hip House is the place to be.

Clinton used to be a roadie for No Sweat. He's a Heavy Metaller, his hair is long, his jeans are tight and his heels are high. He says he's a

new breed of Heavy Metal fan. His heroes are Jon Bon Jovi, Riskie Tempest and Jo Elliot. Harder Metal fans slag Clinton—they say he's a wimp. They say real men are like Metallica, Halloween, Slayer Manowar and Death. Nice lads!

What is a real Cure Head? Michelle claims she is a fully fledged Cure Head. Her hair is gelled skywards. Black eyeliner is her most essential piece of make-up. Her clothes are black and baggy and her footwear is courtesy of Doctor Marten—the air cushion hero. Her boyfriend is David. His favourite song is 'Boys Don't Cry', and you guessed it—he too is a Cure Head.

I met Roy on a Saturday afternoon outside Clive's Skateboard Shop. He's a skater. Roy will not be knocked down on a dark night; his clothes are 'luminous', right from the laces of his Reebok boot sneakers to his headband. His Bermudas show off the make of his skateboard—it's a Powell Peralta Special. His personalised deck has to be seen to be believed. Guns n' Roses and the Hot Chilli Peppers blast out of his Walkman. The music is loud and fast and the ramp is steep.

All the characters listed above are fictional and any resemblance between them and any person living or dead is purely coincidental.

JO-MAXI   JO-MAXI   JO-MAXI   JO-MAXI

Although the programme is primarily aimed at the ten to fourteen age group, RTE discovered that older teenagers are also watching it for bands, fashion items and challenges. Declan explains that they have pitched the programme beyond the ten to fourteen age group so as not to patronise the viewers: 'We have avoided taking the classroom into the studio as we see this as the kids' leisure time and we have put our emphasis on entertainment. We also cover environmental issues, but we don't beat them over the head with civics lessons.' The programme is varied and fast moving, which seems to appeal to its viewers. Both Declan and RTE are very happy with its success so far.

Declan has learned a few things from, and about, young people since he started working on the series. 'Firstly, I've learned that you can't patronise them. Young people want to be treated seriously, and they are extremely honest in their feedback—if they don't like something they say it.' He has found them to be incredibly discriminating consumers, with little loyalty. They will only continue watching the programme as long as it continues to be good and interesting television. He explains that for young viewers, things must be kept moving and short— no item runs more than four to five minutes. Hence the snappy, bitty, varied style of the programme.

What about his role as series producer? 'Basically,' he says, 'the buck stops with me, as I have overall responsibility for the programme and its resources.' The team of producers, presenters, production assistants, researchers and secretary work in a very spontaneous way. 'We are a collection of individuals who do our own thing in close co-operation.' He does not believe that it would work if he took on a 'super-production' role. Declan himself worked previously on another young people's programme called

Borderline, from which he developed some of the ideas that have been used in *Jo-Maxi*.

Declan is lavish in his praise of the film editor and crew who work with the *Jo-Maxi* team. He also speaks with great warmth about the studio 5 crew who 'give everything' to the programme— some of the unseen and unsung heroes of RTE.

How well or badly are young people catered for by RTE in its programming? Declan feels that there is a gap in the fifteen to eighteen year old age group as there is no programme specifically aimed at them. He believes that worldwide television companies have been

Four people at petrol pump

mistaken in portraying a hip and cool image in young people's programmes, as they discriminate against those who are not hip and cool. 'On *Jo-Maxi* we have avoided sticking with any particular image because we want to be available to different kinds of teenagers.' He praises *Nighthawks* as another programme which has experimented with image and avoided any specific one. He also likes the BBC's late night arts show, as it is serious about music and fashion and again has moved away from a rigid 'cool' image. Maybe he's right, and maybe someone in RTE will devise a programme for older teenagers as successful and multi-imaged as *Jo-Maxi*.

WELCOMING TAM INTO YOUR HOME

Teri Garvey explains TAM (Television Audience Measurement) and how RTE gauges that indefinable audience reaction

Whether or not we understand the term, most of us talk about TAM ratings. Ever thought about being a TAM family? Every spring, 2500 families are surveyed by Irish TAM Ltd, a private TV audience measurement company commissioned by RTE and the advertising industry to monitor audience reaction to individual programmes. The houses picked are representative of the whole country, chosen on the basis of age, sex, social class, size of family, type of equipment (two sets, video, teletext etc) and the number of channels, cables and satellites available. 432 houses are carefully selected and are linked to the TAM computer in Dun Laoghaire. Polling takes place between 2 and 5 am each night. The results are analysed by the TAM office and are on screen in RTE by midday, giving them a picture of the previous twenty-four hours' viewing. Each TAM family gets its TV licence paid and is eligible for draws and prizes, but in the main people enjoy the feeling that they are helping RTE monitor viewing.

TAM ratings have been taken since 1962, shortly after RTE opened. Up to now the system of measurement involved quantitative 'headcounting' but this year an appreciation index has been added. This new qualitative approach means that RTE now can know on a daily basis not only what viewers were watching on TV last night but what they thought of it!

The radio audience is measured by door-to-door surveys commissioned by RTE and the Institute of

mathews.

Advertising Practitioners of Ireland. Feedback from TAM and the radio survey goes to the IAPI, the director of programmes, the advertising sales department and to department heads and producers. The information is very important for the planning of programmes, for would-be advertisers and for scheduling. It helps department heads when making adjustments to the content of programmes or personnel. It can even lead to rescheduling of programmes when it is found, for instance, that a programme is going out too early or too late for its target audience, or if it is competing in a time-slot with a programme which would attract a similar audience (eg, a cookery programme and *Coronation Street*).

Audience research, whether it is TAM or a radio survey, means

RTE knows who is watching and listening to what and what they think of it. But if you're not surveyed or you're not a TAM family, you can still let them know what you think. Just ring the Information Office!

AUDIENCE REACTION

If you ring RTE with a complaint about a programme or a query, your call goes through to the Press and Information Office. Here the staff of six deals with all queries of a general nature. It provides information on programmes, gives details about the stars involved, answers questions on future programmes (When are RTE going to show *King Lear*? Why can't we have the *Famous Five* series again?) Every letter gets an answer, often accompanied by information leaflets. The office also prepares listings and publicity releases for programmes, arranges preview screenings of new programmes and deals with press queries.

That doesn't sound too taxing for a staff of six, in an office which is open 363 days a year, from 9.15 am to 12 midnight (shorter hours at weekends), closed only on Christmas Day and St Stephen's Day. Ah yes, but you weren't at the receiving end when the irate woman rang to know what RTE was thinking of by screening such filth as *The Singing Detective* during Holy Week, or the choleric man phoned to complain about the language of a guest on a chat show.

The staff are old hands now at letting callers vent the pent and get rid of the steam that has been building up during a programme, reaching full-boil when the Information Office phone is answered. The staff see themselves as offering a service to the public who are responding to the stimulation of a programme on radio or television. Every call is taken down and logged. If they get a large volume of calls on the same topic (for instance, a drunken or controversial guest on a chat-show), then the staff log the gist of the remarks, otherwise all details are logged. Names and addresses are not asked for unless offered. Often the calls are positive, praising a par-

ticular programme, complimenting a presenter on the handling of a show, admiring a newsreader's change of hairstyle or clothes.

However, human nature being what it is, the negative calls are the most frequent. If it's a good show, then most people sit back and take it for granted. One slip up and we're all on the line to complain, correct the mispronunciation or incorrect fact.

RTE provide the Information Office service on the basis of callers being reasonable (even if irate). They won't divert resources and energy to deal with unreasonably abusive callers. But the staff get used to the regular callers and suspect that there may be many lonely people using the TV, radio and the Information Office as a form of social interaction. Access programmes such as *Mailbag* and *Down the Tube* and the increasing number of phone-in programmes such as *Liveline*, *The Gay Byrne Show*, the *Gerry Ryan Show*, *Examline*, and the phone-in service on *Dempsey's Den*, *The Sunday Game*, the *Late Late Show*, all give the public a great opportunity to air their views on an immediate and direct level. But the phonelines in the Information Office are never still. The calls are recorded in a daily log, then printed and circulated to the RTE authority, senior executives and producers. So you can let RTE know how you feel about things and be sure that your comment will get to the right sources. Must ring in again about that fellow's tie. It's driving me mad!

QUIZTIME
OPERA QUIZ
set by Ray Lynott

1. Why is opera so called?

2. What country is said to be the 'home of opera'?

3. What political significance had Verdi in the mid-nineteenth century?

4. What was Rigoletto's profession?

5. What was Puccini's first name?

6. What opera did Debussy write?

7. Give the English equivalent of the word *aria*.

8. What is the text of an opera called?

9. 'Mary, Mary, quite contrary— how does your garden grow?' Mary _____, the name of an opera singer born in Scotland?

10. Where was Placido Domingo born?

11. Who was 'Maggie from Mayo'?

12. Name the operas of 'The Irish Ring'.

13. When did the Wexford Opera Festival begin?

14. Which founding member of the Wexford Opera Festival died last year?

15. In Ireland, what does OTC stand for?

16. Who sang the title role in Bellini's *Norma* for the Dublin Grand Opera Society this year?

17. Where was the mezzo-soprano Anne Murray born?

(cont. on page 58; answers on page 158)

Napoleon and Josephine: A Love Story

SCHEDULES

Bob Collins, director of TV programmes, explains what the EBU is, and tells how RTE buys and schedules programmes

The EBU (European Broadcasting Union) is an organisation representing all the National Broadcasting Organisations in what is known as the European Broadcasting area—covering all of western and northern Europe and the countries around the Mediterranean. It plays a very important role in representing public service broadcasting on a European basis. The Eurovision network links all the member countries of the EBU and enables exchanges of programmes to take place on a continuing basis. Every day there are exchanges of news material (see Our Katie, p. 4). Viewers will be familiar with the Eurovision Song Contest which is held every year and which is organised under the auspices of the EBU. Similarly, many sports events are co-ordinated, for example, coverage of the Olympic Games is usually a joint operation involving both RTE and the EBU.

The EBU is also involved in bringing programme makers together, in areas such as children's programmes, music and art; in developing programme policy; in evaluating the new broadcasting environment, and in the whole area of technical standards.

THE PURCHASING OF MATERIAL

Every television station in the world makes some of its own programmes and also acquires programmes from other countries. RTE has in recent years made substantial efforts to increase the number of programmes which it makes itself and it has also increased the programmes which it commissions from independent producers. Acquired programmes represent a very important part of RTE's schedules on RTE 1 and Network 2, accounting for about half of total transmission.

The process of acquisition is undertaken very carefully. Every year screenings are held in a number of centres in Europe and America, to which production and distribution companies bring their new and existing programmes so that they can be viewed. In RTE the overall schedule is worked out in advance. Decisions are made about what will be produced by RTE and by independent producers and finally, what will be acquired. Representatives from RTE, from the acquisitions area and the programme departments, attend the screenings and make their selections from what is available.

Of course, not every individual programme that is to be transmitted can be viewed at these screenings. And so there is a group of film acceptance viewers whose task is to view every single acquired programme RTE intends to transmit. This ensures that nothing is broadcast that hasn't been seen and evaluated and any problems which a programme may have, either in terms of its content or for technical reasons, are identified well in advance of its being broadcast.

Meryl Streep at the 1989 Oscar ceremony

John Kavanagh—a great screen or stage actor

Tadhg MacDhonnegáin and Archimedes returning with Eureka *for its third season*

RTE takes considerable care with what it acquires and this is reflected in the quality of acquired programming which it achieves. Many important series have their first ever TV showing on RTE and even more have their first European showing on RTE. Many of our feature films are world premières; *Dallas*, for example, appears on RTE before it can be seen on any other European station and many British productions are shown on RTE before they are available to a British audience.

PROGRAMME SCHEDULING

Perhaps the most difficult thing in broadcasting is to provide a programme schedule which satisfies everybody. It is almost impossible by definition, even with two channels. There will always be occasions when a viewer wishes to see programmes on both channels at the same time; there will always be occasions when a programme is scheduled at a time when a particular viewer has other commitments; there will always be occasions when a viewer cannot maintain continuous attention to a series across the whole of its run.

Every effort is made to minimise these difficulties. As far as possible RTE tries to ensure that programmes appealing to similar audiences are not transmitted at the same time on both channels. With the introduction of Network 2 we have provided as many common junctions as possible, so that a programme on one channel ends as a programme on the other channel is beginning, thus enab-

ling the viewer to make real choices of what she or he wishes to see. Care is taken to ensure that material transmitted when children are viewing is by and large suitable for unsupervised viewing, although parents should never totally abdicate their responsibility for what their children see on television. Every

effort is made to ensure that each day's schedule has a balance of programming within it and that programmes are transmitted at the time when the relevant audience is available to view.

This latter point is an important part of public service broadcasting philosophy, but even if a programme is directed at a comparatively small group it is not relegated to a peripheral time slot on that account. Thus at peak time in our schedule we have Irish language programmes, religious programmes, science programmes, etc. This is an important principle and ensures that the audience gets the best service possible.

The intention of the schedule is to ensure that as many people as possible can watch the programmes RTE transmits, in particular Irish-made programmes. In drawing up the schedule, RTE is aware of the fact that up to 60 per cent of the audience has access to British channels and about 30 per cent has access to satellite channels. This competitive fact of life is taken into account but it is not allowed to determine the way in which RTE's schedules are structured. Those schedules are designed to provide a comprehensive programme service to as wide a section of the audience as possible and to enable viewers to make the widest and most satisfying choice of programming on any day or across any week.

In general, that process works, but it is extremely difficult to find the mix that suits everybody.

with Britt Ekland

with Sue Pollard

The *Late Late Show*,
A handy summer filler by Gay Byrne

If we only hadda known then what we know now . . . Most people who were in at the beginning of any large organisation speak glowingly of those adventurous, heady early days . . . No one too sure of what they were at; people stumbling around in the dark, feeling their way; so it was with the fledgling Telefís Éireann trying to find its feet, its identity and its direction.

In the land of the blind, the one-eyed man is king. And Gaybo was a king. Darn it, I'd had two years flying time on a daily show and news reading for Granada TV in Manchester; a couple of years before that in Radio Éireann, and an early success on the new television service with the *Jackpot Quiz*. So when Tom McGrath wanted to produce an Irish version of America's *Jack Paar Tonight Show*, could he look any further for a host? 'Course not. And he didn't.

Although it was *still* only intended for a handy summer filler. If we only hadda known . . . The rest has been written about, talked about and dissected, as far as I'm concerned, to the point of tedium. My recollections of the highs and lows are all jumbled up together, with dates a total confusion. But I suppose most people in Ireland who've grown up in the past thirty years here have one or two

memories of the *Late Late Show*. 'D'ye remember the night . . .?' All of our special birthday tribute shows were successes: nights of jollity, crack, music and good-will—they came out as they were designed. So many of our other, routine shows did not come out as designed and were disasters. Even as late as this year when we were reaching the stage of believing that if we were no longer turning out award winners, then we were no longer turning out catastrophes either . . . we turned out one of the worst shows, in my estimation, of the past ten years. And it wasn't for want of trying or taking care. It was as if the great god of television (come to think of it, who is the great god of television?) decided to give us a swift smite up our bums to warn us of the dangers of smugness and complacency. Even after twenty-seven years, watch out, fella . . .

I recall the early years of such ferocious controversy, objection and belligerence, when Irish people took their telly so very, *very* seriously. Public hanging was too good for that entire Montrose shower . . . I remember the comedians who took the place apart, and those who tried so hard and died a death . . . So many groups and singers who went on to mighty things, and so many who were never heard of again . . . The extraordinary efforts we made

with some shows to ensure that they would be Important and Significant, only to find them die with a thud from three minutes in . . . and then just for spite taking no care at all the following week and throwing together an evening of Irish rubbish, to find the thing lifting off right from the start and ending up like one of those terrific parties which you can never hope to repeat.

WHEN IT'S TOO LATE FOR REGRETS

What other programme anywhere in the world would talk about death for two hours and get laughs out of it? Even after twenty-seven years, it's a leap into the dark every week. Because there is no knowing how people are going to behave, react and respond on live television, until they're on—by which time it's too late for regrets. Unlike most other similar TV shows in the world, the *Late Late Show* never gets a second chance to do it again. But at its best it has been shown repeatedly that when all the flashing lights are doused; when all the big bands have been silenced; when all the groups have stopped raving; and when all the dancing girls have gone home, television can be at its best just having people talking to each other and telling their own stories in their own way. If they can talk, that is. You need that, y'see, for a Talk Show.

LATE LATE SHOW GUESTS
FROM 1964 TO 1989

A note from the publisher

When the first *Late Late Show* was transmitted twenty-seven years ago, no one knew that it would become the broadcasting institution it now is. Well, maybe, just maybe, Gay Byrne knew...

For twenty-seven years the show has informed, infuriated, and entertained, courtesy of the host, the mixture of guests, panellists and the audiences.

In the following pages we have attempted to list these combined forces since the records of the show began in 1964. The lists speak for themselves—an impressive record of work, a useful source of reference, a memory jogger and a social history of sorts of the past twenty-five years in Ireland.

Year by year the guests are classified as: (pg) panellist or guest, (ent) entertainer, (sp) sports person, (pol) politician, (wr) writer, (med) media person.

Sometimes the categories get mixed up, as, for instance, when an entertainer is on the show as a panellist or guest; or when a politician is also an entertainer . . . (Oops! I mean singer).

These lists are as comprehensive as we could make them, given the records available and our interpretation of them. There are definitely omissions and in some cases there may be errors. We had to take wild guesses on occasions about a particular guest or classification. This is particularly so in relation to the early years. In doing this, we hope no one feels let down. Sadly, we had no space to include the guests who appeared in the 'special shows'. They were just too numerous.

So let's start with—Amongst the guests to appear on the *Late Late Show* during the past twenty-five years were:

Some highlights of the shows

1964

3 October 1964
Rory O'Connor (pg)
Joseph Strick (pg)
Pastor Paul Borchenius (pg)

10 October 1964
Joan Diener (pg)
Madame Eriquetta Aza (pg)

17 October 1964
Earl Jorden (pg)
Sheila Ward (pg)
Sam Thompson (pg)

24 October 1964
Maud Liddy (pg)
Louis Marcus (pg)
Seán Kavanagh (pg)
Kruger Kavanagh (pg)
Proinsias Mac Aonghusa (med)
Cecil Sheridan (ent)

31 October 1964
Proinsias Mac Aonghusa (med)
Cecil Sheridan (ent)
Sheila Walsh (med)
Dr Pat O'Callaghan (pg)
Veronica Dunne (ent)
Rev M Gray-Stack (pg)
Johnny Butler (pg)

7 November 1964
Proinsias Mac Aonghusa (med)
Cecil Sheridan (ent)
Sheila Walsh (med)
Renato Sidoli (pg)
Lorcan Bourke (pg)
Pat Murphy (pg)

14 November 1964
Cecil Sheridan (ent)
Mary Nolan (pg)
Pat Murphy (pg)
Bramwell Fletcher (pg)
Denis Mornaghan (pg)
Isabella Wallich (pg)
Mary Wales-North (pg)
John O'Donovan (pg)
Martin Crosbie (ent)

21 November 1964
Denis Franks (pg)

Pat Murphy (pg)
John O'Donovan (pg)
Maisie McDaniel (ent)
Peggy O'Hara (pg)
Madge O'Neill (pg)
Mrs Marty Mann (pg)
E C Pickering (pg)
L Barry (pg)
Marjorie Harte Barry (pg)
Neill Crawford (pg)
J G Cooney (pg)
Mrs J Davis (pg)

28 November 1964
Madge O'Neill (pg)
Ted Bonner (pg)
John McConville (pg)
Ann Iremonger (pg)
Paddy Bolger (pg)
Lord Altamont (pg)

5 December 1964
Lord Altamont (pg)
Yvonne Voigt Molloy (pg)
Bernard Carr (pg)
Michael Corcoran (pg)
Sgt Major Donald Cosgrove (pg)
Dr Colm O'Lochlann (pg)

12 December 1964
Paddy Bolger (pg)
Séamus Duke (pg)
Frankie Byrne (med)
Danny Gunnery (pg)
Rev Fr McDyer (pg)

19 December 1964
Des Benson (pg)
Ann Rowan (pg)
John O'Donovan (pg)
Desmond O'Neill (pg)
Francis Kendall (pg)
A C McLaughlin (pg)
Sr M Gertrude (pg)

26 December 1964
Pat Murphy (pg)
Margaret O'Neill (pg)
Ted Bonner (pg)
Kitty Eu (pg)
John Kendrick (pg)
Matthew K Osei (pg)
Mairtín Ó Dioláin (pg)
Ivan Beshoff (pg)

1965
2 October 1965
Jane Johnston (pg)
Matthew Doolan (pg)
Patrick Power (pg)

9 October 1965
Trudy Simms (pg)
Godfrey Wynn (pg)

16 October 1965
Bunny Carr (pg)
Carmel Quinn (pg)

23 October 1965
Clement Freud (pg)
Seán Keating (pg)
Frank Leddin (pg)

30 October 1965
Denis Franks (pg)
Mr M Von Mossihizker (pg)
Ray McAnally (pg)
Paul Farrell (pg)

6 November 1965
Brian Devanney (med)
Tom O'Dea (med)
T de Vere White (med)
Brendan Cauldwell (ent)
Maureen Potter (ent)
Rosaleen Lenihan (ent)
Cecil Sheridan (ent)
Fr Walter Macken (pg)
Milo O'Shea (pg)
Mr E Brophy (pg)
Seán Bolger (pg)
Billy Seamons (pg)

13 November 1965
Miriam Woodbyrne (pg)
Kevin Anyanwu (pg)
Veronica Hartland (pg)
Desmond Leslie (pg)

20 November 1965
Gladys Waller (pg)
Matt Doolin (pg)
Patsy Dyke (med)

4 December 1965
Ulick O'Connor (wr)
John Hauxvell (pg)
Naomi Kidney (pg)
Joe Carr (pg)
John B Keane (wr)
Julian Bream (ent)

11 December 1965
Ulick O'Connor (wr)

Naomi Kidney (pg)
Mrs S Kelly (pg)
Honor Blackman (pg)

18 December 1965
Ulick O'Connor (wr)
Naomi Kidney (pg)
Mrs C S Archer (pg)
Ned Sherrin (pg)
Caryl Brahms (pg)
Bridie Gallagher (ent)

1966
8 January 1966
C S Archer (pg)
Sandra Bromley (pg)
Tom Lynch (pg)
Lily Curtis (pg)
Mrs O Clarke (pg)
John Jacobs (pg)
Sen Eoin Ryan (pol)
Sen Garret Fitzgerald (pol)
Sen Owen Sheehy Skeffington (pol)
Michael O'Beirne (pg)

15 January 1966
C S Archer (pg)
Sandra Bromley (pg)
Tom Lynch (pg)
Joyce Gardiner (pg)
Eoin Ó Maghthamhna (pg)
Patricia O'Reilly (pg)
Lady Glenavy (pg)

22 January 1966
C S Archer (pg)
Tom Lynch (pg)
Greta Hodgins (pg)
Marnie Nixon (pg)
Lord Altamont (pg)
Eliza Sherriff (pg)

29 January 1966
Ulick O'Connor (wr)
Greta Hodgins (pg)
Tom Lynch (pg)
Paul Vincze (pg)
Mr W Norton (pg)
Clement Freud (pg)
Norman Vaughan (pg)
Michael Miles (pg)

5 February 1966
Greta Hodgins (pg)
Tom Lynch (pg)
Matt Gallagher (pg)
Esther Mulvey (pg)

Fr Michael Cleary (pg)
Paul Goldin (ent)

12 February 1966
Greta Hodgins (pg)
Joe Lynch (ent)
Matt Gallagher (pg)
Harry Armitage (pg)
Mr Francis O'Flanagan (pg)
Fr de Rocquois (pg)

19 February 1966
Dr J Cooney (pg)
Michael Viney (pg)
Rev D Dargan (pg)
John Keogh (ent)
Mr R Perceval (pg)
Dickie Rock (ent)
James Flannery (ent)
Mr W O'Neill (pg)

26 February 1966
Mrs W Burrowes (pg)
Eoin 'The Pope' O'Mahony (pg)
Major G Moorhead (pg)
Bryan MacMahon (wr)
Maureen Potter (ent)

5 March 1966
Joe Lynch (ent)
Brian Friel (wr)
Mrs W Burrowes (pg)
Robert Carrier (pg)
Tom Jones (ent)
Bowyer Family (ent)
Stirling Moss (pg)

12 March 1966
Mrs M Bowes-Daly (pg)
Joe Lynch (ent)
Hal Roach (ent)
Hilton Edwards (pg)
John Molloy (pg)
Peter West (pg)
Clement Freud (pg)

19 March 1966
Joe Lynch (ent)
Hal Roach (ent)
Mary O'Callaghan (ent)
Dominic Behan (wr)
Joseph Denver (pg)
Nadia Cattouse (pg)
Bunny Lewis (pg)

26 March 1966
Brian Trevaskis (pg)
(cont. on page 48)

AN APOLOGY FOR FARMERS

It was Virgil who wrote: 'Lucky beyond bliss are farmers, if only they knew their own happiness.' Paddy Smith says it might be true, but for the weather . . .

Every time you hear or see a farmer on the radio or on television, he seems to be complaining about something or other. In many people's minds, it has got to the stage where they would collapse with surprise if the leader of one of our farming organisations came on air and said things were going well.

Not that it will be any consolation to these people, but Irish farmers are no different from farmers anywhere else in the world. A politician friend of mine confirmed this for me recently when telling me about his official visits to East Germany and Taiwan. Department of Agriculture officials in each country addressed him and his colleagues at great length about all they were doing for their farmers; my friend—rather mischievously, I suspect—asked if their farmers were happy. His question was greeted with roars of laughter from the officials, who were obviously tickled pink at the very idea that farmers could be content with their lot!

Indeed, I discovered recently that farmers have always been perceived in the same way. The poet/writer Virgil said it all 2000 years ago and even his colloquial Latin could not disguise his bemusement when he declared (in translation, of course): 'Lucky beyond bliss are farmers, if only they knew their own happiness.'

Even in ancient Rome they must have realised that if there is one single factor that causes pessimism and general disgruntlement among farmers, it is the weather: Our own climate may be the envy of the world when it comes to farming, but it is difficult to be convinced of its benefits if you are standing in the rain forking out hay to hungry store cattle on a dark winter afternoon. Statistically, the rainfall figures are 750mm per annum in the east and 1300mm in the west, south-west and north-west. But there is not a farmer in the entire country who would not swear to you that each and every drop of that rain falls on his fields/crops when he doesn't want it. He needs only 400mm of it for his grass to thrive, but that

It rarely arrives when necessary

amount is required at very specific times of the year and, being an average figure, it of course rarely arrives when needed.

A dairy farmer once summed up for me his paradoxical attitude to the weather. He was growing his own barley for feeding to his cows and he definitely didn't want any rain on the bottom field, where the barley stood high and heavy. But there had been no rain for the previous two weeks, so he simply had to have it for the grass, which would otherwise 'melt' away before the summer was over. What that man prayed for at his bedside at night, I never discovered. Those 'local showers' that the weathermen often talk about could hardly be expected to

be so local that they would fall on the fields of grass and leave the cornfield dry. He probably got the rain on the barley and none on the grass—and, being a farmer and knowing in his heart and soul that the worst always happens, he would not have been in the least bit surprised.

The sheer impossibility of my friend getting what he wanted in that particular instance can easily be generalised into a statement that 'farmers are never satisfied'. Well, would you be—if you were so dependent on the vagaries of Irish weather? Me, I get upset if it rains when we bring the kids the forty miles to see their granny (I hate driving in wet weather). But if somebody told me that my monthly salary cheque would be that much smaller because of the inclement weather for the previous four weeks—well now, let's see, what did I do with the number of the union rep?

It is ironic to think that it is the weather that causes one of the primary divisions of understanding between town and country, simply because non-farmers can never fully appreciate the damage that failure to control the elements can have on the already tricky job of growing and producing off the land.

Make no mistake about it, good farming is a skilful business, even more so in an age of specialisation. A couple of years ago, our family went off on a farmhouse holiday in the west and we had a wonderful time, but a major source of disappointment to us was the fact that the drystock farm we stayed

Paddy Smith's quiet rural tones are broadcast to the farmers of Ireland before the 8.00 am news on radio. His unusual approach has won him lots of town and city support.

on was merely that—a beef fattening farm, with no other farm animals whatsoever. The milk we put on our cornflakes each morning was delivered in cartons by a milkman and there were no hens in the yard to lay the eggs we had for breakfast. This specialisation is certainly nothing to complain about from the farmer's point of view, but having all one's eggs in one enterprise basket has to be a source of worry; if things go wrong, as they frequently do, they can go very wrong.

A move towards less intensive concentration on single-enterprise farming has been taking place in the last couple of years, mainly enforced by an EC that has, at long last, begun to succeed in tackling the vexed question of surpluses. A familiar sight at the sheep mart in recent years has been the slightly bewildered dairy farmer who has decided that lamb production is the thing to diversify into, partly because it is profitable but also because it is one of the few areas into which he can expand his otherwise restricted business, due to milk quotas. He is bewildered because he doesn't know the first thing about sheep and is hoping that his ignorance isn't showing. He will spend his

couple of thousand pounds on lambs, have them lorried home and then fret about them as they break out into the neighbour's land through the most carefully built fences. He has too much pride to ask somebody how to manage the little monsters, and you can be sure he won't complain to anybody about his lot.

ENVY, BEGRUDGERY OR FRUSTRATION

The traditional and historical lack of understanding between town and country is as nothing compared to the friction between farmer and farmer that has become a modern-day phenomenon—specifically between dairy farmers and the rest. Call it envy, begrudgery or frustration, it is reaching levels of viciousness and is causing much unhappiness due to the fact that dairy farmers have streaked ahead of everyone else. The much dreaded milk quotas and superlevy have, in fact, turned out to be a veritable boon to dairy producers, who have never had it so good. By 1988 the average net margin per acre from creamery milk was up to six times the margins in the other enterprises.

If you still feel that farmers complain too much, then don't criticise them with your mouth full! They do grow the food you're stuffing yourself with and there is

nothing calculated to annoy them more than unreasonable attitudes among consumers—mainly because the consumer, being the customer, is always right, even when he/she is wrong. This was most obvious in the debate about the use of artificial hormones in cattle, when the EC decided that, even though its own expert committee had carried out a very comprehensive study of the subject and found that there was no cause for unease, hormones should be banned because consumers felt they were harmful—and that was that.

A 1989 survey of Irish consumers' concerns about diet presented the frustrating information that the thing they were most worried about was the presence of antibiotics in beef. The fact that antibiotics are rarely if ever used in beef production is beside the point; if the public's ill-conceived fears turn sufficiently against antibiotics in farming, these products may be banned too. Who does a farmer complain to about that?

So, if things are so bad with farmers, why are they not dying out? Well, the fact of the matter is that they are. Of the 114,000 full-time farmers in Ireland, less than 70,000 will survive on the land by the end of the next decade, according to economists, and the figure will drop to around 30,000 by the year 2030.

Oh, goody, you might say—there will be less of them around to moan. Indeed. But I have a feeling in my bones that those who are left will just complain louder!

QUIZTIME
FARMING QUIZ

set by Paddy Smith

1. The average price of milk is about £1 per gallon to the farmer. What was it in 1973 when we joined the Common Market?

2. When ACOT and the Agricultural Institute (the farm advisory and research services) were amalgamated in 1988, what was the new organisation called?

3. What RTE TV farming programme has won a large number of international awards?

4. Who was Minister for Agriculture when the 25th Dáil was dissolved in May of this year?

5. Which well-known cereal disease has Mike Murphy referred to on Radio 1 as 'a new kind of Irish dance'?

6. What is the Irish for 'ragwort'?

7. Up to 70 per cent of the land being farmed in the EC is rented rather than owned. What is the equivalent figure for Ireland?

8. What plant disease is commonly recorded around the end of May in conditions of over 95 per cent humidity and temperatures greater than 10°C?

9. Boundary fencing of at least 6ft high is recommended for what kind of farming?

10. What month, on average, is the driest month of the year in Ireland?

11. What farm animal can thrive in conditions as cold as minus 20°C?

12. What farm animal cannot survive under 32°C?

13. Who became president of the National Farmers Association in 1967?

14. When rising, does a cow stand first on her hind legs or forelegs?

15. Who were the original 'six' in the EEC?

16. In which product does Ireland have A, B and C quotas?

17. In 1941, Ireland had the last outbreak of which cattle disease?

18. On 1 September 1977, it became obligatory to fit what on all tractors?

19. Which red and white cattle breed was introduced to Ireland in 1775?

20. ERAD is the farm body responsible for what?

21. Which political party leader used to be economic adviser to the NFA?

22. What farm waste produce is 220 times stronger as a pollutant than domestic sewerage?

23. What agricultural body was set up in 1958 with the help of Marshall Aid from the US?

24. In the High Court on 23 July 1982, what was declared unconstitutional after 130 years in operation?

25. The Irish Farmers Association HQ is at the Farm Centre, Bluebell, Dublin, but where were its offices (as the NFA)?

26. Grange, Co. Meath, is the field base for what kind of agricultural research?

27. The average size of a farm in the UK is 172 acres. What is the average in Ireland?

28. And in Germany?

29. And Italy?

30. The second largest farming organisation is the ICMSA. What do the letters stand for?

31. In which city does the ICMSA have its headquarters?

32. Who took over from Michael Lally as agricultural correspondent in RTE earlier this year?

33. When he retired as secretary of the Department of Agriculture, Jim O'Mahony joined the board of which company?

34. Ireland joined the EEC in 1973, but formal application was first made on 1 August of which year?

35. Which Irish county was the first area in Ireland or Britain to be officially declared brucellosis-free?

36. What farm animal will often abandon its young if any human assistance is given at birth?

(Answers on page 158)

WHAT THE STARS HAVE
IN STORE FOR THE STARS

Austin Byrne and Una Rogan, *Live at Three* astrologers, give four predictions for 1990
Teri Garvey reports...

Thelma Mansfield

How many readers look up their horoscope in papers and magazines? Those who do probably accept the promise of a 'windfall' or a 'romantic meeting with a dark stranger' but if the predictions are any less pleasant they tend to dismiss them as rubbish. But are they?

Most horoscopes found in magazines or daily papers are so general they probably are rubbish (otherwise wouldn't a twelfth of the population be off spending the windfall while the other lot would be falling over dark strangers at every bus-stop!). But what of the professional astrologer? How much more accurate are they?

We gave the birth-times (but no other details) of four RTE personalities to astrologers Austin Byrne and Una Rogan, both known to many of you from their appearances on *Live at Three*. This is what we got back.

THELMA MANSFIELD

Austin says:

A very creative person with much centred on her own performance, image and style. Very good actress and would have a first preference for the theatre. Exceptionally generous, surprisingly self-conscious, but her acting and self-projection skills over-ride this tendency with ease. Enjoys cooking and loves to prepare original and exotic dishes.

If she is prepared to change her job in 1990, she will make it highly successful. It will throw up a dilemma, should or shouldn't she stay in broadcasting? An alternative job appears in March and April. Travel in July is beneficial. By the last quarter of 1990 it seems very likely that job status has altered quite considerably. It certainly does suggest that whatever role is taken on, it's very much a higher profile one and mostly along the lines of what she herself would prefer to do, and do even better. So 1990 is going to be a dramatic year.

Una says:

In terms of career some unexpected offers will be made and these should be thought through and negotiated with care and awareness. The summer months are important with the possibility of public recognition or an award in the autumn. There are some wonderful opportunities for expansion on the creative level. A natural gift for creative writing shows very strongly and will be stimulated by planetary aspects in 1990. A combination of inspiration and imagination if followed through and expressed could produce a work that would be a best seller.

CYNTHIA NÍ MHURCHÚ

Austin says:

A talker with a very adaptable nature who can cut losses very quickly. A tendency to change horses mid-stream can highlight versatility. Most likely a writer, certainly someone who would succeed in journalism. The world of communications offers great opportunities. Tends to be linguistic. Fond of cycling, card-games and motor sport. Could have a talent for golf.

The likelihood of making a special discovery figures strongly in this chart and could mean that this person, through persistent effort and willingness to improvise, might strike it very rich indeed.

Can interpret well and is talented at transcribing or adapting scripts. Life as a playwright could show itself to be worthwhile. An interest in studying law always colours the academic persuasion.

Una says:

1990 could see this person ride on the crest of a wave or be totally engulfed by it. The alert, expansive and investigative mind of this individual will be stimulated in a very innovative way. A natural communicator, ready to take on any challenge, this person will certainly be faced with the opportunity to display their talents in 1990, and February, May, June and December will be significant in this regard. Needs to guard against impatience and forcefulness. In terms of relationships there could be a new intense one which will feature strongly.

MYLES DUNGAN

Austin says:

Intense personality and a sharp turn of authority. Loves the night-time and tends very much to be the night owl. Very imaginative,

loves music and poetry, delights in all things artistic. The eyes are a striking feature, deep and penetrating.

A career in music shows strongly. A very successful 'tour of duty' is augured for 1989. 'Name in lights' and that sort of thing. 1990 will be the year for taking the initiative on your own home ground. In January you will benefit from a remarkable success related to sport. An invitation to go abroad advances your career in 1990. Best time for travel and work is November.

Una says:

Some great opportunities on the career level, ambitions will be higher than usual and a project started in June 1989 could begin to show some positive results. Travel could take up a great deal of time but could also produce some outstanding opportunities and bring about a level of excitement and independence this person needs. Health needs careful attention, especially possible allergic reactions.

RONAN COLLINS

Austin says:

This person is gentle, tactful and diplomatic, fashion-conscious, with a lovely home, popular with children, a difficult person to get really annoyed with. Not so sporty, fond of dancing, the ballet is likely to have a special place of interest. This person doesn't like a rough hard-lined approach.

Moving is the keynote for 1990, showing it to be a year when changes of residence over the following four years will be initiated. A more involved area of research is highlighted for 1990; it puts a special emphasis on careers

and may involve having to take over a project, thus saving it from failure.

Work which is connected to a new 'colouring' or 'dyeing' technique will require more study and research. October is a very successful month when it comes to recruiting a work force, getting the right people for the right job, enhancing your standing as a diplomat and negotiator. This could be a major year for discovery if you are prepared to experiment.

Una says:

It is important to establish a strong sense of identity in 1990. Despite being Libran, there is quite a revolutionary side to this person which might hinder their ambitions and endeavours. They need to tune more into the humanitarian, charismatic side where publicity can be of real value both personally and socially. Foundations laid in 1990 are an important basis for the next three to four years and it is important to get them right.

What do our personalities think?

We left Thelma out on the grounds that Austin and Una accidentally discovered her identity before making their predictions.

Myles Dungan felt that it was close enough to be accurate but he thought a career in music was most unlikely—his singing and piano playing are confined to private parties!

Ronan thought his was totally off beam—he has no interest in fashion or ballet. He conceded he was popular with children but said he was neither gentle nor diplomatic.

Cynthia said hers was quite surprisingly accurate. The interest in law studies, in cycling, the linguistic ability, the family in-

terest in golf, all were correct—but she has no interest in motor sports.

What do you think? Whatever about the personality assessments, we'll just have to wait and see how accurately all those career predictions turn out in 1990. You can bet that our four personalities will be keeping an eye on their personal forecasts as 1990 comes along!

(cont. from page 41)

Liz Burrowes (pg)
Matt Doolan (pg)
Mark Grantham (pg)
Wesley Burrowes (pg)
Normah Smythe (pg)
Michael Ó Moráin (pg)
Mary Stewart (pg)

2 April 1966
Liz Burrowes (pg)
Matt Doolan (pg)
Brian Trevaskis (pg)
Vincent Grogan (pg)
Dr Conor Cruise O'Brien (pg)
John Gregson (ent)
Maurice Woodruff (pg)
Seán Whelan (pg)

9 April 1966
Liz Burrowes (pg)
Matt Doolan (pg)
Brian Trevaskis (pg)
Barry Morse(pg)
Louis Rukeyser (pg)
Clancy Brothers (ent)
Des Brannigan (pg)
Gwynford Evans (pg)

16 April 1966
Bryan McMahon (wr)
Andréas Ó Gallchóir (med)
Owen Dudley Edwards (wr)
Louis Lentin (med)
Tim Pat Coogan (med)
Tomás MacAnna (pg)

23 April 1966
Tom Lynch (pg)
Mary O'Callaghan (pg)
Tom Ryan (pg)
Edward Delaney (pg)
Stanley Unwin (pg)
Ted Moult (pg)
Sandie Shaw (ent)
Mr B Sweeney (pg)

30 April 1966
Tom Lynch (pg)
Mary O'Callaghan (pg)
Tom Ryan (pg)
Dan O'Herlihy (pg)
David Hedison (pg)
Peter Murray (pg)

6 May 1966
Tom Lynch (pg)
Mary O'Callaghan (pg)
Tom Ryan (pg)
Val Doonican (ent)
Kadar Asmal (pg)
Diana Collins (pg)
Lelord Kordel (pg)
John H McGrath (pg)
John McCormack (ent)
Jim Norton (pg)
John Farrell (pg)
Mary Farrell (pg)
Mr F Cahsen (pg)
Joseph Moran (pg)

14 May 1966
Sally Ogle (pg)
Ted Bonner (pg)
Ulick O'Connor (wr)
Hughie Green (pg)
Tomás McAnna (pg)
Betty Kenny (pg)

21 May 1966
Sally Ogle (pg)
Ted Bonner (pg)
Rev Fr E Casey (pg)
Herman Donchin (pg)

28 May 1966
Sally Ogle (pg)
Ted Bonner (pg)
Matt Doolan (pg)

Mr E Peters McDermott (pg)
Ernest Jocher (pg)
Mrs E O'Carroll (pg)
W Mullins (pg)

1967

30 September 1967
Julius Katchen (ent)
Freddie Davies (pg)
Atlantic Rowers (pg)
Greville Wynne (pg)
Carmel Quinn (pg)
Dick Cameron (pg)
Ted Bonner (pg)
Séamus McConville (pg)
Kevin Kennedy (pg)

7 October 1967
The Dalys (ent)
Alun Owen (pg)
Hector Grey (pg)
MacAongusa/Brown/O'Leary (pg)
Tony Drennan Group (ent)
Ted Bonner (pg)

14 October 1967
American Indians & Freeman (pg)
Flor O'Mahony (pg)
Castlebar Songs (ent)
Wexford Festival Queen (pg)
Butch Moore (ent)
Brendan Bowyer (ent)

21 October 1967
Fr O'Connor & Clerics (pg)

28 October 1967
Milo O'Shea (pg)
L Constantine (pg)
Jack Hage (pg)
Chester Harriot (pg)
Ted Bonner (pg)
Mary Leland (wr)

4 November 1967
Seán McCarthy (pg)
Seán D Loftus (pg)
Redeway (ent)
Des Fennell (med)
Gerry Lawless (pg)
Leif Reck Group (ent)
Mary Leland (wr)

11 November 1967
Sir Basil Goulding (pg)
Bruce Arnold (med)
Edward Delaney (pg)
Clement Freud (pg)
Kay Johnson (pg)
1st Mate Desmond Murphy (pg)
Liz Willoughby (pg)
Brigeen Gilroy (ent)
Joan Horan (pg)
Danny Doyle (ent)

18 November 1967
Larry Adler (ent)
Miriam Makeba (ent)
Michael Emmerson (pg)
Adam Darins (pg)
Tom Kinsella (pg)
John McGahern (wr)

25 November 1967
Fr Bright (pg)
Spike Milligan (pg)
Claude Cockburn (pg)
Alasdair Gillies (pg)
Charles McCarthy (pg)

2 December 1967
Rural Programme
Fr McDyer (pg)
Eithne Viney (pg)
Tony O'Reilly (pg)

Dick McCarthy (pg)
Brian Daly (pg)
Tremeloes (ent)

9 December 1967
Beth Bryant (wr)
Fr O'Donoghue (pg)
Ken Wood (pg)
Mary Leland (wr)
Bruce Arnold (med)

16 December 1967
Carmel Quinn (pg)
Beth Bryant (pg)
Bridget Hogan O'Higgins (pg)

Angela McNamara (pg)
Ruth Bradley (pg)
Monica McEnroy (pg)
Bernadette McLoughlin (pg)
Pat Cahill (ent)
Backing Group:
Jack Daly
Jim McKay
Rick Walsh
Tony Drennan

23 December 1967
J Ryan (pg)
Frank Dougan (pg)
James Doyle (pg)
John Walsh (pg)
Garda-Sgt Brendan Colvert (pg)
T Harkin (pg)
Abe Weiners (pg)
Mr Mooney (pg)
Mrs Mooney (pg)

30 December 1967
Chris Meredith (wr)
The Pattersons (ent)
Gerry Collins (pg)
Marcus Clements (pg)
Kitty Eu & husband (pg)
Arkel (pg)
Fr Dowling (pg)
Nora Courtney (pg)
Paul Hughes (pg)
Thomas Doyle (pg)
Paddy O'Sullivan (pg)
P J Fortune & Fox (pg)

1968

6 January 1968
Alan Cowle (pg)
Paddy Crosbie (pg)
Frank Crummy (pg)
Sen Brosnahan (pg)
Dr Cyril Daly (pg)
Ulick O'Connor (wr)
Frankie McBride (ent)

13 January 1968
Kate Pratt (pg)
Twins & Co (ent)
Tony Hopkins (pg)
Freshmen (ent)
Cork Musical Society (ent)
John Hauxvell (pg)
Mary Sheridan (pg)
Alan Cowle Band (ent)

20 January 1968
Tony Butler (pg)
Moore Street Traders (pg)
The Sands (ent)
Ger McInerney (pg)
Maeve Allen (pg)

27 January 1968
A J P Taylor (pg)
Desmond O'Kennedy (pg)
Dillon-Mahon (pg)
Kathleen Watkins & Deirdre O'Callaghan (pg)

3 February 1968
Gordon Colleary (pg)

John B Keane (wr)
Kirby Turner (pg)
Oliver J Flanagan (pol)
Anthony Butler (pg)
Larry Cunningham (ent)
Johnny McEvoy (ent)

10 February 1968
Eurofashion-8 models
Gillian Gazalet (pg)
Ralph Moore (pg)
Al Cox (pg)
Seán Dunphy (ent)
Ira Henry & group (ent)

17 February 1968
John O'Hanlon (pg)
Paul Rowan (pg)
Paddy Bolger (pg)
John Murray (pg)
Dick Stevins (pg)
Dana (ent)
Alice Boyle (pg)
Helen Burke (pg)
Greta Sweeney (pg)
John Skehan (med)
Ann Whelehan (pg)

24 February 1968
Dr Boydell (pg)
Dowland Consort (ent)
Miss Malalieu & students (pg)
William Daly (pg)
Vincent Scally (med)

2 March 1968
Val Doonican (ent)
Seán O'Shea (pg)
P Canning (med)
Hughie Green (pg)
Prof Suzuki & Prof Shamitz (pg)

9 March 1968
Angela Collins (pg)
S Baker (pg)
Séamus Kelly (ent)
Maire Keane (ent)
Phyllis Diller (ent)
Peter Law (pg)

18 March 1968
Special from London

23 March 1968
Dr Stanley Browne (pg)

Ann Davis and Glynis Miller (pg)
T P O'Neill (pg)
Proinsias MacAonghusa (med)
Ernest Blythe (pol)
Danny Doyle (ent)

30 March 1968
Joe Rea (pg)
Pat McGeegan (ent)
Arthur Wise (pg)
Angela McNamara (pg)
Wolsey Gracey (pg)
Johnny Johnson (pg)
N S C Winner (pg)

6 April 1968
No Show

13 April 1968
Doc Carroll (pg)
Noel Purcell (pg)
Stanley Dunne (pg)
Denis Bruton (pg)
Obe Egibino (pg)
Cream Crackers (ent)
Dickie Rock (ent)
Irish National Opera (ent)

20 April 1968
Innes Ireland (pg)
Fr Mick Cleary (pg)
Richard Behal (pg)
Cathal Goulding (pg)
Vincent McDovell (pg)
Liam O'Brian (pg)
Tony Lynch (pg)
Lorrian & Sean (pg)
Alma Carroll (ent)

27 April 1968
Fergal O'Connor (pg)
Kevin and Helen Clear (pg)
Dr Mary Hynes (pg)
Dr Karl Mullen (pg)
Pacific Showband (ent)
Anne Bushnell (ent)

4 May 1968
Jimmy Saville (pg)
Fr Ag. Andrews (pg)
Donald Connoly (pg)
Rev. Wormbrund (pg)
Des Fennel (med)
The Johnsons (ent)
Jim Farley (ent)
Liz Willoughby (pg)

11 May 1968
Charles Kidd (pg)
Ulick O'Connor (wr)
Rodd Redving (pg)
James Clavell (wr)
Peter Lennon & film
Michael O'Duffy (pg)
Marian Propst (pg)

18 May 1968
Gordon Clarke/Sherlock Holmes (pg)
Mary Stanley (pg)
A L Choir (ent)
Tina and Maxi (ent)
Kathy Harrup (ent)

25 May 1968
Sheila Scott (pg)
Dr Conor Cruise O'Brien (pg)
Chester Harriot (pg)
Bachelors (ent)

1 June 1968
Michael Aspel (med)
Charles Acton (med)
Mike Meaney (pg)
Emmet Spiceland (ent)
Smokey Mountain Boys (ent)

8 June 1968
No Show

15 June 1968
Sally Ogle (pg)
John Montague (wr)
Tomás McAnna (pg)
Fr A Kennedy (pg)
Thomas Rosengrave (pg)
Movement (ent)
Wolf Tones (ent)
Dermot O'Brien (ent)

22 June 1968
John Kendrick (pg)
Nobby Stiles (sp)
A S Neal (pg)
Paddy Dwane (pg)
Declan Burke-Kennedy (pg)
Bro Minoge (pg)
Harry Hawe (pg)
Dermot O'Brien (pg)
Nazareth House Band (ent)
Dr Strangely Strange (ent)

29 June 1968
Sen Garret Fitzgerald (pol)
Charles McCarthy (pg)
Des Fennell (med)
Joe Foyle (pg)
Bryan McMahon (wr)
Bart Cronin (pg)
Terence de Vere White
   (chairman)
Liz Willoughby (pg)

28 September 1968
John Betjman (wr)
Peter Maloney (pg)
Phil Coulter (ent)
Maureen Toal (pg)
Performing Bear (ent)
Maria Kozchinska (pg)

5 October 1968
Rosemary Hulme (pg)
Andrew Hamilton (pg)
Desmond Cunningham (pg)
J Robert Emmet (pg)
Robert Emmet (pg)
Lee Dunne (wr)
Bill Verrity (pg)
Brenda McManus (pg)
Jack Daly (pg)
Ian Whitcombe (pg)

12 October 1968
Michelman Cox (pg)
Fr Jack Kelly (pg)
Charles McCarthy (pg)
D J Cullinan (pg)
Gay O'Brien & film
Robin Bailie (pg)
Trinity Players (ent)
Don O'Hare Trio (ent)

19 October 1968
Johnny O'Donoghue (pg)
Colm Kelly (pg)
Tommy Power (pg)
Publicans in audience:
Leo Fagan and Mr O'Leary
Festival Queen (pg)
The Pattersons (ent)

26 October 1968
Dan O'Herlihy (pg)
Seán Burke (pg)
Ulick O'Connor (wr)
Eileen Proctor (pg)
Valerie Sheridan (pg)
Bob Gallico (pg)
Jim Norton with a cow
Herb Moulton Trio (ent)
Danny Doyle (ent)

2 November 1968
Peter Brinson (pg)

Terry Wogan (med)
Brendan Balfe (med)
Mike Murphy (med)
B P Fallon (med)
Ruth Buchanan (pg)
Liz Wogan (pg)
Freda McGough (pg)
Benny Cauldwell (pg)
Tom Studley (pg)
Aedin Ní Caoimh (pg)
Rex McGall (pg)
Hoggert (pg)
Noel Carroll (pg)
Mick Dowling (pg)
John M Ferguson Trio (ent)
Dickie Rock (ent)
Reform Quartet (ent)

9 November 1968
Maureen Potter (pg)
Anjelica Huston (pg)
Henry Higgins & film
Fr Desmond O'Brien SJ (pg)
Rev Michael McGrail (pg)
Inez Heron (pg)
The Cotton Mill Boys (ent)
Bill Stapleton and Audio
   Visual Machine (pg)

16 November 1968
Susan Hampshire (pg)
Paddy McClintock (pg)
Calton Younger (pg)
D Brannigan (pg)
Donal McCartney (pg)
'Finian's Rainbow' (ent)
Frankie Ford (pg)

23 November 1968
John Taylor (pol)

John Hume (pol)
Ivan Cooper (pol)
Ian Hill (pg)
William Houston (pg)
Barry Kent (pg)
Betty Sinclair (ent)
Edward Pearl (ent)
Noel Picarda (pg)
Major Bunting (pg)
Ray Bradford (pg)
John Dankworth (pg)
Cleo Laine (pg)
Richard Stilgoe (pg)
Kenneth Tynan (pg)

30 November 1968
Stephanie Sachs (pg)
Emperor Rosco (pg)
Mrs Jim Reeves (pg)
Christine Turnbull (pg)
Tony O'Dalaigh (pg)
D Breathnach (pg)
Johnny McEvoy (ent)
Barry St John (pg)

7 December 1968
Major G Underwood (pg)
Mrs Jessie Nason (pg)
Dr Conor Cruise O'Brien (pg)
Major R Bunting (pg)
Patricia Cahill (ent)
Seán Dunphy (ent)
Mrs Murray (ent)
Desmond Domican Dancers
   (ent)
Prudence Smith (nuns) (pg)

14 December 1968
Joe Lynch (pg)
Frank McCourt (pg)
Patrick Clancy (pg)
David Cassidy (pg)
David D Hurley (pg)
Ruairí Roberts (pg)
Peter Moloney (pg)
The Cameos (ent)
The Gypsies (ent)

21 December 1968
Des Keogh (ent)
Tom Mennard (pg)
Frank Murphy (pg)
Mary Cooney (ent)

Jean Begley (pg)
Inez Heron (pg)
Tim Dennehy (pg)

28 December 1968
Ted Bonner (pg)
Wolsey Gracie (pg)
Clare Boylan (wr)
Ulick O'Connor (wr)
Finbar Dowling (pg)
Tommy Dand (ent)
Tom O'Donnell (pg)
McWhirter Twins (pg)
Pacific Showband (ent)
Homer Knodds (pg)

1969

4 January 1969
Yann Goulet (pg)
Tomás McGiolla (pg)
Winifred Ewing (pg)
Joseph Locke (pg)
Michael Collins (pg)
Rosita Sweetman (pg)
Diana Connolly Carew (pg)
Ted Bonner (pg)
Margo (ent)
Dr Seán Cawley
Dermot Herbert (pg)
Fr Anthony Byrne (pg)
We 4 (ent)

11 January 1969
Margo (ent)
Josef Locke (ent)
Cyril Stapleton (pg)
Seán Wright (pg)
Mide Fagan (pg)
John Feeney (med)
Fr Brian Wilkinson (pg)
Muredach McAndrew (pg)
Mrs P Smith (pg)
Nola McDevitt (pg)
Joseph Doyle (pg)
Harri Pritchard Jones (pg)
Diana Connolly-Carew (pg)
Tomás McGiolla (pg)

18 January 1969
John Feeney (med)
Fr Wilkinson (pg)
Cyril Stapleton (pg)
M McAndrew (pg)
Muriel and David Day (pg)
Gael Linn Cabaret (ent)

25 January 1969
Herbert Haydon (pg)
Ted Connaughton (pg)
Brendan Murphy (pg)
Brendan Smith (pg)
Paddy McClintock (pg)
David Hanly (pg)
Fr White (pg)
Dave Allen (ent)
The Philosphers (ent)
Jon Ledingham (pg)

1 February 1969
Sir Gerard Nabarro (pg)
Charles Simon (pg)
Stanley Archer (pg)
Rev Francis Schaeffer (pg)
June Levine (med)
Inez Heron (pg)
O S Whitehead (Zibbie) (pg)
MacTaggarts (ent)

8 February 1969
Prof Northcote Parkinson
   (pg)
Joan O'Carroll (pg)
Harold Cudmore (sp)
Mrs C Bruen (pg)
Stanley Archer (pg)
Gerry Fitt (pol)
Major Ronald Bunting (pg)
The Harpoons Group (ent)
The Scaffold Group (ent)

15 February 1969
Mr and Mrs Wilson (pg)
Desmond Guinness (pg)
Paul Rowan (pg)
Roger Hussey (pg)
Mary Kenny (med)
Nick Leonard (pg)
Shay Healy (ent)
Des Keogh (ent)

22 February 1969
Eddie Harty (pg)

Brian Trevaskis (pg)
Claire O'Loughlin (pg)
Brian Bourke (pg)
Ray Carroll (pg)
Gerry Finnegan (pg)
D R Mulcahy (pg)
Joe McGough (pg)
Dr Brink (USA) (pg)
Bill Quinn Group (ent)
The Pattersons (ent)

1 March 1969
Prof Edward C Bursk (pg)
Peter Owens (pg)
Carmel Quinn (pg)
Sony Sidar (pg)
Jo Grimmond (pg)
Josephine Scanlon (pg)
Ramon Ramedios (ent)
Albert Healy (ent)
Hedley Kaye (ent)

8 March 1969
Eric de Rothschild (pg)
Willy Woods (pg)
Christabelle Bielenberg (pg)
The O'Grady Sisters (ent)
Richard Stillgoe & Jefferson
   (ent)

15 March 1969
Alan Bestick (pg)
Tim Hall (pg)
Alan Cowle Band (ent)
Doreen Rohan (pg)
June Levine (med)
Tony Butler (pg)
John McConville (pg)
High School Band (ent)
Margo (ent)

22 March 1969
Burt Budin (pg)
Nellie Mulcahy (pg)
Eric Cross (wr)
Muriel Day (pg)
Ronnie Walsh (med)
Matt Doolin (pg)
Alexander Bros (ent)

29 March 1969
No Show

5 April 1969
The Unity Singers (ent)
Jazz & Blues Therapy (ent)
Michael O'Duffy (ent)
Big Tom (ent)
Dot Redmond Irish Dancers
   (ent)
John Carpenter (pg)
Charles Lysaght (pg)

12 April 1969
Prof Williams (pg)
Prof O'Halloran (pg)
Prof Wedell (pg)
Lelia Doolin (med)
Tom O'Dea (pg)
Fr Jack Kelly (pg)
Roy Orbison (ent)
Mary/Jonathan/Tim Corbett
   (pg)

19 April 1969
Jim Plunket Kelly (wr)
Mervyn Clarke (pg)
Michael Ryan (pg)
Lelord Kordel (pg)
Jack Dash (pg)
Albert Healy (ent)
Kathy Harrop (pg)

26 April 1969
Enoch Powell (pol)
Myles McSwiney (pg)
Rosita Sweetman (wr)
Patrick Lindsay (pg)

Alan Freeman (pg)
Leoine Baxter (pg)
Jean Marc Heidsiech (pg)
Anna McGoldrick (ent)
Jack McGinn Trio (ent)
Anne Moran (pg)
Jenny Reddin (med)

3 May 1969
Jimmy Saville (ent)
Cunarder Fashion Collection
   & models
Tom Corbett (pg)
Fathat Bartholomew (pg)
Danny Keany (pg)
'Phone call from Val
   Doonican
Sandie Jones (Royal Earls)
   (ent)
Joe Dolan and Mrs Brown
   (pg)

10 May 1969
John Lawrence (pg)
Paddy Crosbie and old folks
   (pg)
Noel Jones and J L Field (pg)
The Freshmen (ent)
The Johnsons (ent)
Monica Mae (pg)

17 May 1969
Sir Gerald Nabarro (pg)
Sir Roland Penrose (pg)
Ulick O'Connor (wr)
June Levine (med)
Prionsias MacAonghusa (pg)
Chris Smith (pg)
The Sands (ent)
The Young Dublin Singers
   (ent)

24 May 1969
Ernest Joker (pg)
Fr O'Sullivan (pg)
Judy Cornwell (pg)
John McDarby (pg)
Larry Cunningham (ent)
Tommy Makem (ent)
Ray Durham and The
   Steadfast Brass Band (ent)

31 May 1969
Susannah York (pg)
Willie Watt (pg)
Brian Cleeve (med)
Phyllis Doyle (pg)
Colm Madden (pg)
Siobhán McKenna (pg)
June Levine (med)
Ted Bonner (pg)
The Taste (ent)
The Irish Rovers (ent)
Thelma Ramsey
   accompanying Willie Watt
   (ent)

7 June 1969
Quintin Hogg (pg)
Dr Paul Dudley White (pg)
Bernadette Devlin (pol)
McDyer and Gogan (pg)
The Dreams (ent)
John McNally (ent)
The Mountaineers (ent)
Celine Hession Irish Dancers
   (ent)

13 June 1969
Clayton Love (pg)
Roy Bulson (pg)
Brian Friel (wr)
Michael Craig (pg)
Lewis C Franks (pg)
Roly Daniels (ent)
Anne O'Dwyer (ent)

21 June 1969
Libby Morris (pg)
Spike Milligan (pg)
Brian Phelan (pg)
Benny Cauldwell (ent)
Claire Mullen (pg)

28 June 1969
State of the Nation Special

4 October 1969
Michael York (pg)
George Pratt (pg)
Mr E O'Byrne (pg)
Frank Harris (pg)
Mary Casey (ent)
Ivan Cooper (pol)
Mr D J Jones (pg)
Terry Rogers (pg)

11 October 1969
Milo O'Shea (pg)
Fr Fergal O'Connor (pg)
Kiaran Kilroy (pg)
Jack Henry Moore (pg)
Rev W M Wynne (pg)
Dr Norman Moore (pg)
Agnes Bernelle (ent)
Tony Sidar (ent)

18 October 1969
Thomas Pakenham (wr)
Kenneth Williams (ent)
Peter Eade (pg)
Prionsias MacAonghusa (pg)
Des Rush (pg)
Hugh Leonard (wr)

Caption for this photograph on inside back cover

25 October 1969
Special Tribute to Micheál
   MacLiammóir

1 November 1969
Fr Eamonn Casey (pg)
Brian de Salvo (pg)
Robin Knox-Johnston (pg)
Anne Comyn (pg)
Memories (ent)
Michael O'Duffy (ent)
Maynard Ferguson (ent)

8 November 1969
Bob Quinn (med)
Jack Dowling (med)
Lelia Doolan (med)

15 November 1969
Danny Doyle (ent)
Jessie Nason (pg)
Hammond Innes (wr)
Mr J E Hoofnagle (pg)
Tiny Tim (ent)
Jimmy Shand Band (ent)
Maxie, Dick and Twink (ent)

22 November 1969
Special on Travellers

29 November 1969
Norman St John Stevas (pol)
Betty Sugru (pg)
Harvey Matusow (pg)
Mrs Brita Durley (pg)
Peter Bull (pg)
Fr Fergal O'Connor (pg)
B P Fallon (pg)
Dr Strangely Strange (ent)

6 December 1969
Quintan Hogg (pol)
C J Barry Richardson (pg)
Mr H Maclear Bates (sp)
Sr M Candida (pg)
Peter Cosgrove (pg)
Chem Chenutengwende (pg)
Ted Bonner (pg)

13 December 1969
Miriam Hederman (pg)
Henry Kelly (pg)
Dermot Ryan (pg)

Jeremy Thorpe (pg)
Penny Sinclair (pg)
Liam Maguire (pg)
Marie Wilkinson (ent)
Paco Pena Spanish Flamenco
   (ent)

20 December 1969
Alison Larimie (pg)
Mr and Mrs J Gleeson (pg)
Bridget Gleeson (pg)
Pam Collins (med)
Maeve Binchy (wr)
Jean Begley (pg)
Celine Hession (ent)
Recordites (ent)

27 December 1969
Tony Fitzpatrick (pg)
The Mummers (ent)
Celine Hession Dancers (ent)
Tony Sidar (ent)
Jimmy Shand (ent)
The Sandmen (ent)
Noel Byrne (ent)
Gaelic League Choir (ent)
Patrick O'Brien (ent)
Alan Cowle Band(ent)
Jackie Farn (ent)

1970

3 January 1970
Garret Fitzgerald (pol)
Justin Keating (pol)
Michael O'Kennedy (pol)
Uinsin MacEoin (pg)
Maureen Burke (pg)
Fr Jerome O'Herlihy (pg)
The Sandmen (ent)
Anna McGoldrick (ent)

10 January 1970
John Wade (ent)
Brendan Bowyer (ent)
Linguard Goulding (pg)
Alan Cowle (pg)
Éamon de Buitléar (pg)
Gerrit Van Gelderen (pg)
Mary Kenny (med)
Ulick O'Connor (wr)

17 January 1970
Brian Cleeve (pg)

Fr Corlishly (pg)
Fr Desmond O'Donnell (pg)
Joan O'Sullivan (pg)
Ruth Bradley (pg)

28 February 1970
Jack Benny (ent)
Kaye Hart (pg)
Mr Richard Pierce (pg)
Richard Harris (pg)

7 March 1970
Bernadette Devlin (pol)
Monica McEnroy (pg)
Dermot Clarke (pg)
Maureen Ahern (pg)
Finbar Slattery (pg)

Kathy Harrup (pg)
Patrick O'Hagan (ent)

14 March 1970
Caitlin Scallon (pg)
Peter Walshe (pg)
Carmel Campbell (pg)
Tom Kiernan (sp)
Rev Clarence Duffy (pg)
Anne Bushnell (ent)
Tremeloes (ent)
Dana (ent)

21 March 1970
No Show

28 March 1970
Tony Johnston (pg)
Joe McGough (pg)
Peter Keehan (pg)
Derry Lindsay (pg)
Jackie Smith (pg)
Robb Smith (pg)
Dana (ent)
Dubliners (ent)
Noel Ginnity (ent)

4 April 1970
Joey Lomongino (pg)
Stevie Coughlan (pg)
Tom Tobin (pg)
Vincent Browne (med)
John Feeney (med)

11 April 1970
Special on Nuns

18 April 1970
Michael O'Leary (pol)
Sally Trench (pg)
Rev G Reynolds (pg)
Ulick O'Connor (wr)
Jimmy Breslin (pg)

25 April 1970
Ann Harris (med)
Spike Milligan (ent)
Dick Brandon (pg)
Rev Con O'Donovan (pg)
Dermot Egan (pg)
Paddy Maguire (pg)
Johnny McEvoy (ent)

2 May 1970
Alannah Tandy (pg)
Jimmy Saville (ent)
Al Parker (pg)
Ann Sidney (pg)
Tom Mennard (ent)
Carmel Quinn (ent)
James Mason (pg)

9 May 1970
Most Rev P Birch (pg)
Most Rev E Casey (pg)
Very Rev Dean C Gray-Stack
   (pg)
Most Rev E Milingo (pg)
John Stewart (pg)

16 May 1970
Jackie Stewart (sp)
Rosemary Brown (pg)
A J Potter (pg)
Chester Marriot (ent)
Noel Burns (ent)

23 May 1970
Dr Edward de Bono (pg)
Seean Burke (pg)
Mona Byrne (pg)
Jimmy Breslin (pg)
John McNally (ent)
Christy Brown (wr)

30 May 1970
Mr J McHugh (pg)
Jim Kemmy (pol)
Dr J Fernandez (pg)
Liam Tarrant (pg)

Mr J Dore (pg)
Mr J Mills (pg)
Dick Pierce (pg)
Tom Riordan (pg)
Seán Loftus (pol)
Mary Bourke (pg)

3 October 1970
Shirley Temple (pg)
Katie Boyle (pg)
Arthur Fiedler (pg)
Paddy Reilly (ent)
Máirín Johnston (wr)
Pat Scully (pg)
Maurice Walsh (pg)
Owen Moriarty (pg)
Dermot Mulhane (pg)
John MacConville (pg)
June Levine (med)
Mary Maher (med)
Mary Kenny (med)
Nell McCafferty (med)

10 October 1970
Mothers & Daughters:
June Levine and Diane (pg)
Elizabeth Hannon and Ingrid
  (pg)
Moira Bastable and Siona
  (pg)
Yuri Ustimenko (pg)
Moira Woods (pg)
Slim Whitman (ent)

17 October 1970
Elmer Bernstein (ent)
Joseph Foyle (pg)
Tony Johnston (pg)
Michael Sweetman (pg)
John Maguire (pg)
Rev James McDyer (pg)
Rev Con O'Donovan (pg)
Mr O Lionsoigh (pg)

24 October 1970
Fr Borelli (wr)
Anton Clifford Wallich (wr)
Al Jolson (ent)
Roger Whittaker (ent)
Prof Mellanby (pg)
John Healy (pg)
Lord Longford (pg)
Hiroshi Maede (pg)
Ray Millichip (pg)
Peter Norfold & Trio (ent)
Labby Siffre (ent)

7 November 1970
J K Galbraith (wr)
Jemmy Colgan (pg)
Dora Bryan (pg)
Peter Moloney (pg)
Rob Kaurmont (pg)
Gene Stuart and the Mighty
  Avons (ent)

14 November 1970
Frank Grimes (sp)
Pat Golden (pg)
Bryan Flanagan (pg)
Phil Ochs Yippies! (pg)
Kathleen Watkins (ent)
Andy Stewart (ent)

21 November 1970
Patrick Moore (pg)
Roy Croft (med)
Pat Quinn (pg)

28 November 1970
Gyles Brandreth (pg)
George Best (sp)
G Tyndell (pg)
Ladies Soccer Team-Civil
  Service (sp)
Sinéad Cusack (pg)

5 December 1970
Liam Nolan (med)

Fr McGlinchey (pg)
John Mulcahy (med)
Ann Woodworth (ent)
Judy Woodworth (ent)
Brendan Bowyer (ent)

12 December 1970
Supermarkets
Marriage Guidance
The Freshmen (ent)
The Swarbriggs (ent)

19 December 1970
Antiques Special

1971

2 January 1971
Joanne Mollereaud (pg)
Alex Sanders (pg)
Brian Phelan (pg)
Michael Clery (pg)
Margaret Barry (ent)
Tom McCuaig (ent)
We 4 (ent)
John Curran band (ent)

9 January 1971
State of the Nation—special

16 January 1971
Delia Murphy (ent)
Count de Geoffre (pg)
Brian Byrne (ent)
Louis Stewart (ent)

23 January 1971
Special on Farmers
Darby O'Gill (ent)

30 January 1971
Special on the Tourist
  Industry
Rory O'Connor Dancers (ent)
Dana (ent)

6 February 1971
Myles McWeeney (med)
June Levine (med)
Nuala Fennel (med)
Ulick O'Connor (wr)
Mary Anderson (pg)
Jeananne Crowley (pg)
Chester Harriot (wr)
McDonald Bailey (pg)
Cait Ní Guish (ent)
Dr Collis (pg)
C Brown (pg)

13 February 1971
Finbarr Nolan (pg)
Dr John McConnell (pg)
Dr Manny Berber (pg)
Dr Davin Power (pg)
Margaret Powell (pg)
The Mountaineers (ent)
Paschal Poge (ent)

20 February 1971
Alan Bestick (pg)
Supply Demand & Curve
  (ent)

27 February 1971
No Show

6 March 1971
Special on Women's
  Liberation
Alexander Bros (ent)

13 March 1971
Theatre Festival
John Gregson (pg)
Jack Leonard (pg)
Norman Beaton (pg)
Oliver J Flanagan (pol)
Val Doonican (ent)
Jim Doherty Band (ent)
The Johnstons (ent)

20 March 1971
John Horgan (med)
John M Kelly (pg)
Justin Keating (pol)
Fr Denis Faul (pg)
Bernadette Devlin (pol)
John Hume (pol)
Roly Daniels (ent)
Fairport Convention (ent)

27 March 1971
Rosemary Smith (sp)
Maurice Craig (wr)
Pat Lynch (pg)
Casterbridge Union (ent)
Angela Farrell (ent)

3 April 1971
No Show

10 April 1971
Paddy Crosbie (pg)
Niall Toibín (ent)
Roy Orbison (ent)
Kenny Ball Band (ent)
Chubby Checker (ent)

17 April 1971
Joey Lomongino (pg)
Fr Pelletier (pg)
Hal Roach (ent)
Bishop N Dingan (pg)
Fr Egan (pg)
F Flannery (pg)
Red Hurley (ent)

24 April 1971
Lord Longford (pol)
Ernest Blythe (pol)
Margery Forester (pg)
Máire Comerford (pg)
Hannie Collins (pg)

1 May 1971
Management & Workers
  Special
The McKennas (ent)
Anne Byrne (ent)

8 May 1971
Bryan McMahon (wr)
Jimmy Saville (ent)
Anton Diffring (pg)
Peter Bander (pg)
Don Pistoni (pg)
Alan Stivell (ent)
O'Gradys (ent)
Frank Patterson (ent)

15 May 1971
Norman Wisdom (ent)
Michael Cahill (pg)
Nita Norry (ent)

22 May 1971
Juanita Casey (pg)
Peter Bander & Co (pg)
Austin Williams Prisoners
  (pg)
The Liberty Belles (ent)
Phil Butler (ent)

29 May 1971
Special on the Horse
  Industry
Tom Connors (pg)

5 June 1971
Niall Toibín (ent)
Aker Bilk (ent)
Paul Jones (ent)
Major Wylie (ent)
Phil Butler Quartet (ent)
Bill Codding (ent)
Val Fitzpatrick (ent)

1971

1 October 1971
Pierre Salinger (pg)

Liam Nolan (med)
The Bachelors (ent)
Tom Paxton (ent)
Basil Payne (wr)
Mary Leland (pg)

9 October 1971
Richard Condon (wr)
Lord John Surtees (pg)
Vincent Manning (pg)
The Sands (ent)
Frank Carson (ent)

16 October 1971
David Hossoff (pg)
Fr Brophy (pg)
Ciaran Carty (med)
Hugh Leonard (wr)
Dermot Flynn (pg)

Mrs Ireland (pg)
Hildegarde Kneffe (pg)
Arun Chattergee (pg)
The Cotton Mill Boys (ent)
Patricia McCarry (ent)

23 October 1971
Jackie McGowran (pg)
Eamonn Andrews (pg)
Peter Sellers (pg)
Barbara Kelly (pg)
Trevor Howard (pg)
Sir Matt Busby (sp)

30 October 1971
Roddy Carr (sp)
Gordon Thomas (wr)
Eamonn McCann (med)
James Young (ent)
Simon Winchester (med)
Colin Brady (med)
Patricia Cahill (ent)

6 November 1971
John B Keane (wr)
Fr Brophy (pg)
Hanna Grealy (wr)
Ann Comyn (pg)
Ivor Browne (pg)
Mick O'Malley (pg)
Maire Comerford (pg)
Prof J O'Meara (pg)
Niall Toibín (ent)
Lord Mustard (ent)
Gene Stuart (ent)
Lindsay Singers (ent)

13 November 1971
Mairéad Allen (pg)
Michael Byrne (pg)
Pat Quinn (pg)
Patrick Murphy (pg)
Clement Freud (med)
Dorothy Walker (pg)
Anne Crookshank (pg)
George Dawson (pg)
Paul Funge (pg)
Alice Hanratty (pg)
Michael Kane (pg)
The Skillets (ent)

20 November 1971
Bishop Piu (pg)
Brian Cleeve (med)
John Hume MP (pol)

Austin Currie MP (pol)
Ted Bonner (pg)
Ulick O'Connor (wr)
Tina (ent)

27 November 1971
Special on Being Disabled in
  Ireland
Michael McGarr (ent)
Barley Cove (ent)
Tir na nÓg (ent)

4 December 1971
Michael Vaughan (pg)
Ernie Evans (pg)
J A Corr (pg)
Bobby Kerr (pg)
John Feighery (pg)

Frank Fennelly (pg)
Gabrielle Williams (med)
The Freshmen (ent)
Des Keogh (ent)

11 December 1971
Larry Lyons (pg)
George Waters (pg)
Martin O'Malley (pg)
Bill Nolan (pg)
Tim Dudman (pg)
Nuala Fennell (med)
Fr Con O'Donovan (pg)
Nell McCafferty (med)
Seamus Ó Tuathail (pg)
Patricia Lawlor (ent)
Tex Withers (ent)

18 December 1971
Dermot Hegarty (ent)
Geraldine (ent)
The Rebels (ent)
Patrick O'Hagan (ent)
Albert Healy (ent)
Kathleen Watkins (ent)
Tom Gregory (ent)
Des Keogh (ent)
Tadgh de Brún (ent)
Liam Devalley (ent)
Brendan O'Reilly (ent)
Chris Curran (ent)
Tom Hickey (ent)
Jack Cruise (ent)
Maureen Potter (ent)
Ulick O'Connor (wr)
Brendan Cauldwell (pg)
Niall Toibín (ent)

25 December 1971
No Show

1972

1 January 1972
Ulick O'Connor (wr)
Tom Hickey (ent)
Brendan O'Reilly (pg)
Liam Devalley (pg)
Frank Hall (med)
Brendan Cauldwell (ent)
Jack Cruise (ent)
Maureen Potter (ent)
Chris Curran (ent)
Kathleen Watkins (ent)
Patrick O'Hagan (ent)

Niall Toibín (ent)
Des Keogh (ent)
The Rebels (ent)
Dermot Hegarty (ent)
Geraldine (ent)

8 January 1972
Ernest Blythe (pg)
Gabriel Fallon (pg)
Lelia Doolan (pg)
John Slemon (pg)
David Thornley (pol)
Charles McCarthy (pg)
Bryan MacMahon (wr)
Tom Murphy (wr)
Philip O'Flynn (pg)
Maire Ní Dhomhnaill (pg)
Vincent Dowling (pg)
Tomás MacAnna (pg)
Peadar Lambe (pg)
Kathleen Barrington (pg)
Joe Dowling (pg)
Terry Prone (wr)
Brendan Smith (pg)
Ronan Wilmot (pg)
Wesley Burrows (wr)
Tom Kilroy (wr)
Séamus Kelly (pg)
Harry Brogan (pg)
Seán Page (pg)
Criostóir Ó Floinn (pg)
Noeleen Dowling (pg)
Piet Kameran (pg)
John Boland (pol)
Eugene McCabe (wr)
Sheelagh Richards (pg)
Carolyn Swift (wr)
Jonathan Marsh (pg)
Ruby Murray (ent)
Noelle Callinan (ent)
Bernard Geary (ent)

15 January 1972
Peter Black (wr)
Mary Whitehouse (wr)
Fr Fergal O'Connor (pg)
Danny Gunnery (pg)
Frank Ryan (pg)
Miss Walker-Frascati (pg)
Madame Helene (pg)

22 January 1972
Séamus Ó Tuathail (med)
Donal Foley (med)
Liam Bergin (med)
Michael Mills (med)
Vincent Browne (med)
Mary Cummins (med)
Conor O'Brien (med)
Brigitta Pierre (med)
John H Murdoch (med)
Bill O'Donovan (med)
Brian Phelan (ent)
Roly Daniels (ent)
Billy Brown (ent)

29 January 1972
No Show

5 February 1972
Mike Murphy fill-in

12 February 1972
Ted Bonner fill-in

19 February 1972
Spike Milligan (ent)
Tony Gray (med)
Hugh Leonard (wr)
Joan O'Brien (pg)
Julie Felix (ent)
Danny Doyle (ent)

26 February 1972
Michael Winner (pg)
Billy Duffy (pg)
Larry Dillon (pg)

Ian Broad (pg)
Mr Feely (pg)
Bill Keating (med)
Tracy (ent)
Planxty (ent)

4 March 1972
Michael Donnelly (pg)
John Carroll (pg)
Mr D E Williams (pg)
Frank Flynn (pg)
Mattie Merrigan (pg)
Peadar Kelly (pg)
Tessie Burns (pg)
Fr Michael Cleary (pg)
Fr Fergal O'Connor (pg)
Nuala Fennell (pol)

11 March 1972
Judge Kingsmill Moore (pg)
Donal Barrington (pg)
Tom Finley (pg)
Paddy O'Keeffe (pg)
Miriam Hederman (pg)
Daniel Murphy (pg)
Franz Freschmuir (pg)
Garret Fitzgerald (pol)
Tony Coughlan (pg)
John Carroll (pg)
Mrs McLiam (pg)
Fr McDyer (pg)
Justin Keating (pol)

18 March 1972
Michael Dillon (pg)
Din Joe (pg)
Rose Tynan (ent)
Pam Collins (pg)
Wolf Mankovitz (pg)
Sandie Jones (ent)
Joe Cuddy (ent)
Des Smyth (ent)
Donovan (ent)

25 March 1972
No Show

1 April 1972
Veronica McSweeney (ent)
Tommy O'Brien (pg)
Dana (ent)
Joe Loss (ent)
Michael O'Dea (ent)
Swarbriggs & Friends (ent)
Stanley Archer (wr)
Harry Thuillier (pg)

8 April 1972
Old Folks Special

15 April 1972
Ray Webb (pg)
Donald Bunting (pg)
Dave Guiney (pg)
Mahatma Saffranang (pg)
Breta Strong (pg)
Joe O'Donnell (pg)
Sandie Jones (ent)
D J Curtin (ent)
The Mountaineers (ent)
Carmel O'Byrne (ent)
Robert Boyle (ent)

22 April 1972
Robert Kee (wr)
Dr Conor Cruise O'Brien (pg)
Prof John A Murphy (pg)
Val Doonican (ent)
Ken Campbell Road Show
  (ent)
Brendan McShane (ent)

30 April 1972
Gilbert O'Sullivan (ent)
Joe Lamont (pg)
Daniel Leonard (pg)
Sam McGreedy (pg)
Cathal O'Luain (pg)
David Synnott (pg)
William Martin (pg)

Kathleen O'Neill (pg)
Alma Carroll (ent)
Red Hurley (ent)

6 May 1972
Milo Rockett (pg)
Nicholas Leonard (pg)
Paddy Boland (pg)
John Briscow (pg)
Liam C Martin (pg)
Jimmy Saville (ent)
St Mary's School Choir (ent)
Candy Devine (ent)
The Dubliners (ent)

13 May 1972
Peter Barry (pol)
Pat Power (pol)
Dick Burke (pol)
Jim Tunney (pol)
Dr John O'Connell (pol)
Dr David Thornley (pol)
Rod McKuen (ent)

20 May 1972
Brian Cleeve (med)
Tommy O'Flaherty (pg)
Mr Murphy (pg)
Mr McGrath (pg)
Dr Graham (pg)
Laurie O'Sullivan (pg)
Jimmy Serwer (pg)
Michael Legar (wr)
Gregory (ent)
Dick (ent)

27 May 1972
Peter Bander (pg)
Anna Dolan (pg)
Leslie Flint (pg)
Madeleine Montalban (pg)
Herbie Brennan (pg)
Peter Prescott (pg)

3 June 1972
Neil Blaney TD (pol)
Most Rev Cathal Daly (pg)
Desmond Fennell (med)
John Healy (med)
Sen J M Kelly (pol)
J J Maher (pg)
Rev Horace McKinley (pg)
Dr Conor Cruise O'Brien TD
  (pol)
Michael O'Kennedy TD (pol)

Douglas Gageby (med)
Robert Babbington MP (pol)
Canon John Barry (pg)
Robert Cooper (pg)
John Hume MP (pol)
Dr Ian Paisley MP (pol)
Fr Des Wilson (pg)
Seán O'Toole (pg)
Kevin McCorry (pg)
Thomas Passmore (pg)

7 October 1972
Richard Widmark (pg)
Matt Doolan (pg)
Prof Liam O'Briain (pg)
Frank Hall (med)
Mary Kenny (med)
Hilton Edwards (pg)
Mícheál MacLiammóir (pg)
Josef Locke (ent)
Christy Brown (wr)
John B Keane (wr)
Ulick O'Connor (wr)
Mary Leland (pg)
Stanley Archer (pg)
Brian Phelan (pg)
Paddy and Eileen Fox (pg)
Angela O'Doherty (pg)
Oliver J Flanagan (pg)
Mrs Mullins (ent)
Ted Bonner (pg)
June Levine (med)
Fr Fergal O'Connor (pg)
Ken Grey (med)
Tom O'Dea (pg)
Brian Devenney (pg)
Hugh Leonard (wr)
Danny Cummins (pg)

14 October 1972
June Levine (med)
Lord Longford (wr)
Malcolm Muggeridge (wr)
Alan Bestick (pg)
Miss Ireland
Terry and Gay Woods (ent)
Peter Skellern (ent)

21 October 1972
Edna O'Brien (wr)
John Hume MP (pol)
Dr Conor Cruise O'Brien
  (pg)
Bishop Lamont (pg)
Family Pride (ent)

28 October 1972
Mother Teresa (pg)
Leslie Pine (pg)
Dick Pierce (pg)
Neil Coll (pg)
Niall Toibín (ent)

4 November 1972
Matt Doolan (pg)
Donal Donnelly (pg)
Catherine McGuinness (pg)
Mena Cribbin (pg)
Winnie O'Dea Group (ent)

11 November 1972
Lord O'Neill (pg)
Catherine McGuinness (pg)
Michael Gill (pg)
Bishop Colin Winter (pg)
Ian Whitcomb (ent)
Brendan Shine Band (ent)
Kevin Hayes (Coasters) (ent)

18 November 1972
Des Broadberry (pg)
Garret Fitzgerald TD (pol)
Dr Eric Woodhouse (pg)
Anne Ladbury (pg)
Gabrielle Kearns (pg)
Mary Cassidy (pg)
Mary Keane (pg)

Deirdre McGlinn (pg)
Paolo Soleri (pg)
Louis Stewart Quartet (ent)
Rathmines & Rathgar
  Musical Society (ent)

25 November 1972
No Show

2 December 1972
Toy Show

9 December 1972
Cecil King (pg)
Tim Phillips (pg)
Jeremy Cooper (pg)
Fr Michael Kane (pg)
John B Keane (wr)
Patrick Aherne (pg)
Willie Finucane (pg)
John McElligott (pg)
Tom Leary (pg)
Spanish Flamenco Dancers
  (ent)

16 December 1972
Carol Shaw (pg)
Darine McCluskey (pg)
Patricia McElhone (pg)
Gretta Dunleavy (pg)
Michael Conlon (pg)
Pat Adam Smith (pg)
Nuala Fennell (med)
Jimmy Reilly (pg)
Colette Delaney (pg)
Betty (behind screen) (pg)
Ann (behind screen) (pg)

23 December 1972
Irish Traditional Music
  Special

30 December 1972
No Show

1973

6 January 1973
Special on Seán Keating

13 January 1973
Miss World—Eva
  Rueberstaier (pg)
Chay Blyth (sp)
A R Johnston (pg)
Desmond Hourie (pg)
Vivian Ray (pg)
Kieran Kilroy (pg)
(Members of audience)
John McNally (ent)
Deirdre O'Callaghan (ent)
Horselips (ent)

20 January 1973
Bob Bartlett (pg)
Tony Harnett (pg)
Dr Joyce Delaney (wr)
Douglas Bennett (pg)
Nenner Hoidale (wr)
Stage 2 (ent)
Al O'Donnell (ent)
Tommy Makem (ent)
Rosaleen Linehan (ent)

27 January 1973
Dublin City Growth
Ruairi Quinn (pol)
Fr Paul Freeney (pg)
Eleanor Fitzgerald (pg)
Bernadette Joyce (pg)
Marion Moggan (pg)
Murphy & the Swallows
  (ent)
Fossetts' Lions (ent)
Bavarian Band (ent)

3 February 1973
Fr Fergal O'Connor (pg)
3 American millionaire girls
  (pg)

Seán Ganley (pg)
Fr Finnegan (pg)
Brian Cox (pg)

10 February 1973
Programme on Health

17 February 1973
Nora Relihan (pg)
Holiday Magic (ent)
Uri and Irene Ustimenko (pg)
Nickey Barry (ent)
Sea City (ent)

24 February 1972
No Show

3 March 1973
Jean Moriarty (pg)
Barbara Mullen (pg)
Ulick O'Connor (wr)
Clement Freud (pg)
Jonah Barrington (sp)
Brendan O'Dowd (ent)

10 March 1973
Prof Jack Weingreen (pg)
Layi Oluwa (pg)
Antonia Healy (pg)
Karanbir Singh Gill (pg)
Sr Leslie Shepart (pg)
Dr Jal Fanny Bunda (pg)
Bishop Eamon Casey (pg)
Des Wilson (pg)

17 March 1973
Programme on Brussels

24 March 1973
Joe Kennedy (med)
Vincent Jennings (med)
Dr Conor Cruise O'Brien (med)
John Feeny (med)
Jazz Coasters (ent)
Jimmy Helims (ent)

31 March 1973
John Huston (pg)
Horst Buckholzt (pg)
Milo O'Shea (pg)
Clement Freud (pg)
Tina (ent)
Maxi (ent)

7 April 1973
No Show

14 April 1973
Anthony J Cronin (wr)
Geo Crosby (pg)
Jack Brierley (pg)
Paddy Malone (pg)
Mich Hand (pg)
Tony Wilson (pg)
Bobby Charlton (sp)
Alun Williams (pg)

21 April 1973
Donal Nevin (pg)
Paddy O'Keeffe (pg)
John Doyle (pg)
Diarmuid O'Neill (pg)
Joe McPartland (pg)
Jim Motherway (pg)
Tom Roche (pg)
Dublin Grand Opera Society (ent)

28 April 1973
Jimmy Saville (ent)
Derek Jameson (med)
Eric Leggit (med)
Otto Herschan (med)
Matt Doolan (med)
Mary Kenny (med)
Brendan Grace (ent)
Danny Doyle (ent)
Dickie Rock (ent)

5 May 1973
Herman Kahn (pg)
Fr Fergal O'Connor (pg)
Ivor Browne (pg)
Dr John Cullen (pg)
Dr Aubrey Cagan (pg)
Dr Seymour Levine (pg)
Thin Lizzy (ent)

12 May 1973
Georgian State Dancers (ent)
Brian Inglis (wr)
Jack Ashley (pg)
Ellen Peck (pg)

19 May 1973
Dr Issels (pg)
Prof Thorns (pg)
Dr Pippet (pg)
Dr J J Fennelly (pg)
Gordon Thomas (wr)
Marion Montgomery (ent)

26 May 1973
Dr Malachi Martin (wr)
Frank Sheed (pg)
Suzanne Murphy (pg)
Milo O'Shea (ent)
Kitty O'Sullivan (ent)

2 June 1973
A Bennett (pg)
Basil Payne (wr)
Mairéad Allen (pg)
Molly Cranny (pg)
Sheila Kennedy (pg)
Betty Morrissey (pg)
Major Wiley (ent)
Family Pride (ent)

29 September 1973
John McIvor (pg)
Johnny Speight (pg)
Eddy Byrne (pg)
The Mountaineers (ent)
Nancy Cole (pg)
Harding Lamay (pg)

6 October 1973
Siegfried Berz (pg)
Mrs T Morley (pg)
Dominique McEvoy (pg)
Ted Bonner (pg)
Frank Carson (pg)
Sam Crea (pg)
Sam McCaughey (pg)
Rowel Francis (pg)
Teresa Morley (pg)
June Levine (med)
Audrey Ellis (pg)
Bernadette Ní Ghallachóir (pg)
Don Maclean (ent)
Geraldine Kane (pg)

13 October 1973
J P Murray (sp)
Noel Carroll (pg)
Marie Herbert (pg)
Mary Maher (med)
Emer Bowman (pg)
John Kendrick (pg)
Vincent Jennings (pg)
Sonny Knowles (ent)
Shades of McMurrough (ent)

20 October 1973
Dr Cooney (pg)
Dr Brian McSharry (pg)
Dr McQuade (pg)
Nell McCafferty (wr)
Dame Marjorie Corbett-Ashby (pg)
Jan Tomaschevski (sp)
Mary Maher (pg)
Emer Bowman (pg)
Anne Lough (pg)
Marie Mullarney (pg)

Col Doherty (pg)
Johnny McEvoy (ent)
Army Band (ent)

27th October 1973
May Hobbs (pg)
Fitzgerald/Faulkner link up
Rona Fields (pg)
Denis Lehane (pg)
Martin Dillon (pg)
Alma Carroll and B Track (ent)

3 November 1973
T J Maher (pg)
John O'Connell (pg)
Hugh Munro (pg)
John Molley (pg)
Larry Adler (pg)
Brendan Bowyer (ent)
Sepulchre (ent)

10 November 1973
Alan Gibson (pg)
Fred O'Donovan (pg)
Hilton Edwards (pg)
Pat Quinn (pg)
McStenson (ent)
Dr Paul Marx
Frankie Vaughan (pg)
Charlie O'Brien (pg)
Tom Barrett (pg)
Dana (ent)
John O'Conor (ent)

17 November 1973
Jimmy Reid (pg)
Adriana Stapanopulous (pg)
Judith Keith (pg)
Paul O'Dwyer (pg)
Dickie Rock (ent)
Jonathan Kelly (pg)
William Clauson (pg)

24 November 1973
Barry McArdle (pg)
Niall Toibín (pg)
Chris Curran (pg)
Dr Jim Loughnan (pg)
Dr Gus Davis (pg)
Catherine McGuinness (pg)
Treasa O'Reilly (pg)
Peter Keegan (pg)
Angela Jenkins (pg)

1 December 1973
Joanne Mollinaux (pg)
Toy Airport (ent)
Pat Reade (pg)
Hangan (pg)
Gene Stewart (pg)
Dermot O'Brien (ent)
Fintan Stanley (ent)
Gayle Nelson (ent)

8 December 1973
Peter Hain (pg)
Myles Tierney (pg)

Hugh McGrillen (pg)
Michael Maguire (pg)
Tom O'Neill (pg)
Michael McDone (pg)
Planxty (ent)
Candy Devine (ent)
Rev Ian Paisley (pol)
William Craig (pg)
John Laird (pg)
Vincent Browne (med)
Kieran McKeon (pg)
John Mulcahy (med)

15 December 1973
John Behan (pg)
Hugh MacDiarmuid (wr)
Fr Gavghaun (pg)
Dick Piersi (pg)
Bryan McMahon (wr)
Rowel Friers (pg)
Ryan O'Neal (pg)
Ted Bonner (med)
Angela Bonaick (pg)
Glen Curtin (ent)
Pumpkin Head (ent)

22 December 1973
Noel Purcell and guests celebrate his 73rd birthday

1974

5 January 1974
Fr Noonan (pg)
Barney McCool and Eamon Kelly
Ed Custer (pg)
John Hume (pol)
Patti O'Hagan (pg)
Courtney Kenny (pg)
Peggy Dell (ent)

12 January 1974
Fr Fergal O'Connor (pg)

Ivor Brown (pg)
Nuala Fennell (med)
Mary Leland (wr)
Maura Wall (pg)
Kathleen O'Higgins (pg)
Sylvia Meehan (pg)
John McManus (pg)
John O'Brien (pg)
Frank Hamilton (pg)
Jim O'Reilly (pg)
Anne Fray (pg)
Danny Doyle (ent)
Irish National Opera (ent)

19 January 1974
John Horgan (med)
Ruairi Graham (pg)
Seán Brosnahan (pg)
Bro Declan (pg)
Pierce Purcell (pg)
Séamus O'Conghaile (pg)
Fr Leo Quinlan (pg)
Trevor Dagg (pg)
Geraldine O'Grady & Eily

26th January 1974
Enda Kennedy (pg)
Patrick LeChene (pg)
Tom Whiteham (pg)
Seán Maher (pg)
John Coleman (pg)
Madeleine Bell (pg)

2nd February 1974
Wyatt Watson (pg)
Harold Loughton (pg)
Miriam Woodbyrne (pg)
Grace O'Shaughnessy (pg)
Patti Howard (pg)
Christina Murphy (pg)
Anne Byrne and Paddy Roche (ent)
The Derry Chair (ent)
Johnny Dawson (ent)

9th February 1974
No Show

16 February 1974
Eilish Dillon (wr)
Rose Robertson (pg)
Fr Owen Murphy (pg)
Bridget O'Brien (pg)
Judith Casten (pg)
Jim Ryan (pg)
Barney McKenna (ent)
Teddy Palmer (pg)

23rd February 1974
Prof John Godkin (pg)
Dr Sally Parsonage (pg)
Dr Willie O'Flynn (pg)
Enda Ryan (pg)
Hugo Duncan (pg)
Pan Butter Band (ent)
John Norris (pg)
Neil Toner (pg)

2nd March 1974
Geoffrey Moorehouse (pg)
Mrs Raymonde Hawkins (pg)
Henry Pleasants (pg)
Jonah Barrington (sp)
Gerry O'Flaherty (ent)
Frankie McBride (ent)
Snake Hips (ent)
Virginia Pleasants (pg)

9th March 1974
Tony Buzan (pg)
Judy Hayes (pg)
Phil Silvers (pg)
Spike Milligan (pg)
Lord Longford (wr)
Roly Daniels (ent)
Val Fitzpatrick (ent)

16 March 1974
Tom O'Neill (pg)
Ben Rafter (pg)
Michael Ware (pg)
Conor Cruise O'Brien (pg)
David Greene (pg)
Ruairi Brugha (pg)
Maurice Healy (ent)
Ken Barry (ent)
Ena O'Sullivan (ent)
Donal Crosbie (ent)
Pat Craig (pg)
Donal Moylan (pg)
Lady Valerie Goulding (pg)
Tony Hegarty (pg)
Billy Brown (ent)

23 March 1974
Gary Glitter (ent)
Dr Ben Graves (pg)
Rosmary Smith (sp)
Lord Altamont (pg)
Lourdes choir (ent)
Labbi Sifre (ent)

30 March 1974
Henry Cooper (sp)
Richie Ryan (pg)
John Bristow (pg)
Bruce Arnold (med)
Tina (ent)
Veronica Jochum (ent)

8 April 1974
No Show

13 April 1974
Stanley Morgan (pg)
Tony Quinn (pg)
Eddie Mahon—Divine Light
   (pg)
Zacharia—L. of God (pg)
Kieran O'Neill—V. Family
   (pg)
Fr Paul Gallaher SJ (pg)
Fr Eamon Breslin (pg)
Dr Jo Fernandez (pg)
Denis Leahy (ent)
DGOS (ent)

20 April 1974
Nicky Furlong (pg)
Sr Stanislaus (pg)
Ray Fuller (ent)
Michal Lorimer (ent)
Laelitia Van Wayenburg (ent)
D J Curtin (ent)

27 April 1974
Mary Peters (sp)
Hughie Greene (pg)
Glynn Langston (pg)
Dr Daly (pg)
Paddy Whalley (pg)
Jim Brady (pg)
Mrs Moore (pg)
The Pattersons (ent)
Mary Sheridan & Philip
   Byrne (ent)
Festive Ensemble (ent)
Cyril Daly (pg)

4 April 1974
Lyall Watson (sp)
Fernando Parrado (pg)
Roberto Canassa (pg)
Ray Fuller (pg)
Chips (ent)
JSD Band (ent)

11 May 1974
Erin Pitsey (wr)
Eileen O'Gorman (pg)
Bishop C Daly (pg)
Aef McCreary (wr)
Gordon Burns (pg)
Prof Harris (pg)
Tommy Makem (ent)

18 May 1974
Fr Fergal O'Connor (pg)
Fr Paul Gallagher (pg)
Leslie Shepherd (pg)
Kevin Clear (pg)
Prof Lanczos Cornelius
Paddy and Betty Bryne (pg)
Tony Buzan (pg)
Harry Kernoff (pg)
Wexford Light Opera Society
   (ent)
Donal Crosbie (pg)

28 May 1974
Fr Fergal O'Connor (pg)
Paul Gallagher (pg)
Leslie Shepherd (pg)
Kevin Clear (pg)
Prof C Lanczos (pg)
Dermot Ryan (pg)
Thomas Wiseman (pg)
Victor Bewley (pg)
Willie O'Brien (pg)
Colm O'Doherty (pg)
Andy and David Williams
   (ent)

1 June 1974
Bruce Arnold (med
Anthony Lejeune (pg)
Noel Harris (pg)
Tom Redmond (pg)
Fr C Ned-Smith (pg)
Rev Stanley Baird (pg)
John Gibson (pg)
The Times (ent)

8 June 1974
Dr Conor Cruise O'Brien
   (wr)
Michael Garvey (pg)
Ruairi Brugha (pg)

28 September 1974
James Cameron (wr)
Barbara Stoney (pg)
Andrew Oldham (pg)
Libby Morris (ent)

5 October 1974
John Kennedy (pg)
William O'Sullivan (pg)
Dr George Simms (pg)
Mrs D Scannell (pg)
Edna O'Brien (pg)
Brotherly Love (ent)

12 October 1974
Alan Benson (pg)
Gerald Davis (pg)
Gladys Factor (pg)
John Finkel (pg)
Maurice Abrahamson (pg)
Rev Ginnsberg (pg)
Gerald Goldsberg (pg)
Percy Diamond (pg)
Barbara Feldman (pg)
Maurice Cherniak (pg)
Bernard Share (pg)

19 October 1974
Moore McDowell (pg)
Colm Rapple (pg)
Martin O'Donoghue (pg)
Clannad (ent)
Louis Browne (ent)
Cathal Dunne (ent)

26 October 1974
Dr Karl Mullen (pg)
Fergus Slattery (sp)
Tom Clifford (pg)
Edmund Van Esbeck (pg)
Gordon Thomas (pg)
Margaret Bramwell (pg)
Maura O'Dea (pg)
Joe Gavin (pg)

2 November 1974
Ulick O'Connor (wr)
Kenneth Griffith (pg)

Noel Pearson (pg)
Ray Edmonds (pg)
Pascal Burke (pg)
Mr A Lefik (pg)
Mary Peters (sp)
Rosaleen Linehan (ent)

9 November 1974
Dermot Foley (pg)
Charles Acton (med)
Deirdre Ryan (pg)
Cedric Woods (pg)
Christina Murphy (pg)
Tom McDevitt (ent)

16 November 1974
Mary Kenny (med)
Stanley Archer (pg)
Dr David Robinson (pg)
Cedric Woods (pg)
Tom Maher (pg)
Rosaleen Linehan (ent)
Des Keogh (ent)
Don Summers (pg)
Dr Ivor Browne (pg)

23 November 1974
Thomas Webster (pg)
Dr Ivor Browne (pg)
Declan Bree (pg)
Sr Maura Clune (pg)
Fr John Feyreey (pg)
Larry Hogan (pg)
Kevin Clear (pg)
Alun Williams (sp)
Sam McGready (wr)

30 November 1974
Roger McGough (pg)
Rolf Harris (ent)
John Simpson (pg)

7 December 1974
Brian McCarthy (pg)

14 December 1974
Robert Molloy (pg)
Bridie O'Flaherty (pg)
John Meehan (pg)
Fr Staunton (pg)

21 December 1974
Derek Crozier (pg)
Michael Herity (pg)
Clare Boylan (wr)
Ted Bonner (pg)
Ted Nealon (pg)

31 December 1974
New Year's Eve Special

1975

4 January 1975
Bernie Dillon (pg)
Deirdre Reddy (pg)
Conor O'Driscoll (pg)
Anita Leslie (pg)
Commander W King (pg)
Fr D P Noonan (pg)
Peter Boate (pg)
Sheelagh McGowan (pg)
Mary O'Hara (ent)

11 January 1975
Larry Slattery (pg)
Raymond O'Donoghue (pg)
Ted Bonner (pg)
Des O'Neill (pg)
Joe Carroll (pg)
Seán McEntee (pg)
Lt Gen Michael J Costello
   (pg)
Charles Kelly (pg)
Spud (ent)
Ronnie Drew (ent)

18 January 1975
Catherine McGuinness (pg)

Anna Raeburn (pg)
Maureen Johnston (pg)
Sr Benvenuta (pg)
Gemma Hussey (pg)
Jean Moorehouse (pg)
Eileen Desmond (pol)
Michael O'Leary (pol)
In audience:
Una Claffey
Peter Cassells
Mary Anderson (Cherish)
Mr Dunne

Mrs Lemass
Margaret Bocle
Hilda Tweedy

25 January 1975
Seán D Loftus (pg)
Arthur Reynolds (pg)
Thomas Watt (pg)
Dr John Kelly (pg)
Dr James McGill (pg)
Maureen Killeavey (pg)
Takashi Ochi (ent)
Jazz Coasters (ent)
Hilary Boyle (pg)
Tom Hudson (pg)
Noel Broderick (pg)
Deirdre Greer-Delaney (ent)
Walter Trohan (ent)

1 February 1975
Frederick Forsythe (wr)
Jean Moorehead (pg)
Catherine McGuinness (pg)
Maureen Johnson (pg)
Mairead Allen (pg)
Gemma Hussey (pg)
Mary O'Dwyer (pg)
Paddy O'Flynn (pg)
Jerry Rooney (pg)
Niall Meegan (pg)
Dusty Millar (pg)
Hugh McCullough (pg)
Soft Ware (ent)
J Deegan (ent)
P Phelan (ent)
The Tumblers (ent)

8 February 1975
No Show

15 February 1975
Julie Felix (ent)
Matt Munroe (pg)
Joan Turner (pg)
Joe Lynch (pg)
Boys of the Lough (ent)
Donovan (ent)
Herbie Brennan (wr)
Jo Hughes

22 February 1975
Ib Jorgensen (pg)
Patricia Jorgensen (pg)
Brendan Coffey (pg)
Seán D Loftus (pg)
Thomas Watt (pg)
John Kelly (pg)
Arthur Reynolds (pg)
Ann Tolan (pg)

1 March 1975
Education Special

8 March 1975
Rathmines and Rathgar
   Musical Society (ent)
Lord Kilbracken (pg)
Bal Moan (ent)
Geoffrey Buckley (ent)
Robert Nichol (pg)
Peter Kelly (pg)
Russell Winn (pg)
Henry Murdoch (pg)
Frank Mason (pg)
Bob Poole (pg)

John Browne (pg)
Fred Nolan (pg)
Mr Cobbe (pg)

15 March 1975
The Swarbriggs (ent)
City Waites (ent)
Geraldine Brannigan (ent)
Catriona Yeats (ent)
Julian Hodgson (sp)
Hilary Healy (sp)
Henry Higgins (sp)
Ann Shouldice (sp)
Des McCarthy (sp)
Mrs Robinson (pg)
Bill Darman (pg)
Lady Wicklow (pg)
Jock Maguire (pg)
Fionnuala Brennan (pg)

22 March 1975
No Show

29 March 1975
The Non-Stop Connolly
   Show (ent)
Lee Dunne (wr)
Danny Cummins (ent)
The Wolfe Tones (ent)
Etienne Rynne (pg)
Jean Holmes (ent)
Dr John Rush (ent)
Desmond Leslie (wr)
Maurice Abrahamson (pg)
Fr Quigley (pg)

5 May 1975
Ian Whitcomb (pg)
Clifford T Ward (ent)
Red Hurley (ent)
Dublin Grand Opera Society
   (ent)
Prof Clemens Benda (pg)
Mr Rex Brinkworth (pg)
Mr John Connolly (pg)
Patricia Jorgenson (pg)
Thérèse Nelson (pg)
Rosemary Smith (pg)
Ted Bonner (pg)
Dr Karl Mullen (pg)
Suzanne McDougall (pg)
Eamonn Cannon (pg)
Lady Antonia Wardell (pg)
Ian Whitcomb (pg)
Lord Jeremy Altamont (pg)
Noel Carroll (pg)
Mrs Susan Philips (pg)

12 April 1975
Oswald Mosley (pg)
Prof Maurice Manning (pg)

Johnny McEvoy (ent)
Jack Cruise (ent)
Bothy Band (ent)
Dermont Walsh (pg)
Michael Vaughan (pg)
Nancy Fitzgerald (pg)
Angela Muckley (pg)

19 April 1975
George Melley (ent)
St Louis Group (ent)
Paddy Crosbie (ent)
John David Biggs (pg)
Mrs Biggs (pg)
Jack Kyle (sp)

26 April 1975
Tom Savage (pg)
Brendan Coffey (pg)
Pat O'Loughlin (pg)
Fr Michael Cleary (pg)
Loudest Whisper (ent)
Enzo Plazzota (pg)
Dr Helen Roseveare (pg)

3 May 1975
Jimmy Saville (ent)
Lady Plowden (pg)
Jan Morris (pg)
The Memories (ent)
Shawaddy Waddy (ent)

10 May 1975
Olympia Theatre Special

17 May 1975
Sammy Cahn (ent)
Broderick Crawford (pg)
Anne Bushnell/Jack McGinn
  Quartet (ent)
Des Smith (pg)
Frank Sutcliffe (pg)

24 May 1975
Mr George Colley T D (pol)
Richard Harris (pg)
Eavan Boland (wr)
Kevin O'Farrell (pg)
Lief Reck Group (ent)

31 May 1975
Special on Michael O'Hehir

7 June 1975
Simon Williams (pg)
Dermot Breen (pg)
Jane Seymour (pg)
Carol Cleveland (pg)
Jackie Tongue (pg)
Pat Wayne (pg)
Peter Jenkinson (pg)
The Janacheks (ent)
Niall Toibín (ent)
Susan Milch (ent)

11 October 1975
Asachi Controversy

18 October 1975
John Ryan (pg)
Clement Freud (pg)
Erich Von Daniken (pg)
Tanya Tucker (ent)
The Swarbriggs (ent)
Richard Blore (ent)

25 October 1975
Tony Buzan (pg)
20 Danish Gymnasts (ent)
Sandra Brown (pg)
Chris de Burgh (ent)
Grace O'Shaughnessy and
  models (pg)
Kalman Dobos (pg)
Pat Fanning and 4 Christian
  Bros (pg)

1 November 1975
Jimmy Chipperfield (pg)

Bud Freeman & Group (ent)
Charles Aznavour (ent)
Dr Paddy Leahy (pg)
Nurse of the Year
  Competition

8 November 1975
Ulick O'Connor (wr)
Terry Prone (pg)
Gerry Davis (pg)
Milo O'Shea (ent)
Barrie Cooke (pg)
The Stylistics (ent)
Tony Kenny (ent)
The Corriamo Choir (ent)

15 November 1975
Special on Divorce
Rathmines & Rathgar
  Musical Society (ent)
Pumpkinhead (ent)

22 November 1975
Margaret Powell (pg)
Gemma Craven (ent)
Shay Healy (pg)
Young Lindsay Singers (ent)
Veronica McSwiney (ent)
James Galway (ent)
Mary Cole (pg)

29 November 1975
David Bellamy (pg)
Evelyn Reed (pg)
Shay Healy (pg)
Rosaleen Linehan (ent)
Des Keogh (ent)
Patricia Cahill (ent)
Champagne (ent)
Donovan (ent)

6 December 1975
Marie Walsh (pg)
John Rush (pg)
Tony Malone (ent)
Ray McAnally (pg)
Ronnie Masterson (pg)
Brendan Cauldwell (pg)
The Chieftains (ent)
David Niven (pg)

13 December 1975
Toy Show

20 December 1975
No Show

27 December 1975
The Occult Special
Geraldine Brannigan (ent)

1976

3 January 1976
Emmanual Shinwell (pg)
Gordon Thomas (wr)
Michael O'Duffy (pg)
John O'Connor (ent)
Children's Theatre Company
  (ent)
Frank Harte (pg)

10 January 1976
Dr Conor Cruise O'Brien (pg)
Prof John A Murphy (pg)
Tim Pat Coogan (med)
Sen Eoin Ryan (pol)
Dr James Fairly (pg)
Fr Dan Noonan (pg)
Dickie Rock (ent)
Trinity (ent)

17 January 1976
Liz and Phil Mooney (pg)
Greta Hughes (ent)
Bothy Band (ent)
Mary O'Hara (ent)
Aidan Grenell (pg)
Colin Smith (pg)

Dr Richard Mackarness (pg)

24 January 1976
Special on the Budget

31 January 1976
50 Years of Radio Special

7 February 1976
(?)

14 February 1976
Special on Sex
Rosaleen Linehan (ent)
Aileach (ent)
Danny Doyle (ent)

21 February 1976
Marianne Faithful (ent)
John McNally (ent)
Larry Adler (pg)
Howard Kinny (pg)
Ronan Wilmot (pg)
Jeremy Thorpe MP (pol)
Gerhardt Lensen (pg)

28 February 1976
Bobby Beasley (sp)
Noel Purcell (pg)
Dermot Kelly Quartet (ent)
Pat Quinn (pg)
Packy Hayden (ent)
Breda Foley (ent)
Joe Cuddy (ent)
Los Paraguayos (ent)
Pritu Vashti (pg)

6 March 1976
The Wombles (ent)
Nancy Kominsky (pg)
Brendan Bowyer (ent)
Eddie Moore (pg)
Bernard Share (pg)
The New Excelsior (ent)
Talking Machine (ent)
Dr Glen Doman (pg)
Paul Brady (ent)
Shanty Nairdoo (ent)

13 March 1976
Special from Limerick
Mick Delahunty (ent)
Tommy Drennan & Choir
  (ent)
Jabberwocky (ent)
Pageant Choir (ent)

20 March 1976
Shaft Band (ent)
The Bards (ent)
Des McHale (pg)
Sharon Gmelch (pg)
Gabriel Estarellas (ent)
Seán O'Cearbhaill (pg)
Dr McCarthy (pg)
Nuala Fennell (pg)
Moira Woods (pg)
Des O'Neill (pg)
Judith Cahill (pg)

27 March 1976
Red Hurley (ent)
Brendan Grace (ent)
Richard Condon (pg)
Minnie Clancy (ent)
June Crocker (ent)
John Gibson (pg)
Dr Francis O'Connor (pg)
Constance Behan (pg)
Mrs Hughes (pg)
The Jim Doherty Trio (ent)
Ted Bonner (pg)

3 April 1976
(?)

10 April 1976
Eamonn Cannon (pg)
Emer O'Kelly (med)

Pat Quinn (pg)
Ted Bonner (pg)
Naomi Kidney Palmer (pg)
Mike Murphy (med)
Karl Mullen (pg)
Constance Behan (pg)
David Cabot (pg)
Patricia Jorgensen (pg)
Rosemary Smith (pg)
Pamela Mant (pg)
Christy Moore (ent)
Eileen Reid (ent)

17 April 1976
Marcella Bernstein (pg)
Mr R Condon (pg)
Veronica McSweeney (ent)
John Oates (ent)
Dervla Murphy (wr)
Yehudi Menuhin (ent)
Maureen Hegarty (pg)
Philip Greene (pg)
Our Lady's Choral Society
  (ent)
Roly Daniels (ent)
The Pint Machine (ent)

24 April 1976
Michael Parkinson (med)
Roger Leon (pg)
Deirdre McSharry (med)
Mary Kenny (med)
Kelly's Heroes (ent)
Derek Bridges (pg)
Patricia Kavanagh (pg)

1-22 May 1976
No shows

29 May 1976
Maureen Potter (ent)
D J Curtin (ent)
David Langton (pg)
Dinah Sheridan (pg)
Niall Murray (pg)
Douglas Fairbanks Jr (pg)
Kathleen Nolan (pg)

5 June 1976
Nicola Kerr (ent)
Clare Boylan (wr)
Rosemary Smith (pg)
Emer O'Kelly (pg)
Kay Toal (pg)
Five 'Mr Late Late'
  contestants (pg)
Brendan Shine (ent)
Thomas O'Hanlon (pg)
Gemma Hassen (ent)
Rosaleen Linehan (ent)
Des Keogh (ent)
Liam Ó Murchú (pg)
Tony Butler (pg)
Catherine McGuinness (pg)

2 October 1976
Tony Summers (wr)
Tom Mangold (pg)
Paddy Doherty (pg)
Group of Flamenco Dancers
  (ent)
Theodora Fitzgibbon (med)
Eamon Coughlan (sp)
Deirdre Ryan and models
  (pg)
Anna McGoldrick (ent)

9 October 1976
Joe Cuddy (ent)
Jim Fahy (med)
Jean Vanier (pg)
Donal Donnolly (pg)
Mary O'Hara (ent)
Tony Buzan (pg)

16 October 1976
Elizabeth Harris (pg)

Group from 'Maritana' with
  Austin Gaffney (ent)
Terry Reid (pg)
Louise Browne (pg)
Colman Pierce (pg)
Pam Ayres (wr)
Jim Farley (ent)
David and Nonie Phillips
  (pg)

23 October 1976
Frank Muir (pg)
Shirley Conran (wr)
Stirling Moss (sp)
Joe Grimond (pg)
Kevin Johnson (pg)
The Wolfe Tones (ent)

30 October 1976
Special from Co. Wexford

6 November 1976
Albert Gubay (pg)
Alan and Hazel Fletcher (pg)
John Seymour (pg)
Peter and Jill Mullet (pg)
Donald and Mary Grant (pg)
Nana Mouskouri (ent)

13 November 1976
Peter Murray (pg)
Dr Risteard Mulcahy (pg)
Des McHale (pg)
Rathmines & Rathgar
  Musical Society (ent)
Terry O'Connor (pg)
Carmel Moore (pg)
Atfuko Hibiki (pg)
Tina (ent)
Semprini (ent)

20 November 1976
Alexander Bros (ent)
Harry Lorayne (pg)
James Hunt (sp)
John Watson (pg)
Dickie Rock (ent)
Sandie Jones (ent)
Mairéad Corrigan (pg)
Betty Williams (pg)
Ciaran McKeown (pg)

27 November 1976
Dick Katz (ent)
Ray Azala (pg)
John Carroll (pg)
Michael Crowe (pg)
Jilly Cooper (wr)
Rita Killian (pg)
Jack Cruise (ent)
The Cotton Mill Boys (ent)
Joanne Mollereau (pg)
Sylvia Meehan (pg)
Una Claffey (pg)
Chris de Burgh (ent)
Alice Glenn (pg)

4 December 1976
Faith Browne (ent)
The Jim Doherty Trio (ent)
Maeve Binchy (wr)
The Bothy Band (ent)
Dr Magnus Pike (pg)
Derek Bowskill (pg)
Nana Mouskouri (ent)
Hugh Leonard (wr)
Jimmy Magill (pg)

11 December 1976
The Indians
Ken Hamilton
Bugsy Malone (Child Star)
Pam Ayres
The Courtneys
Jim Doherty

18 December 1976
Special on Maureen Potter

25 December 1976
No Show

31 December 1976
New Year's Eve Special

1977

8 January 1977
Fred Astaire (pg)
Ava Astaire (pg)
Peter Ustinov (pg)
Louis Stewart Quartet (ent)

15 January 1977
Up With People (ent)
Lady Harlech (pg)
Brendan Coffey (pg)
Michael O'Beirne (pg)
Hans Kung (pg)

22 January 1977
Paul Griffin (pg)
Peter Kowlher (pg)
David Cabot (pg)
Tommy Makem (ent)
Liam Clancy (ent)
Des Colgan (pg)
A J Went (pg)
Jim Mitchell, Lord Mayor of
  Dublin: (pol)
Ned Brennan (pg)
Colm Ó Briain (pg)
John Stephenson (pg)

29 January 1977
Food Special

5 February 1977
Lord and Lady Dunraven
  (pg)
Brendan Shine (ent)
Maura O'Dea (pg)
Lil Smith (ent)
The Jim Doherty Trio (ent)
Dick Emery (ent)
Fr Peter Lemass (pg)
Gordon Heald (pg)
Nick Robinson (pg)
Niamh Cusack (ent)

12 February 1977
Larry Cunningham (ent)
Jack Marrinan (pg)
Dame Ruth Railton (pg)
Mr and Mrs J Murphy (pg)
Catherine Gaughan (pg)
Christopher Cox (pg)
'Cherish'
Dana Wynter (pg)
David Kennedy (pg)
Paul McGuinness (pg)
Dylan Todd (pg)
Honor Moore (pg)
Jimmy Flahive (pg)

19 February 1977
No Show

26 February 1977
Colin and Rosie Swale (pg)
Tim Severin (sp)
Lady Arran (pg)
Gudmundur Kjaernsted (pg)
Brendan O'Kelly (pg)
Joey Murrin (pg)
John O'Connor (pg)
Brian Love (pg)

5 March 1977
Special from Co. Sligo

12 March 1977
John Carroll (pg)
Paul Johnson (pg)
Paddy Lane (pg)
Peter Cassells (pg)
Bert Weedon (ent)
Mr Teahan (pg)
Albert Gubay (pg)

Pat Quinn (pg)
Danny Doyle (ent)
Kate O'Callaghan (pg)
Brendan Coffey (pg)
Michael O'Beirne (pg)
Hans Kung (pg)

19 March 1977
Val Doonican (ent)
The Drifters (ent)
Tim Rose (pg)
Joan Armatrading (ent)
Ian Whitcomb (pg)

26 March 1977
Moira Anderson's Trio (ent)
Kieran Moore (pg)
Stuart McDonald with Noel
  Healy and Duo (ent)

Dr Winning (pg)
Dr Worlock (pg)
Dr Birch (pg)
Dr C Daly (pg)
Eamonn Casey (pg)

2 April 1977
The Garda Choir (ent)
John Dean (pg)
Dr John Hanson (pg)
Dr Carmody (pg)
Jim and Marion Lenihan (pg)
Hugh O'Brien (pg)
Vincent Banks (pg)
Catherine Keane (pg)
Red Hurley (ent)
Tony Adams (pg)
Rosita Sweetman (pg)

9 April 1977
Sandie Jones (ent)
Tony Malone (pg)
Kyung Wha Chung (pg)
Guinness Choir (ent)
Bernie Flint (ent)
Floyd Patterson (pg)
Tony Brutus (ent)
Bernadette Greevy (ent)
John Kavanagh (pg)

16 April 1977
Tess Kelly Doran (pg)
Sister Gabriel (pg)
Irene Penton (pg)
Catherine McGuinness (pg)
Betty Williams (pg)
Supply Demand and Curve
  (ent)
The Furey Bros (ent)

23 April 1977
Brendan Hatigan (pg)
Martin O'Donoghue (pg)
Myles Staunton (pg)
Dr Brendan Walshe (pg)
Des Norton (pg)
Alan Matthews (pg)

30 April 1977
The Swarbriggs plus 2 (ent)
Cakes and Ale (ent)
David Nixon (ent)
Jimmy Saville (ent)
Take Four (ent)

Inspector Walker (pg)
Crystal Gayle (ent)
Marie Soden (pg)

7 May 1977
No Show

14 May 1977
Eamonn Cannon (pg)
Mary Finan (pg)
Pat Kenny (pg)
Patricia Jorgensen (pg)
Eamon Coughlan (pg)
Miriam Woodbyrne (pg)
Ted Bonner (pg)
Alma Carroll (pg)
Paddy Leahy (pg)
Dr Karl Mullen (pg)

Gemma Craven (pg)
Fergus Slattery (pg)
Sacha Distel (ent)
Ciarán MacMathúna (pg)
Atrium Musicae (ent)

21 May 1977
Gina and Dale Hayes (ent)
Michael O'Connor (pg)
St Brigid's School Choir (ent)
Denis Larkin (pg)
Elsie O'Donovan (pg)
Seán Mealy (pg)
Tony Ryder (pg)
Bill O'Connell (pg)
Mon Murphy (pg)
Mary Whitehouse (pg)

28 May 1977
Fashion Special

4 June 1977
Gemma Craven (ent)
Loretto O'Connor (ent)
Tony Kenny (ent)
Ballybunion Bachelors (ent)
Dorothy Nelson (pg)
John M Hutchings (pg) (?)
Anna Fenton (pg) (?)
Raymond Brophy (pg) (?)
Jim Doherty (ent)
Eamonn Campbell (ent)
James A McKay (ent)
Trevor Power (pg)
Deirdre Ryan (pg)
Noel Pearson (ent)
Oliver Barry (ent)
Martin St James (pg)
Murray Boland (pg)
Mr Protheroe-Brynon (pg)
Cathy Nugent (pg)
Aine O'Connor (pg)
Grace O'Shaughnessy (pg)
Jean O'Reilly (pg)
Marguerite MacCurtain (pg)
Willie Kinsella (pg)
Dessie Lynch (pg)
Mrs Feldman (pg)
Michael Pill (pg)
Catherine Cotter (pg)
Kay Clerkin (pg)
Cecile Morgan (pg)

For this particular section the
records are poor and the
guests are listed to the best
of our ability.

1 October 1977
The Boomtown Rats (ent)
Hugh Leonard (wr)
Antonia Wardell (pg)
Tony Ensor (sp)
Philomena Collins (pg)
Mick McCarthy (pg)
Cara Evans (pg)
Des McHale (pg)

8 October 1977
Dorothy Nelson (pg)
Mike Murphy (pg)
Joe Dolan (ent)
Mary Woodworth (pg)
Heather Perdue (pg)
Margaret Barratt (pg)
Muriel Gallagher (pg)
Helen Robinson (pg)
Anne Shumate (ent)
Alo Donegan (pg)
Brendan Madden (pg)
O'Sullivan Brothers (ent)
Brad Ashton (pg)

15 October 1977
Frank Carson (ent)
Dorothy Nelson (pg)
Michael Ponder (pg)
Linda Byrne (pg)
Sheila Cassidy (pg)
Patrick Masterson (pg)
David Berman (pg)

22 October 1977
Cast from The Riordans (ent)
Wesley Burrows (med)
Dorothy Nelson (pg)
Colm C T Wilkinson (ent)
The Glasnevin Musical
  Society (ent)
Paddy Masterson (pg)
David Berman (pg)
The Duanes (ent)
Greta Hughes (pg)

29 October 1977
Siobhán McKenna (pg)
Niall Buggy (pg)
Members of the National
  Dairy Council (?)
Duo (ent)
Joe Byrne (ent)
Denis Johnston (wr)
Noel Griffin (pg)
Seán Kelleher (pg)
Patricia Fehily (pg)
John Rooney (pg)
Garret Mac Ainmhire (pg)

5 November 1977
Myrtle Allen (pg)
Parrots and the Adairs (ent)
George Melly (ent)
Hank Locklin (ent)
Billy Boyle (ent)
Philomena Begley (ent)
Juniper Green (ent)

12 November 1977
Mrs Jimmy Carter (pg)
Pat Lovell (pg)
Eddie Kehir (pg)
Des Moines Jazz Band (ent)
Tommy Reilly (ent)
James Moody (ent)

19 November 1977
Programme on alcoholism

26 November 1977
Lord George Brown (pg)
Angela Williams (pg)

David Berman (pg)
Fr Michael Ledwith (pg)
Paddy Masterson (pg)
Steven McCarthy (pg)
Veronica McSweeney (ent)
Des Smyth (pg)

3 December 1977
Desmond Morris (wr)
Ronnie Delaney (sp)
Tony Buzan (pg)
Derek Daly (sp)
Daly & Wayne (ent)
Mary Woodworth (pg)
Stefan Grappelli (ent)
Trinity (ent)

10 December 1977
Toy show

17 December 1977
Neil Boyle (pg)
John Le Mesurier (pg)
Pierce Hinkston (pg)
Joe Conroy (pg)
Daniel Kaufman (pg)
Tony Drennan Band (ent)
Patricia Cahill & Ciaran (ent)
Pat Crowley (pg)
Mary Finan (pg)
Thelma Mansfield (pg)
Grace O'Shaughnessy (pg)
Susane McDougald (pg)
Anne Rehill (pg)
Anne O'Brien (pg)
Terry Keane (pg)

24 December 1977
No Show

31 December 1977
Anne Bushnell (ent)
Jim Doherty Quartet (ent)
Sheeba (ent)
Jazz Coasters (ent)

1978

7 January 1978
Rod Taylor (ent)
Mr and Mrs Tom McGrath
  (pg)
Dave Guiney (pg)
Terence Molloy (ent)
Veronica McSwiney (ent)
Dave Gunnery (pg)
Na Filí (ent)
Joanne Mollereaux (pg)
Dee Ryan (pg)
Norman Hamilton Farmer
  (pg)

14 January 1978
Charles Lynch (ent)
Patricia McCarry (ent)
Denise Kelly (ent)
Albert Bradshaw (pg)
Veronica McSweeney (ent)
Doris Keogh (ent)
Thérèse Timoney (pg)
Brigid Dolan (pg)
The Carlow Union Choir
  (ent)
John Gibson (pg)
The Georgian Brass
  Ensemble (ent)
Madeline Bradley (pg)
The Capriol Consort (ent)
Anne O'Brien (pg)
Michael O'Rourke (pg)

21 January 1978
The Bothy Band (ent)
The McCartan Brothers (pg)
Ted Nealon (pol)
Frank Dunlop (pol)
Eileen Lemass (pol)
Niall Andrews (pol)
(cont. on page 63)

OUTSIDE AND ABOUT

Joe Barry explains the innovation and expertise behind an outside television broadcast

A TV outside broadcast is a complex operation, and particularly so when covering major national events. RTE TV outside broadcasts have an outstanding record, stretching back to the first live OB in Dublin's O'Connell Street on New Year's Eve, 1961, launching the new TV service. Many will remember the live TV coverage of President John F Kennedy's visit to Ireland, and the subsequent visits of Pope John Paul II and, more recently, Presidents Reagan

and Gorbachev. The great national sporting occasions seen live in Ireland and in many parts of the world are TV outside broadcasts, as are other major events such as the Telethon, Live Aid and, of course, the Eurovision song contests. All of these have helped to establish RTE world-wide as a progressive and innovative broadcasting organisation.

To achieve this level of professional expertise requires the input of many talented technological and operational experts working with the most sophisticated of modern broadcasting equipment and software.

Mounting an outside broadcast means developing a comprehensive plan. In a typical OB situation, such as a football or hurling match, the OB unit manager and a director visit the location and set up the technical and operational plans. These establish the disposition of an agreed number of cameras around the ground. Approximately six cameras, including mobile cameras, are used on big games. While most of the action is shot on two main centreline cameras on towers or platforms, the additional cameras are strategically placed to enhance the production.

Computer graphics and team information are all a standard part of the production. All of these resources are provided not only to ensure that our standard of coverage compares favourably with the very best that our competitors, such as the much larger BBC, can achieve, but if possible, to surpass it.

The operational core area for any operation is the outside broadcast unit. This is a custom-built vehicle containing the control systems and operational equipment for vision, sound and communications. It is compartmentalised to accommodate a sound control room, a

Outside and About
(cont. from page 57)

vision and engineering control room and a production control room. Additional vehicles house videotape, editing and slow-motion facilities, and commentary control equipment to handle international commentators. The capital cost of a large OB unit is approximately £1.5m. It is crammed with the most modern technology and operated by highly skilled technicians. In the OB unit, sound and vision signals are processed in their respective areas. In the production area, the director makes the selection of camera pictures, which is either recorded on videotape machines or fed into microwave link transmitters which carry the signals to distant pick-up receivers. The vision and sound are inserted into the RTE network, fed out to the transmitters and broadcast to RTE viewers.

The Carroll's Irish Open Golf outside broadcast at Portmarnock involves laying many miles of cables, buried at various places to protect the public. RTE OB riggers and scaffolding contractors are first on the site. They set themselves up the previous week and lay camera, video and sound cables at various positions selected around the course. All these cables are connected to two OB units, which are used in a master/slave role to provide extensive coverage. Thirteen cameras are used, some on various high scaffolding towers and Simon's hoists, giving elevation of up to 80ft. A roving-eye radio camera, mounted appropriately enough on a golf buggy, provides enhanced coverage, with close-up shots on fairways and greens.

The video signals from the slaved or remote OB unit, which is located 'out the course', are transmitted to the main OB unit by microwave links. Here the incoming vision is interswitched with the cameras operating through this unit, which is usually placed beside the eighteenth green. Sound effects from various points at each hole covered are

passed back to the main OB unit and mixed with the commentary, as required.

The commentators are housed in a large Portakabin-type commentators' box, mounted on a scaffolding platform to give a good view of the area, particularly the eighteenth green. The commentators are provided with TV monitors showing the on-air pictures on which they comment. A number of sophisticated independent communication systems are provided that ensure information on a selective basis is available to all operational areas. All technical and directorial information is accomplished through the OB units.

A sophisticated scoring information system, using radiophones, provides up-to-date information from the course to the commentators, and also to the graphic computer for the master OB unit, where all the information is assembled and switched out 'on-air'.

Standby generators are provided to protect against a power outage. Security is also of considerable importance. The various camera towers attract the more adventurous spectators and there is always the possibility of serious accidents when large numbers are involved. Towers are protected from enthusiastic climbers in order to minimise shake problems while cameras using telescopic lenses hold tight focus on a golfer on a distant tee, half a mile away.

At least thirty people are directly involved in the operation and more than £3m of capital equipment is provided for this type of outside broadcast.

RTE do, on average, five outside broadcasts per week. Many of these are multi-day operations. This translates into a programme output of more than 800 hours per annum, or over two hours per day. How's about that then!

QUIZTIME
OPERA QUIZ

set by Ray Lynott

(cont. from page 37)

18. Name the composer living in Ireland whose most recent opera was a success in Copenhagen.

19. Name a play by an Irish author which has been made into an opera.

20. Did Luciano Pavarotti sing an opera role in Dublin?

21. How many of Verdi's operas are based on plays by Shakespeare?

22. Where was Bellini born?

23. What Irish singer took part in the first performance of *The Marriage of Figaro* by Mozart?

The late Tommy O'Brien

24. Who wrote 'Idomeneo'?

25. What was Wagner's first name?

26. Where did Wagner build his own opera-house?

(Answers on page 158)

SELLING UP-FRONT

Sales teams for RTE: on the left, the TV sales force, and below, the radio sales personnel

Television sales:

(left to right) Mary Courtney, Paul Mulligan, Colm Brophy, Aidan Burns (seated front), Leslie Hall, Tom Devine, Sheila Horan, Catherine Nolan, Hilda Clabby

Radio sales:

(left to right) Breda Brennan, Jacinta Kelly, Margaret O'Farrell, Dara Meaney, Ann Burke, Brian Bates (seated), Val Bates, Collette Manning

WORKSHOP WORKFORCE

Here's the team that works hammer and nails to make the sets you see

(left to right, front ground) Joe Doyle, Jim Davy, Gay Coates, Bill Farrell, Brian Comiskey, Michael Smith; (left to right, back) Michael O'Connor, Jim Mooney, Frank Healy, Pat Tigh

TRANSMITTING A GENERAL ELECTION OVER THE AIRWAVES

Ann O'Donnell examines the difficulties and complexities of making election results known nationwide

No doubt you have heard it said that the best way to follow general election results is to sit in front of the TV, with the sound turned down, and listen to the radio. You can then turn up the TV when you see your favourite TD, or the TD to whom you are allergic, appear on the screen.

John O'Connor, the head of radio production facilities and communications, explains why the radio can communicate election results more rapidly than the TV. Unlike television, radio is a highly mobile and flexible medium of communication—one man and his mike can go to mow a meadow (or at least record it being mowed). This, of course, is a slight simplification in the context of recording and transmitting election results. However, because of the relative simplicity of radio communications, results can and do come into the main election studio in the RTE Radio Centre as soon as they are available, and are transmitted to the public almost immediately. Television transmission is much more complex and therefore cannot convey this information as quickly or easily as radio.

At general elections RTE, as part of its public service broadcasting obligation, must provide outside broadcast radio units at every count centre in the country. A corporate decision was taken about ten years ago by RTE that the quality and extent of election coverage was to be of the highest calibre. As a result of that decision, operational and technical manuals on how to broadcast elec-

tions were drawn up. Now a protocol exists, based on those manuals, which is followed for all elections.

Long before polling day, John O'Connor starts the process of ensuring that we all receive the most up-to-date radio information and results from all over the country. Detailed lists of returning officers, technicians, reporters, Telecom contacts and other relevant data are drawn up for each constituency. Further lists are prepared with information as specific as the type of sound equipment to be used by each reporter. The more detailed these lists, the more likely it is that everything will go smoothly on polling day. Every count centre is in direct communication with one of the RTE studios in Donegal, Castlebar, Tralee, Sligo, Galway, Limerick, Waterford, Cork or Dublin. Each provincial studio has a full production team producer, presenter and technical staff. RTE in Dublin acts as the main switching centre through which all the

provincial studios transmit their coverage.

Information from provincial studios is fielded to one of the four election studios in Donnybrook, one of which (Studio 10 usually) is the main election studio. The producer in Studio 10 is responsible for the production of the entire radio election coverage. Information from all the provincial studios and the other Dublin studios is passed to Studio 10, where decisions are taken about which studio will transmit to the public at any particular time. You can begin to understand just how complex is the transmission of election results and coverage on radio.

THERE IS MASSIVE PRE-PLANNING

What we eventually hear on our radio sets is dependent upon massive pre-planning in relation to the establishment of high-quality programme circuits (which carry the sound of voices over the air) all over the country. Some areas of the country have better circuits than others. Where no adequate circuits, or an insufficient number of such circuits are available, trunk links or direct exchange lines (telephone lines) are used as back-ups. Since the mouthpiece in the ordinary telephone distorts sound, the RTE and Telecom staff remove the entire phone and attach high-quality microphones to the telephone wire. Telecom Éireann works in very close co-operation with RTE in the pre-planning for elections, as it is Telecom which provide all the circuits requested by RTE. All circuits leading into every count

THEY MAY GREET YOU ON ARRIVAL

Receptionists

(left to right) Maura Mitchell, Laura Hyland, Yvonne Doran

centre, provincial studio and Dublin studio, must be in perfect working order before election day.

John O'Connor tells a story of a pre-election technical nightmare which happened a few years ago. The day before polling day a JCB ripped up all the circuits leading into the Portlaoise count centre. Thanks to the swift and skilled action of Telecom technicians the circuits were restored to working order in time for the election.

Yet another layer of complexity in this already highly technical operation is ensuring that all incoming results are speedily fed into the computer, based in the main switching centre in the Dublin studio building. The computer results come in on radio circuits and are fed out to the radio and TV studios. RTE uses very modern computer equipment to this end. A number of years ago, John O'Connor came across the now redundant magnet boards (owned by Telecom) in seeking the most effective switch system to link in with the computer. Some readers will remember these old magnet boards in post offices, which were used for holding and transferring calls on manual exchanges. John discovered that these were the most suitable system for feeding election results into the computer, as they are exceptionally simple and flexible, despite being so old.

When next you listen to election results on your radio, you will know that both old and new technologies are involved in letting you know who will be running the country.

THEY MAY FEED YOU BEFORE YOU LEAVE

Canteen Staff

(left to right, standing rear) Mark Dickinson, Tony Campbell, Catherine Mullen, Jean Tracy, Danny Gallagher, Ciara Fotrell, Fran Gaffney, Mary Davin, Fergus Murphy; (left to right, seated front) Pamela Rooney, Marion Leahy, Maureen Condon

THE REGIONAL CORRESPONDENTS

Tommie Gorman finds that ordinary people display great dignity under pressure

Right: Tommie Gorman, Sligo: correspondent for the north-west

There's a line in T S Eliot's *Love Song of J Alfred Prufrock* which goes 'I have measured out my life in coffee spoons...'

The life of the regional correspondent is measured in ninety-second radio and television reports. While the material is being pursued and processed, it seems the most vital matter in the world. Gathered under pressure, transmitted as soon as possible, and in most instances, soon forgotten. The fruits of one's labour may serve as background noise in a pub or the stuff that helps to shorten a car journey. Why do we do it? Why is the next story the most important of all? Interesting questions.

It's a complex, demanding life. Logistics are as significant as the news items being pursued—can we make Buncrana and back in time for the six o'clock news?; if we get there, will someone talk to us? RTE's regional team in Sligo is compact—Tony and Michael on camera and sound; Jimmy and Gerry in studios; Catherine and Rory keeping us in order. Fortunately we're friends as well as colleagues because there is no room for divisions.

There's a sense of privilege in trying to give ordinary people their place in news bulletins and features. Ireland is small enough for us all to have our place. But it's a constant struggle. Compressing a point of view or personality into thirty seconds is difficult to say the least. In modern Ireland it's accepted that rule-bending right through to greed and corruption are the ways things get done.

Should the media be doing more about this or are we, unwittingly or otherwise, sometimes part of it?

In quiet moments, memories often return, but not necessarily from the big stories (Don Tidey, the hunger strikes, deaths at sea). Ordinary people sometimes display great dignity under pressure. Truth has its own eloquence. A woman once explained poverty by showing me an empty fridge; another woman in Derry, angered by Section 31, accused me of betraying the pursuit of truth.

Six of us work in the regions— Michael Ryan, Tom McSweeney, Jim Fahy, Michael Lally, Gerry Reynolds. Every so often we gather and curse our sense of isolation and the lack of understanding shown by the dinosaur, RTE, to our problems.

Then we go back to our patches...the phone rings and the game is on again. The phone hopping in the middle of the night usually means important work. When that sound ceases to get the adrenaline running, it's time to move on.

THE OTHER REGIONAL CORRESPONDENTS ARE:

Europe: Eamonn Lawlor

Athlone: Gerry Reynolds

Belfast: Jim Dougal

Limerick: Michael Lally

Waterford: Michael Ryan

London: Mike Burns

Galway: Jim Fahy

Cork: Tom McSweeney

(cont. from page 56)
John Boland (pol)
Michael D'Arcy (pol)
Ruairi Quinn (pol)
Al O'Donnell (ent)
D J Curtin (ent)

28 January 1978
Anne Brogan (pg)
Eddie Macken (sp)
The Spinners (ent)
Rudolf Wenter (pg)
The Bomas Dancers (ent)
Carolyn Faulder (pg)
Paul Brown (pg)
Tom Savage (pg)
Dr Charlie Smith (pg)
Jim Barnes (pg)
Maeve Bolger (pg)

4 February 1978
Anne Brogan (pg)
Mary O'Hara (ent)
Dana (ent)
Lithuanian Dancers (ent)
Theodora Fitzgibbon (med)
Micheline McCormack (pg)
Anne Mather (pg)
The Bomas Dancers (ent)
Gemma Craven (pg)

11 February 1978
Rev Stanley Baird (pg)
Bernadette Quinn (pg)
Dr Paddy Leahy (pg)
Barbara Shiffer (pg)
Sr Eileen Keoghan (pg)

18 February 1978
Colette Proctor (ent)
Peters and Lee (ent)
Horace Dobbs (pg)
John Stokes (pg)
Stacc (ent)
Dr Colin Martin (pg)
Betina Lowman (pg)
Mairéad Corrigan (pg)
Ian Whitcombe (ent)

25 February 1978
Tony Hatch (ent)
Jackie Trent (ent)
Rathmines and Rathgar
  Musical Society (ent)
Carmel Moore (ent)
Mme Nuaha Al Hegelan (pg)
Geraldine (ent)
Philip Cleary (pg)
Chips (ent)
Tony Malone Pipe Band (ent)
Ben Briscoe (pg)
Dr Masud Hoghugi (pg)

4 March 1978
No Show

11 March 1978
Roly Hatfield (pg)
John Carroll (pg)
Tom Sharkey (pg)
Anne O'Dowd (pg)
Trevor Power (pg)
Judy Toner (pg)
Dolores Rockett (pg)
Anne McGuinness (pg)
Alvis Crawford (pg)
Liz McWeeney (pg)
John Healy (pg)
Lyla Kennedy (pg)
Tony Stevens (ent)
Lucky Numbers (ent)
Gary Trimble (pg)

18 March 1978
Brendan O'Reilly (pg)

Thomas Boyle (ent)
Fr Noel Holden (pg)
Terry O'Connor (ent)
Jack McGinn (ent)
Mary Woodworth (pg)
Walter Bowart (ent)
Brian Kennedy (ent)
John McGuffin (pg)
George Dyke (ent)

25 March 1978
P M Todd (pg)
Deirdre Tierney (pg)
John Tierney (pg)
Terence McParland (pg)
Angela McParland (pg)
Fionnuala Wallace (pg)
Maurice Cassidy (pg)
Monica Cassidy (pg)
Clara Clarke (pg)
Connie Merriman (pg)
Loretto O'Connor (ent)
Tony Kenny (ent)
Danny Cummins (ent)
Denis O'Sullivan (ent)
Kristin O'Donovan (pg)
Patricia Keilthy (pg)
Cheryl Freeny (pg)
Geraldine Brand (pg)
Eilis Cloherty (pg)
Michael Fitzgerald (pg)
Mary Connolly (pg)
Grace O'Shaughnessy (pg)
Maureen Ahearne (pg)
Jennie Slevin (pg)
Sharon Bacon (pg)
Noelle Campbell-Sharp (med)

1 April 1978
Hughie Greene (ent)
Jury's Cabaret (ent)
Noel Nutley (pg)
Ned Brennan (pol)
Fergus O'Brien (pol)
Ald Kevin Byrne (pol)
Gervaise Keogh (ent)

8 April 1978
Tony Kenny (ent)
Des Smyth (ent)
Nicola Kerr (ent)
Angeline Butler (ent)
Rosaleen Linehan (ent)
Loretto O'Connor (ent)
Brendan Balfe (med)
Dale Alexander (pg)
Alan O'Grady (pg)
Aideen Dynan (ent)
Kathleen Behan (pg)
Dominic Behan (pg)
Jimmy Tarbuck (ent)
Rory Furlong (pg)
Noel Pearson (pg)

15 April 1978
Joe Linnane Special

22 April 1978
No Show

29 April 1978
Ronnie Stewart (ent)
Louis Stewart (ent)
Eamonn Andrews (pg)
David Frost (pg)
Red Hurley (ent)
Diana Dors (pg)
Donald Woods (pg)

6 May 1978
Twink (ent)
Floyd Patterson (sp)
Johnny Logan (ent)
Christine and Jacinta Hyland
  (ent)

Dr M Berber (pg)
Dr L Vella (pg)
Mme Bailey (pg)
Colm O'Doherty (pg)
Fr Seán Fagan (pg)
Angela McNamara (pg)
Pastor Robinson (pg)

13 May 1978
The Eric Sweeney Singers
  (ent)
Tim Severin (wr)
Brendan Quinn (ent)
Sir John Peck (pg)
Ian Wilson (pg)

20 May 1978
Sandie Jones (ent)
David Hamilton (pg)
Bart Ball (pg)
Rose Martin (pg)
Elder Fowler (pg)
Elder Flynn (pg)
The Foyle Choir (ent)
The Inaba Children (ent)
Inez Heron (pg)
Margaret Barry (pg)
Máire Ní Chatháin O'Malley
  (pg)

27 May 1978
Phil Lynott (ent)
Dolores Rockett (pg)
Liz McWeeney (pg)
John Healy (pg)
Lyla Kennedy (pg)
Anne McGuinness (pg)
Alvis Crawford (pg)
Mai Challoner (pg)
Sunshine (ent)
Lewis Leith (pg)
John Horgan (pg)
Eamonn Gilmore (pg)
Con Power (pg)
Fr Paul Andrews (pg)
Harry Chapin (ent)

3 June 1978
John Donegan Trio (ent)
Wendy Boland (pg)
Julie Anne Farnham (pg)
Caroline Going (pg)
Sharon Murphy (pg)
Grace Emmanuel (pg)
Barbara Clusky (pg)
Cassandra (pg)
Wendy Dagworthy (pg)
Barbara Kinley (pg)
Elizabeth Cleary (pg)
Patricia Kielthy (pg)
Kathleen Watkins (pg)
Winnie Butler (pg)
Cathal Dunne and Trio (ent)
Nell McCafferty (wr)
Margot Ahearn (pg)
Eileen O'Connor (pg)
Pierce Finnegan (pg)
Margaret McMenamin (pg)
Brenda Kenny (pg)
John Muldoon (ent)
Niall Toibín (pg)
Barbara Egan (pg)
Iris Michel (pg)
Valerie Furlong (pg)
Susan Hallinan (pg)

30 September 1978
Pádraig MacMathúna (ent)
Paddy Keenan (pg)
Prof Frank Brannigan
Hurricane Johnny & Jets (ent)
Brendan Shine (ent)
Gabrielle Walsh (pg)
Michael McDonagh (pg)

Dr E Hudson (pg)
Ronnie Delaney (pg)
Kevin O'Flanagan (pg)

7 October 1978
Alfonso Orbello (pg)
Up With People (ent)
Mike Carter (pg)
Robert White (ent)
Colman Pearce (ent)
Estelle Parsons (pg)
Monica Dickens (wr)

14 October 1978
The American Airforce Band
Bill Reilly & The Friendship
  Force (ent)
Eamonn O'Farrell (pg)
Murray Beates (pg)
Basil Payne (wr)
Shay Healy (ent)

21 October 1978
David Bromberg (ent)

Bart Bastable (pg)
Frank Patterson (ent)
Eily O'Grady (pg)
Lorraine O'Connor (ent)
Leo Rowsome (ent)
Bridget Boland (pg)
Wendy Cooper (pg)
Robert Harrison (pg)

28 October 1978
Shirley Lord (pg)
Bronwyn Conway (pg)
Jean O'Reilly (pg)
Glasnevin Mus. Society (ent)
John Corrigan (pg)
The Boys of the Lough (ent)
Daire Fitzgerald (ent)
Brendan Hyland (pg)
Prof J Bonar (pg)
Denis McLean (pg)
Geraldine Meegan (pg)

4 November 1978
Johnny McEvoy (ent)
Michael Conlon (pg)
Micko Russell & Friends (pg)
Gareth Edwards (pg)
Deirdre O'Callaghan (ent)
Noel Healy (ent)
Irish National Opera (ent)
Mr Charles Pocock (pg)
Prof Cedric Wilson (pg)
Elizabeth Cullen (pg)

Anthony McNamara (pg)
Mrs Loughman (pg)

11 November 1978
Conor Brady (med)
Derek Nally (med)
Howard Greer (pg)
David Broome (pg)
Harvey Smith (sp)
Paul Darragh (pg)
Ian and Ruth Walker (pg)
The Lookalikes (ent)
The Fureys (ent)
Coleen McCullagh (wr)

18 November 1978
Barbara Woodhouse (wr)
Bob Geldof (ent)
The Avoca Céilí Band (ent)
Jackie Collins (wr)
Lee Dunne (wr)
Frank McCaffrey (pg)
Valerie Riches (pg)

25 November 1978
Patrick O'Connell (pg)
Chris de Burgh (ent)
Nana Mouskouri (ent)
David Essex (ent)
Dr Eileen Byrne (pg)
Sylvia Meehan (pg)
Jessie Matthews (pg)
Wilfred Hyde White (pg)
Greta Hughes (pg)

2 December 1978
No Show

8 December 1978
Toy Show
The Lambert Family (pg)
The Kavanagh Family (pg)

16-30 December 1978
No Shows

31 December 1978
The Jazz Coasters (ent)
Brendan, Daragh and
  Siobhán Muldowney (ent)
Olive O'Neill (pg)
Susie Byrne (pg)
Adam Penney (pg)
Denise Nolan (pg)
Donie Farmer (pg)
Rozelle Cronin (pg)
Mary O'Neill (pg)
Glen Collins (pg)
Paul Collins (pg)
Jack Cruise (pg)

Jack Leonard (pg)
Jacinta White (pg)
Jean O'Reilly (pg)
Mary Woodworth (pg)
Frank Kelly (med)
Gabriel Byrne (pg)
Paul Darragh (pg)
June Levine (med)
Aine O'Connor (pg)
Tina (pg)
Ted Bonnar (pg)
Kevin Marron (pg)
Dave Heffernan (pg)
Caroline Erskine (pg)

1979

6 January 1979
Tony Walsh (pg)
Irene Rynhart (pg)
P Guiney (pg)
Margaret McCurtin (pg)
Rodney Rice (pg)
Ernie Evans (pg)
Seán Kinsella (pg)
George Keeley (pg)
John O'Beirne (pg)
Mary Purcell (sp)
Jim McCann and two
   musicians (ent)
M.A.S.H. (ent)
Eamonn McGirr (pg)
Young Scientist (ent)
Sr Nina Murphy (pg)

13 January 1979
Ray Bourke (pg)
Seán Coakly (pg)
Dr Bob Cuffe (pg)
Lucas Collins (pg)
Paul Blau (pg)
Petra Kelly (pg)
Dr Robert Blackith (pg)
Marie Creed (pg)
The Early Grave Band (ent)

20 January 1979
The Aces (ent)
Norman St John Stevas (pol)
Edna Jackman (pg)
Colman Pearce (ent)
Bernadette Greevy (ent)
Madeleine Berkley (pg)
Des Keogh (ent)
Rosaleen Linehan (ent)
Albert Healy (ent)
Eric Byrne (pg)
Paddy Lane (pg)
Peter Cassels (pg)
Dr Michael Woods (pol)
Michael Keating (pol)
Frank Fahy (pol)

27 January 1979
Geraldine Brannigan (ent)
Charlotte Rampling (pg)
Jean Michel Jarre (ent)
Christine Ortez (pg)
Father Alessio (pg)
Tommy Makem (ent)
Liam Clancy (ent)
Peter Ustinov (pg)
The Chieftains (ent)

3 February 1979
No Show

10 February 1979
Ivor Browne (pg)
Prof Norman Moore (pg)
The Lindsay Singers with
   Eithne Barror (ent)
Cathy McDowell (pg)
Theo Goyvertz (pg)

17 February 1979
Peters and Lee (ent)
Robert Powell (pg)
The Fureys (ent)
Michael Crowley (pg)
Damien O'Callaghan (pg)
Karin Dubsky (pg)
Gerrard Grennell (ent)
Box Car Willie (ent)
Colette Proctor (ent)
Ursula Fleming (pg)

24 February 1979
Noel Gilmore (pg)
Gina (ent)
Anne Bushnell and her son
   (ent)
Jenny Agutter (pg)
Bernard Share (pg)
Joe McGough (pg)
Paddy Crosbie (pg)
Eamonn MacThomáis (wr)
Doreen Wallace (pg)
Dr John Fleetwood (pg)
Matt Doolin (pg)
Tom Higgins (pg)

3 March 1979
Don Baker (ent)
Mary Black (ent)
Johnny Norris (ent)
Christy Geoghan (pg)
Martin O'Donoghue (pg)
E J Kellegher (pg)
Mick Rafferty (pg)
Larry Whelan (pg)
Seán Damer (pg)
Frank McGuire (pg)
John Creegan (pg)
Tony Gregory (pg)
Martha Reilly (pg)
Teresa Whelan (pg)
Jem Kiernan (pg)

10 March 1979
Val Doonican (ent)
Roger Richards (pg)
Mary O'Hara (ent)
Dave Gold (pg)
Desi Reynolds (pg)
Des Moore (ent)
John Drummond (pg)
Johnny Curran (pg)
Jakki Moore (pg)
Vanessa Pano (pg)
Hazel Kenny (pg)

17 March 1979
The Sands (ent)
Michael York (pg)
Veronica Dunne (pg)
Geraldine O'Grady (ent)
Linda Byrne (pg)
Stephen O'Shea (pg)
Three harpists (ent)
Emerald Girls Band (ent)
Bill Golding (pg)

24 March 1979
Cathal Dunne with Group
   (ent)
Sheila and Arthur Hailey
   (wr)
Gloria (ent)
Terry Williers (pg)
Margaret Ryan (pg)
Michael Kelly (pg)
Corrine Giacometti (pg)
Gary Keogh (pg)
Dana Andrews (pg)

31 March 1979
No Show

7 April 1979
Ailish Ní Phaidin (ent)
Lief Reck Group(ent)
Joan Denise Moriarty (pg)
Seán O'Dowd (ent)
Eileen Kieran (pg)
Joe McGough (pg)

14 April 1979
Stephane Grapelli with trio
   (ent)
Trapeze artists (ent)
Deirdre Cooling Nolan (ent)
Jennie Reddin (pg)

Seán O'Siocháin (pg)
Pat Whelan and group (ent)
Susan George (pg)
Oliver Reed (pg)

21 April 1979
Frankie Vaughan with trio
   (ent)
Robert White (ent)
John O'Conor (ent)
Michael O'Carroll (pg)
Dr Noel Hickey (pg)
Con Power (sp)
Fr Brian Hearne (pg)
Fr Declan Coyle (pg)
Jose Comblin (pg)

28 April 1979
Stocktons Wing (ent)
Courtney Kenny (ent)
Det Insp Denis Mullins (pg)
Dr Brian O'Shea (pg)
Stephen Meany (pg)
Jim Farley (ent)
Brendan O'Dowda (ent)

5 May 1979
The Nolan Sisters (ent)
Frank Kelly (ent)
Tony Kenny (ent)
The Jim Doherty Trio (ent)
Sandie Jones (ent)
Vince Hill (ent)
Adele King (Twink) (ent)
Red Hurley (ent)
Harry Armstrong (pg)
Valerie Jelley (pg)
Tony Buzan (pg)

12 May 1979
Brendan Shine (ent)
Brazil Tropical (ent)
Peter Healy Group (ent)
Canon James Horan (pg)
Moonjer Veggily Group (ent)
Mark Lewis (pg)
Mairéad Reynolds (pg)
Philip King (pg)
Rita Connolly (ent)
Fr Seán Fagan (pg)
Dr David Berman (pg)
Michael O'Sullivan SJ ((pg)

19 May 1979
Chinese Dancers (ent)

Alan Shatter (pg)
Muriel G Walls (pg)
Noel Clancy (pg)
The Wolfe Tones (ent)
Fr Daniel Berrigan (pg)
Glen Curtin (ent)
Maureen Concannon O'Brien
   (pg)
Russ McDermott (pg)
Dr Miriam Moore (pg)
Linda Hopkins (ent)

26 May 1979
Din Joe (pg)

Eric Benson (pg)
Dana (ent)
Harry Chapin (ent)
Phoebe Proskey (pg)
Imelda McCarthy (pg)
Sylvia Leahy (pg)
Master Thomas St Charles
   (pg)

2nd June 1979
Michael Kelly (pg)
Margaret Ryan (pg)
Corinne Giacometti (pg)
Gary Keogh (pg)
Terry Willers (pg)
Sonny Knowles (ent)
John Kavanagh (ent)
Adele King (Twink) (ent)
Terri Neason (ent)
Jim Doherty Quartet (ent)

6 October 1979
Billy John Armstrong (pg)
Fr Michael Cleary (pg)
Dr P Leahy (pg)
Monica Barnes (pg)
Gerry Fitt (pol)
Eamon McCann (med)
Angela McNamara (pg)
Joe Dolan (ent)
Virgin Prunes (ent)
Louden Wainright (ent)
Dave Allen (ent)

13 October 1979
Mr and Mrs Brown (pg)
Louise Browne (pg)
Dr Robert Harrison (pg)
Fr Dermod McCarthy (pg)
Teresa McCarthy (pg)
Kim Newport (ent)
Tommy Ware (pg)
Mrs Russell (pg)
Dr Vance Day (pg)
Joyce Grenfell (ent)
Colette Proctor (ent)
Magnus Magnusson (pg)
Japanese Flute Player (ent)

20 October 1979
Horslips (ent)
Brendan McCann (pg)
Seán Cooney (pg)
John D Carroll (pg)
John McNulty (pg)

Joe Dillon (pg)
Fr Andy Shane (pg)
Fr Eddie Griffin (pg)
Chris Fitzpatrick (pg)
Margaret Ryan (pg)
Stephen Kennedy (pg)
John O'Boyle (pg)
Elizabeth Byrne (pg)
Finola Stevans (pg)

27 October 1979
Billy Brown (ent)
Judith Elmes (ent)
Rosaleen Linehan (ent)
Des Keogh (ent)
Betsy White (pg)
Denis Allen (ent)
Terry Murphy (pg)
Stephen Pyle (pg)

3 November 1979
James Baldwin (wr)
Burlington Hotel Cabaret
   (ent)
Robert Ballagh (pg)
Charles Duke (pg)
Al Ryan (pg)
Hector Crory (pg)

10 November 1979
Magic (ent)
Tim Phillips (pg)
John O'Shea (pg)
The Atrix Group (ent)
Joe Keeton (pg)
Anne Dowling (pg)
Nick Skelton (pg)
Mr and Mrs O'Keefe (pg)
Mr and Mrs D'Arcy (pg)
Fr Michael Cleary (pg)

17 November 1979
Brendan Shine (ent)
Noel Carroll (pg)
Fr Michael Cleary (pg)
Mrs A Glynn (pg)
Mr and Mrs O'Keeffe (2pg)
Mr and Mrs D'Arcy (2pg)
Freddie White (ent)
Justin Keating (pol)
The New Seekers (ent)
Six Radio 2 DJs (pg)
Rocky de Valera and the
   Grave Diggers (ent)
Mary Kenny (pg)
Anne Connolly (pg)

24 November 1979
Sheeba (ent)
Dan Kiely (pg)
Eithne Robinson (pg)
Aisling Heneghan (pg)
Jeffrey Archer (wr)
Andy Smith (pg)
Mr Scanlon (pg)
Tracey and the Morman Airs
   (ent)
Elizabeth Shannon (pg)
Freddie Forsythe (wr)

1 December 1979
Sandie Jones (ent)
Barbara Watson (pg)
Ubi Dwyer (pg)
Lena Blair (pg)
The Spinners (ent)
Leslie Halliwell (pg)
Tina King (pg)
Mrs Hinks (pg)
Nancy Hazel (pg)

15 December 1979
The Dooleys (ent)
Mr and Mrs Stokes (pg)
Mr and Mrs Hornett (pg)

Mr and Mrs Reil (pg)
Valerie McGrath (pg)
Jill Hermon (pg)
Bunny Carr (med)
Seán Connors (pg)
Sunshine (ent)
Tony Thursby (pg)
Michael O'Beirne (pg)
Hubert Lambert (pg)
Neville Wiltshire (pg)
John Brady (pg)
John Ryan (pg)
Roy Taylor (pg)
Karen Black (pg)
John Curran (pg)
Keith Donald (pg)
John Tate (pg)
Paddy Colman (pg)
Lindsay Armstrong (pg)
Madeleine Berkeley (pg)
Mike Nolan (pg)
Paul Goldin (ent)
St Patrick's Cathedral Choir
    (ent)
John Dexter (pg)

22 December 1979
John Skehan (ent)
Val Fitzpatrick (ent)
Danny Cummins (ent)
Brendan Grace (ent)
Brendan O'Reilly (ent)
Noel Purcell (ent)
Paddy Crosbie (ent)
Chris Curran (ent)
Michael Buckley (ent)
Romance (George O'Reilly)
    (ent)
Joe Linnane (pg)

1980
The listings for 1980 are
poor; there are several gaps
between weekly dates.

5 January 1980
The Concert Orchestra (ent)
The Young Dublin Singers
    (ent)
Dolores Clinch (pg)
John O'Boyle (pg)
Tim O'Leary (pg)
Amanda Gibson (pg)
John McKenna (pg)
Fiarcre Gaffney (pg)
Margaret Ryan (pg)
Mairín de Búrca (pg)
Séamus Brennan (pol)
Gabriel J Byrne (pg)
Fr Des Wilson (pg)
Dr Garret Fitzgerald (pol)
Justin Keating (pol)
Dana Wynter (pg)
Uinseann Mac Eoin (pg)
U2 (ent)
Joe Keaton (pg)
Hughie Greene (ent)
Des Smyth (pg)
Anne Bushnell (ent)

12 January 1980
Frank Hess and Allegro (ent)
Fr Eddie McDonagh (pg)
Margaret Wade (pg)
John O'Connor (ent)
Jacques Lobelle (pg)

26 January 1980
The Paco Ruiz Flamenco
    Troupe (ent)
Dr Conor Cruise O'Brien
    (pol)
Fr Des Wilson (pg)
Foster and Allen Duo (ent)
John Corrigan (pg)

Jarleth Downes (pg)
Anthony Malone (pg)
Chris Tallon (pg)
P J McCann (pg)
Thomas Landy (pg)
Pat Cassidy (pg)
Dan O'Mahony (pg)
Robert White (ent)
Monica Cowley (pg)
Jerome Kirwan (pg)
Alice Maud O'Hanlon (pg)
Paul Burton (pg)
Mary Coughlan (ent)
Beatrice Duggan (pg)
Mary O'Mahony (pg)
Geraldine Murphy (pg)

2 February 1980
Noel Gilmore with guests
    (pg)
Dickie Rock (ent)
Brendan Fitzgerald (pg)
Richard Byrne (pg)
Tom Darby (pg)
Gina and Dale Hayes (ent)
Wendy Leigh (pg)

9 February 1980
Colette Proctor (pg)
Wendy Boland (pg)
Mia Murphy (pg)
M Conlon (pg)
M McMenamin (pg)
Sharon Bacon (pg)
Jakki Moore (pg)
The Whistle Binkies (ent)
Eamon Gibney (pg)
Jack Donnelly (pg)
Paddy Fitzpatrick (pg)
Bobby Kerr (sp)
Lee Kidney (pg)
Alan Stivel (ent)

Hildegard and Veronika
    Fenerstein (ent)
The UCD Footlights (ent)
Fergus Bourke (pg)
Joan Sheerin (pg)

16 February 1980
Colette Proctor (ent)
The John Desmond Singers
    (ent)
Dr Richard Mackarness (pg)
Amanda Gibson (pg)
Sammy Elliott (pg)
John Ware (pg)
The Bards (ent)
Dr R Mulcahy (pg)

23 February 1980
Maggie MacNeal (pg)

Angela Rippon (med)
Dusty Springfield (ent)
Richard Keel (ent)
Boomtown Rats (ent)

28 February 1980
Frances Biggs (pg)
Rita Whelan (pg)
Kitty Soff (pg)
Seán Richardson (pg)
Ronan Tynan (pg)
Kenny Harris (pg)
Jown Powell (pg)
Michael Mulligen (pg)
Des Kenny (pg)
Martin Crummy (pg)
Anne Claffy (pg)
Laurie Jacobson (pg)
Mary Duffy (pg)
Joan Carr (pg)
Martin Donoghue (pg)
Michael O'Brien (pg)
Deirdre Fincher (pg)
Sr Kevin and Optacon (pg)
Joe Dolan (ent)
The Furies (ent)
Stanely Jones (ent)
Syl Fox (ent)

1 March 1980
Programme on the Budget
2 Families (pg)

5 March 1980
Derek Jameson (med)
Peregrine Wosthorne (pg)
Warren Sillitoe (pg)
Peter Taylor (pg)
Patrick Cosgrave (pg)
Michele Dillon (pg)
Liam Brady (sp)
Denise Nolan (pg)

The Bogey Boys (ent)
John Joe O'Neill (sp)
Ivor Davis (pg)

22 March 1980
Lonnie Donnegan (ent)
Sonia Martin (pg)
Bryan McMahon (wr)
Douglas Gunn Ensemble
    (ent)
Ivan Karl (pg)
Mr Patrick Semple (pg)
Shirley Butler (pg)
Finbarr Dineen (pg)
Anne Buggy (pg)

29 March 1980
Dave Smith (pg)
Donnacha Ó Corróin (pg)

Brendan Shine (ent)
Donal Cashman (pg)
Dan McCarthy (pg)
Pearl Holt (pg)
Jim Canning (pg)
Peter Cassels (pg)
Noel Dowling (pg)
Margaret Geany (pg)
Fergus Whelan (pg)

5 April 1980
Gillian Nevin (pg)
David Richardson (pg)
Justin McCarthy (pg)
Paul Farrell (pg)
Gavin Barrett (pg)
Fab Vinnie (med)

12 April 1980
Johnny Logan (ent)
Henry Cooper (sp)
Violet Mayon (pg)
The Wolfe Tones (ent)
Marian Finucane (med)
Joanne Mollereau (pg)
Brian Cleeve (pg)
Fr James McPolin SJ (pg)
Pastor Chris Robinson (pg)
Shay Healy (pg)
Dermot Morgan (pg)
Gretta Hughes (pg)

26 April 1980
Bagatelle (ent)
Frank Hall (med)
Rose Tynan (ent)
Chuck Colson (pg)
Opera Trio (ent)
Aine Ní Dhubhaine (ent)
Johnny Logan (ent)
Shay Healy (ent)
Tony Barry (pg)

Angela Harding (pg)
Brian Murray (pg)
Bertram Tyner (ent)
Benny Caldwell (ent)
David Kelly (ent)

3 May 1980
Tony Kenny (ent)
Dory Previn (ent)
Art Farmer and Trio (ent)
Mairéad Byrne (pg)
Lorna Marks (pg)
Rose Smith (pg)
Cliona Ó Tuama (pg)
Susan Slane (pg)
Róisín Conroy (pg)
David Gates (ent)
Colette Doherty (pg)
Marilyn French (wr)

17 May 1980
Daddy Cool and the
    Lollipops (ent)
Tony Dowling (ent)
Tony Cully Foster (pg)
Katherine Kelly (pg)
Gerard Mannix Flynn (wr)
Limerick Grannies (pg)
Solid Gold (ent)
Tony Summers (pg)

24 May 1980
Jimmy Saville (ent)
The Marleys (ent)
Upton Steam Ralley
    Members (pg)
Dr Jack Dominion (pg)
The Roches (ent)
Lady Goulding (pg)
Tom Allen (pg)
Vivian Candy (pg)
Lady Miranda Iveagh (pg)
Eddie Kidd (pg)

31 May 1980
June Levine (med)
The Bards (ent)
Henry Kelly (med)
The Gibneys (ent)
Percy Edwards (pg)
Doris Stokes (pg)
Frank Patterson (ent)
Eily O'Grady (ent)
Julia Morley (pg)
Gina Swinson (pg)

7 June 1980
Martin Dempsey (ent)
Donall Farmer (ent)
Eilís Daly (pg)
Maisie O'Brien (pg)
Michael Kelly (pg)
Mary Nolan (pg)
The Butler Dempsey Band
    (ent)
John B Keane (wr)
Anthony O'Reilly (pg)
John Clive (pg)
John Doyle (pg)
Vivian Doyle-Kelly (pg)
Children from the Gaiety
    (Annie) (ent)
Anne O'Briain (ent)
Andrew McQuillan (pg)

4 October 1980
Brian Budd (pg)
Bagatelle (ent)
Katie Boyle (pg)
Séamus Brennan (pol)
Frank Kelly (ent)
The Wolfe Tones (ent)
Patrick O'Hagan (ent)
Johnny Logan (ent)
Val Doonican (ent)
Billy Whelan (ent)

11 October 1980
Gwynfor Evans (pg)
Riobárd Mac Górain (pg)
Henry Kelly (pg)
Paulyn Quinn (pg)
Rosaleen Linehan (ent)
Fergus Lenihan (pg)
Jim Doherty (ent)
Teresa Dwyer (pg)
Helen Connolly (pg)
Dr Jim Behan (pg)
Prof Tom Fahey (pg)
Nikki (ent)
Frank McNamara Trio (ent)

18 October 1980
Michael Scott (pg)
Carmencita Hederman (pg)
(cont. on page 134)

BRINGING THE SONG AND DANCE BACK INTO THE ARTS

Anne O'Donnell talks to senior producer Colin Morrison about *The Arts Show*

Colin Morrison, senior producer on *The Arts Show*, can never remember 'an audience reaction to an evening radio programme as good as *The Arts Show*'. There was considerable scepticism initially to the idea of Mike Murphy presenting this programme. Mike has always had 'a song and dance image' says Colin. However, Colin and his colleagues on the production team firmly believe that Mike is the perfect presenter for this show. The show is aimed at the widest possible audience and concentrates on the pleasure, escapism and entertainment which the arts can provide. While not trivialising the arts, the team avoids meaningful broadcasting like the plague. Colin explains that the show must be accessible to the public as it is not their job to write an academic essay on the arts.

He goes on to point out that artists themselves generally want to simplify their own work. In this context he refers to Patrick Kavanagh's poem *Who killed James Joyce*, in which certain academics and their work are criticised. Colin believes that traditionally the arts

have been surrounded by pretentiousness—a pretentiousness which excludes the majority of ordinary people. *The Arts Show* attempts to axe the idea that only highly educated people can appreciate the arts. Where possible, the production team uses reviewers for films, plays and other events, whose real lives are touched by the subject matter of the production. It also seeks out ordinary people who have an interest in certain artistic works or events. For example, a taxi driver who is a James Joyce expert and fanatic was interviewed about *Finnegans Wake*.

SHE FAILED TO SEE ANY ARTISTIC VALUE IN SOME OF WHAT SHE SAW

The producers are anxious to promote the 'feeling' aspect of the arts—the emotional effects of artistic works or events on people. They look for naïve, honest and open responses to the arts, and seek reviewers accordingly. For one programme they brought

Eileen Reid to the Rosc exhibition. She talked in a direct and honest manner about the exhibits that she liked but also expressed amazement at the fact that some of them ever found their way into an art exhibition. No doubt some of the show's listeners were delighted to hear someone honestly stating that she failed to see any artistic value in some of what she saw.

The production team has a 'first division' list of people it regularly calls upon to participate in the show. Members of this first division have included Michael D Higgins (TD), Michael Colgan of the Gate Theatre, Michael Dwyer and others. Colin explains that these are great talkers and have a wide-ranging interest in the arts. All of them also 'gel' well with Mike, which is essential to a good show. The team members go out of their way to balance the programmes so that there will be material relevant to different interest groups every night. For example, if on a particular show they have a poetry item and a theatre one, they will lighten the programme by covering some zany or unusual artistic event or endeavour. Many of its early sceptics have been converted to the value of the show, possibly because there is no doubt that Mike Murphy is very knowledgeable about the arts and is eminently capable of discussing items with sensitivity and skill.

Sitting in on a weekly programme-planning meeting, I was struck by how well-informed the production team is about current and future arts events. Séamus Hosey,

'A TREAT TO WORK WITH'

Deirdre Purcell talks to Mike Murphy, *The Arts Show* presenter

It's not all Golden Movies, you know. Life is serious. Really? Well, not *really*. If there is one thing Mike Murphy is not serious about, it is life. Take the long number of years he had to get up at the crack of dawn to come in to the studio so that people could be eased into the day with a bit of nice music and a bit of chat. Remember that? Remember the Panzer Division with the 'Erika March' and all the 'yowsa yowsas'?

For those of tender years who may not remember, Mike and his long-time producer on *Morning Call*, Gene Martin, broke new ground on early morning Irish radio, which had been very gentle and very serious up until they arrived. They were responsible, for instance, for shooting the 'Erika March'—complete with jackboots—from nowheresville to top of the request charts. They would play a record, usually something pretty awful, and over it they would play a little sound effect, a faint echo of a derisory voice shouting 'yowsa! yowsa!' It became a catchcry all over Ireland. It follows him still. He enjoyed that show, but once the joints began to creak after a few years, he was off to something new.

There was *The Mike Murphy Show* on television where he broke new personal ground again with his dancing. He enjoyed that while it lasted. He enjoyed *Murphy's America* and *Murphy's Australia*. He enjoyed lunchtime radio, looking with compassion at those who struggled with the 'terribly serious programmes' as he passed through the radio centre on his

---

one of the producers, has encyclopaedic knowledge about the arts in general, but in particular about theatre events. 'Séamus loves the theatre—it is his hobby as well as his work,' says Colin, 'he has a great feel for how to bring a topic to a general audience.' The entire team seems to be immersed in the arts and artistic activities. They get their information from arts magazines and newspapers as well as from the vast quantity of advance publicity which is sent into the programme. It is vitally important that the team members are up to date with the advance plans of the other radio programmes, to ensure that they don't overlap on an item.

The members of the production team work extremely well together. Every week one of the four producers—Colin Morrison, Séamus Hosey, Dick Warner and Pat Leahy—has full responsibility for and takes the decisions about what items will be included in that week's programmes. Colin Mor-

rison, as the senior producer, has ultimate responsibility for the team and its programmes and he could theoretically step in and object to the decisions of a producer. To date he has never had to do so. He prefers the collective approach to the autocratic one. Colin stresses that all four producers, as well as researcher Maura Lee, are from very different backgrounds and have different interests—a fact which he believes strengthens the team and the show. However, disagreements and arguments are regular occurrences which is inevitable with five such different people, all with strong views on the programme.

Among the team, there is a high level of support, respect and affection for Mike himself. Colin emphasises that Mike is open, honest and direct—and does not harbour grudges. Mike really believes in the philosophy of the programme and works very closely with the team. 'Every member of the team is behind Mike,' says Colin, 'he's a treat to work with.'

way to his own studio, where he burbled happily away and kept the nation amused. He thoroughly enjoys *The Arts Show* which has increased the listenership at that time of the evening to a level it has not enjoyed since the advent of television.

This is the key. Enjoy. It's no longer enjoyable? You move on. And you never, ever move back. Life is too short. 'You keep moving. Once a thing is over, it is *over*.' And that way you keep at bay the little grey men who spend their lives doing little grey things and would like to put you into their little grey boxes. You keep surprising them. Just when they think they have you categorised, you quit what you are doing and start something new. Like your own production company, Emdee.

But you are loyal too, to the people who matter. 'There are some very good people in RTE, there will continue to be very good people in RTE. The competition that has arisen and will arise within the next couple of years will be very good for RTE and the station will

HIGHLY COMPETITIVE ENVIRONMENT

survive. They are going to realise they are in a highly competitive environment yet again and, as they have done in this situation before, they will come out shining. In golfing terms, it will be ''play your own game and let the other fella make his mistake''.'

It is not, of course, as if Mr Murphy has not had Big Offers. When the independents came in and

everyone was getting Big Offers, Mike had a Big Offer too—by telephone. The offer was to come in with a consortium and to go for a licence. He hummed and hawed. 'Apart from anything else, I had major reservations about the possibility of these people getting a licence.' The caller, undeterred by the humming and hawing, piled on the pressure. He said that his consortium would be willing to offer Mike 25 per cent of the equity. But Mike still hedged. 'At this stage of my life, did I really want to go and do a daytime show, lasting three hours, and I'm playing records and having meaningful conversations about quizzes?' He said to the caller that on balance he really thought he would not be interested. There was a pause. 'All right,' said the caller, 'do you know anybody who would?'

Mike's ultimate ambition has nothing to do with Big Offers. 'It is to be able to have a relatively relaxed final stage of my life, where there is nothing that I want or *need* to do. It's to create something for my own future—I never did that—or put something aside, I was always a bit adventurous and a bit less than careful about what I did. At this stage I would like to consolidate, also to be a real player in the future of telecommunications.'

And there is one more criterion for Murphy's Life. You never worry what people think, for instance, that just because you are cheerful and chatty, you are a lightweight. Let 'them', particularly the little grey men, think what they like. 'I enjoy being underestimated!'

'SURE WE'RE ALL GOD'S CHILDREN'

Deirdre Purcell spoke to Terence...

Terence discovered quite early on in life that he had this strange talent for listening. (All hairdressers have it of course: 'We're sworn to secrecy. It's like confession when they're having their hair done!') But even for a hairdresser, Terence heard more than his fair share. For instance, take the tragic case of the woman whose husband has a soother. 'He had it when he was small and he never gave it up. When he got married his Mam said he could bring it with him. He keeps it inside his bedside locker. If they have a lover's quarrel last thing at night he turns and takes the soother out of the locker and sucks it away and consoles himself!' Naturally the woman confided in Terence, and to this day that woman swears that the advice he gave her changed her whole marriage. Unfortunately Terence is bound by his hairdressers' oath not to reveal what that advice was...

As the whole nation now knows, Terence's own life changed the day he took all of his considerable courage in his hands—he is a shy man—to ring *The Gerry Ryan Show*. His employers were not amused and gave him the sack. But the story had a happy ending when the powers-that-be at 2FM stepped in and offered Terence a regular Monday morning stint on Ryan's show, *Tell It To Terence*, on which the Cork lad could employ his considerable sympathetic advising skills to the nation as a whole.

● **What to do when your quiff won't stand up straight?**

● **Your Mam won't let you take Elvis for your Confirmation name?**

● **You're 14 and in love with your 72-year-old neighbour?**

Terence gives each problem his total and undivided attention. He even has a cure for the common cold. 'My Uncle Gerry told me this now, he's from Cork, he's a very crude man, God help us, but he's a heart of gold (sure we're all God's creatures!). He said to me, ''First of all, you drink a glass of water, then a glass of whiskey, then you turn your backside to the fire and when the water boils up in you you're cured!'' '

He might never have discovered his great confessional gift had his Mam not brought him to Ballinspittle one time. 'It was a miraculous intervention! Before that I was a very quiet and retiring type. I was always getting mocked when I was small'—for instance, when he would run the wrong way with the hurling ball on the Christian Brothers' pitch... (Typically, however, Terence will not say a bad word about the Brothers. 'They're God's children too, aren't they? Maybe their blood pressure was up or something...')

Terence, who is an only child, is a big sturdy lad, fair-haired and blue-eyed. Women like him, he admits, half-mortified. Take Helga. Helga is the muscular, six-foot German, who dived into the swimming pool in the Canaries to rescue Terence when some English yobbos, scornful of the duffle-coat and lace-up shoes his Mam made him wear to ward off possible chills, pushed him in. The pockets and hood of the duffle-coat were filling dangerously with water, dragging him under, but Helga (topless 'but sure we're all God's children!') pulled him out safely. And from that day Helga, obviously inflamed by the proximity to Terence's body, never let him alone. 'I had to promise that if she left me alone, I'd write to her...'

But there is really only one woman in his life. That's his Mam. Tragically, his Dad walked out on the pair several years ago. 'He went out to get the *Echo* and never came back! ''Good riddance to him!'' that's what me Mam says... ' Terence pauses, deep in sad contemplation. The memory of his father is clearly distressing. 'He was a bit uncouth, like, he didn't have a couth in his body!' But typically, the lad is majestic in his charity: 'I forgive him!'

Terence admits that he has his little eccentricities, which only his Mam would put up with ('like if the eggs weren't boiled properly I might get mad...') so there is another delicate question which must be broached—how will Terence cope when his beloved Mam passes on? He admits it is one which troubles him greatly in the vastness of the black nights. 'I'll get a dog or something...' Instantly contrite, he begs for discretion: 'Be careful, because if me Mam hears she's going to be replaced by a dog her heart will be broken!'

BRUSH SHIELS

The talking head talks

Radio 1, I used to be more into it, but the problem is that I do so much talking myself that now everybody's talking. There is a tendency to bring people on who might not be that hot to trot. I find the ordinary people who come on the *Gay Byrne Show* seem to have a better slant on things because they're not selling anything. When you get people who are selling bits and pieces on every show. When you watch Oprah Whitney, for instance, on the other channel, and she has someone on selling a book, she gets a great panel together in relation to the whole book and you get a really good hour and a half. But there are certain people brought on now, including myself, who are talking about things they shouldn't be talking about. I shouldn't be at the Abbey for instance or I shouldn't be sent to see Kenneth Branagh and the Renaissance Theatre Company where I can only stay for ten minutes, even though I know they're great at what they do. My problem about the theatre is there's too much acting in it...

I understand that I'm basically there a lot of the time when people are not too sure how it's going to go and when worst comes to the worst, they'll ask me something, anything, and it doesn't matter what I talk about so long as it changes the direction of the actual question in the first place, which usually didn't mean anything. I know that my job in the first place is the 'talking head' sort of thing but you'd want to be careful that you wouldn't wind up like someone like Spike Milligan

who's very funny but every time he mentions the ozone layer, everybody laughs...

The problem about people laughing at you when you're talking is when you're serious, they all go asleep. I can understand it if I'm trying to be serious about anything; I remember I did a gig for the Birmingham Six at the Spa Hotel in Lucan and the only thing I can say about a Birmingham Six gig is that if the Birmingham Six were around they probably wouldn't go to it themselves, there are so few people there. But there was a group of dancers on from Russia called the Kalinka Dancers. And they'd organised the Russian ambassador to come. Half-way through the night, when I introduced the Russian ambassador, all the crowd started laughing. Because of course they thought it couldn't be the Russian ambassador! Of course then I made matters worse by saying that his parents were originally from the midlands and were called Boris In Ossory...

INTELLIGENT OR FAIRLY SHREWD?

I can see that this can happen very easily when I'm on a show where I have to talk about anything from Christian mysticism to rheumatoid arthritis but I couldn't see myself on too serious a discussion about anything. Basically all I would be is a 'colourful character' for people who wouldn't know any better. 'Zany' is another word I've come across. 'Unique' if you like me, 'eccentric' if you don't.

They can't make up their minds whether I'm highly intelligent or fairly shrewd...

So I keep playing all that. You could be on the television every week. I think Gay is a fantastic guy, he always makes me look good. Talking on television is a funny thing and it's a lot to do with the sound. When you're listening to BBC2 the sound is much better. The sound is very important to the atmosphere. When you take Robin Day on their *Questions and Answers* and our one on a Sunday night, on our one it kind of sounds as if the guys have got squeezed into the Ballroom of Romance in Mayo somewhere and someone had a mike out in the toilet but on the BBC one when the guy talks into his mike his voice is much deeper and there's a reverb on it and the sound means the guy has a sort of authority...

I'll just tell you a very sad story and it shows you in a way what talking on television really is... There was a guy on Pat Kenny's show, talking about scuba-diving off Rathlin Island, and one of the lad's wives came on and I thought ''I know that voice'', and they were talking about a benefit gig and so on, but I was listening and I wasn't listening if you know what I mean and I just thought no more about it... And then I got a phone call the following week asking me did I know that a pal of mine had died in a diving accident, the first guy I was ever in the band with. They were actually talking about him on Pat Kenny's show and it never even occurred to me. It just shows, you can be watching and not listening. I certainly think RTE will hold its own with any new stations coming in. The only thing that will hit them, I think, will be good films...'

More Brush Shiels on page 103

Painting, watching

Paint shop:
(left to right, front) Seán Fox, Des Davis, Tony Feeney, Kevin Hogg (front), Dermot Ralph (back), John Healy, Mark Lynch; (left to right, on stairs) Andy Hersey, Frank Healy, Martin O'Shaughnessy, Richard Lynch, Paddy Hodson

Security:
(left to right) Anthony MacMurrough, Anthony Hackett, Hugh Brennan, Pat Morey

2FM   2FM   2FM   2FM   2FM   2FM   2FM

Gerry Ryan

Cathal McCabe

Larry Gogan

No radio station can be all things to all people and throughout the 1970s, as the youth population in Ireland continued to grow in numbers, there was mounting pressure on RTE to cater for them. The RTE executives were sensitive to the demands of this new and affluent group of music consumers but the licence for an all-music station was a long time coming.

Eventually the organisation was granted permission for a national pop station and Radio 2 was launched on 31 May 1979. Originally to be called Radio Dhá, it was heralded by an advertising campaign which used the slogan 'Cominatcha Radio 2', which rolled rather uncomfortably off the tongues of the new station's executives, all stalwarts of Radio 1, and perhaps advertising the fact that the station had an initial crisis of identity. This was shown very clearly when on the first full day of broadcasting, Declan Meehan was doing his breakfast programme. Outside the studio, in the control room, was his producer, Louis Hogan, a senior member of the station who had moved across from Radio 1. Declan gave a time check: 'It's nineteen after eight.' The producer came into the studio: 'You don't say nineteen after eight in RTE, you say nineteen minutes after eight o'clock.'

The very first voice on the new station was that of Brendan Balfe. He introduced the Minister for Posts and Telegraphs, Pádraic Faulkner, who formally opened the station. Larry Gogan was the first disc jockey on Radio 2. He had wanted to start the station with an Irish song. The one that was in the charts at the time was the Boomtown Rats' 'Banana Republic'. The producers decided that it was inappropriate and that a compromise was needed, so the station was launched with 'Like Clockwork' from the same band.

Jimmy Greely and Mark Cagney

There was a great variety of programmes in the first Radio 2 schedule; the station was trying out new ideas, receptive to anything which might work. The scheduling, therefore, was a mix of the obvious and the innovative. Pop programmes were the staple, but for the first time the country got a rock show which ran into the small hours, as well as documentaries, current affairs and a consumer programme which Gerry

Ryan, with his background in law and his contacts with free legal aid advisers, presented on Saturdays. Ryan was one of the new breed of DJ, recruited from the pirates, along with colleagues Dave Fanning, Declan Meehan, Marty Whelan and Ronan Collins. Some presenters were recruited from Radio 1: Larry Gogan, Vincent Hanley, Brendan Balfe and Ken Stewart came down the corridor from the senior station. Mark Cagney and Pat Butler came up from Cork Local Radio. In all, fourteen of the twenty-five people who initially came to Radio 2 had previous RTE experience.

'Quiet, firm administrator'

The first controller of Radio 2 was Billy Wall. Experienced, middle-aged, restrained and self-effacing, he came to Radio 2 with a background as a producer on *The Gay Byrne Show*, and was a quiet but firm administrator. His instinct was to accommodate all sides of an argument, sorting out the best compromise. Rooted in the tradition of public service broadcasting, he aimed to steer Radio 2 from being a music station towards being a comprehensive all-round channel for young listeners in a musical context. He did not want simply to mimic BBC Radio 1, but to build a station which served Irish needs and sought to address wider audience needs than those which would be served in a strictly commercial context. Therefore, he was prepared to run programmes like Bryan Day's jazz show, which appealed to minorities, and to finance costly current affairs programmes.

Billy was also willing to give Dave Fanning his head. Dave Fanning was typical of the newcomers. After leaving college he had drifted somewhat aimlessly between pirate stations. He was qualified to teach but at the time he was editing a magazine called *Scene*. His late night rock show on

Gerry Wilson at the 'Comp Op'

one of the pirates earned him £12 a week, too little even to pay his taxi fare home. But his pirate work earned him an audience, and when Radio 2 came to recruit pirate disc jockeys, it was the ones with large audiences who were hired. Fanning took his audience with him, and soon had a national listenership of 100,000, a figure which flabbergasted Billy Wall. Fanning's adventurous style surfaced most conspicuously in his live interviews, often chaotic, frequently riveting. Some of the interviews were first rate. The members of U2 regarded their Fanning interviews so highly that when they became famous they refused to be interviewed by any radio presenter other than Fanning. Even now, U2's manager sums up Dave Fanning as 'the best DJ in the world'. Other interviews which Dave conducted were less successful. Johnny Rotten, formerly of the Sex Pistols, managed to put the station off the air one morning when he spilt lager over the sound mixing console.

On another occasion, the notoriously reticent British band

New Order granted an interview only to spend it alternating between mumbles and silence. Fanning spluttered and choked with embarrassment, but, as his long time producer Ian Wilson, who recently moved onto other programmes, points out, it made entertaining radio: 'There are things that might seem embarrassing at the time, when you're made a fool of, but in retrospect they're kind of great crack, and the punters probably thought they were hilariously funny. Like that New Order interview. It took a lot of footwork by me to get them to come in at all, and the interview was a shambles, but everybody was talking about it for months.'

The main difference the presenters found when they started on 2FM was 'comp-op' (compère operated)—the self-operated panel of buttons and switches which got them talking into a microphone and playing records live. That is still the staple of 2FM. Its success has depended on its broadcasters. And, unlike much of its competition over the years, where colloquial accents were replaced by vague, mid-

2FM   2FM   2FM   2FM   2FM   2FM   2FM

Atlantic accents, the most popular of 2FM's crew have that quality which Terry Wogan identified as good radio: that the listener believes that he or she is being addressed directly. The listener certainly responds.

That evening she cooked a special dinner for both of them

Carol is typical. She telephoned the *Gerry Ryan Show* and told Gerry how the rudeness of her partner, Liam, was ruining her life. Liam would come in from work, sit on the sofa and watch television for the evening. He seldom spoke to her, and when she spoke to him he mostly ignored her. She loved him, she said, but she could not take any more of his behaviour. Gerry asked her what was she going to do. Carol said she didn't really know what to do but that she would give Liam one more chance.

That evening she cooked a special dinner for both of them. Liam arrived in late from work and said he had already eaten. Then he sat down and watched television for the evening. This was the last straw for Carol, so she wrote a note to him and left it on the hall table. She lay awake all night, and by the time he got up she was trembling, hoping he would read the note and realise things had gone sour between them. Liam said nothing to her, and just got ready for work. But on his way out he stopped in the hall and roared abuse up the stairs at her.

The next day Carol got on the *Gerry Ryan Show* again. She was standing crying in her hall, her packed suitcase beside her. She said that she was leaving for her mother's there and then and that she would not return. 'I'm just going. I don't care what excuse he has, I'm not coming back. He can go and stuff himself. I don't care what he does. He'll understand, oh yes. Listen, I have to go. And thanks, you've been awfully nice.'

Dave Fanning — his late-night show on one of the pirates earned him £12 a week

DAVE FANNING GERRY RYAN MICHAEL McNAMARA LARRY GOGAN THE HOTLINE

Gerry Ryan is the cutting edge of 2FM's programming. As senior producer Bill O'Donovan says: 'It's not always understood how risky it sometimes gets. When you have a live, open line to the public you simply do not know what's going to happen next. Anything might be said, it might be slanderous, it could be blasphemous, and you have to have somebody there who can handle it. We had one extreme example when a woman phoned in using appalling language like I wouldn't even use myself. The usual response from a producer would be to cut her off fast but Gerry talked her down and away from it onto some other subject. And we didn't have a single complaint. Not one.' Gerry Ryan has become the new voice talking to the under-thirty-five population of Ireland, pushing back its cuticles, looking under its fingernails, in much the same way Gay Byrne did with an earlier generation.

By the time Billy Wall stepped down as controller of Radio 2, after five years in the job, the station had gathered a huge audience: 57 per cent of fifteen to twenty-four year olds listened to the station at weekends, for instance, according to a survey by the body which publishes twice-yearly surveys on media audience and readership, Joint National Media Research (JNMR). This was despite competition from no fewer than sixty illegal stations, by their nature less encumbered with bureaucracy and, because they were local, better positioned to respond to local needs. Wall attributed the success of the station to the introduction of its own news service, separate from Radio 1's. The station was struggling to keep ahead of its competitors in Dublin, but elsewhere it was comfortably the market leader.

In its early years one in every four records the station played was Irish. However, because the quality of new Irish records being released was often judged by producers to be poor and they were not played on Radio 2, Irish bands and their managers began to get ratty about the station. The producers in Radio 2 were too busy fighting their own corner to take any offence. For years, some said, the showbands and balladeers had got more promotion on RTE than they merited. Unless Radio 2 stood firm against them, it too would be swamped with poor quality Irish records. Their resolve was steely: no diddley-aye music on Radio 2. The producers were backed up by management at the time.

RADIO DOWNTOWN BURBANK

When the Furey Brothers' manager, Jim Hand, said that Radio 2 should be renamed Radio Downtown Burbank, Louis Hogan, who took over from Billy Wall as controller of Radio 2, responded that Irish bands should listen to Radio 2 and make records to fit its sound. 'The kind of records churned out on Radio 1 during the seventies will not be played on Radio 2,' Hogan said. 'Times have changed and the industry has to change with it. We don't ignore the fact that there are illegal stations and that they have an audience. The dominant sound of Radio 2 is adult-oriented rock and pop—that's what people want so that's what we're going to give them.'

Within the station, criticism came most consistently and constructively from Ian Wilson, who nevertheless did not get bogged down in internal squabbling but worked on developing the sessions, where bands record songs in RTE for transmission on the rock show. Wilson's field of expertise is rock, away from the mainstream, for which he holds little regard: 'I think pop radio is pretty appalling. I think it's atrocious. I don't listen to much daytime radio.' For Wilson, the sessions embody the commitment to public service broadcasting which Radio 2 claims to have. 'Public service broadcasting,' says Wilson, 'is a type of broadcasting which is dictated by public need rather than by the desire to create large audiences by any means possible and to make large amounts of money. In other words, you decide from the outset that quality—which is very difficult to define—is the first thing you should be worried about. The second thing to make sure is that you cover, as a network, a wide cross-section.'

2FM 2FM 2FM 2FM 2FM 2FM 2FM

*2FM presenters
Barry Lang and
Ian Dempsey*

An overhaul of the station's programming was undertaken last year by Cathal McCabe, who took over from Billy Wall, and senior producer Bill O'Donovan. The pair believes in market forces determining broadcasting output. The biggest change they made was the launch of Gerry Ryan's morning programme. Their decision to commit producers and researchers to the show paid off quickly. 'We gave him a very specific brief,' says Cathal McCabe. 'The figures show that by about September our audience in Dublin had increased by 50 per cent.'

'The initial brief for Radio 2 in 1979 was wrong'

McCabe acknowledges that the main competition for 2FM is Century Radio so, in preparation for the new competition, another part of the shake-up was to break the day's programming into segments and give responsibility for them to particular producers: Pat Dunne in the daytime, Seán McKenna in the evening, Ian Wilson after midnight and Pat Morley at the weekends. By doing this, more careful attention could be given to keeping coherence and consistency in the programming. The big

change which McCabe and O'Donovan spearheaded was the shifting of the station's views about what it should be. When Radio 2 started out it held to the idea that it would best serve the public by presenting a wide variety of programmes. Cathal McCabe's view now is that the station's main responsibility is to win the biggest audience it can.

'In my view, quite frankly, I believe that the initial brief for Radio 2 in 1979 was wrong,' says McCabe. 'All those years ago I said that the station should be an entertainment station. I think the only way you can ultimately judge our performance in relation to the public is whether the public buy it or not, and they only do that by listening to you. That's the ultimate test. I fulfil my public service broadcasting responsibility by trying to attract the largest numbers of the public to listen to it. That's my job.' The station still acknowledges its obligation to public service broadcasting—to entertain, educate and inform—only now, the emphasis is on entertainment.

Earlier this year the station's name was changed from Radio 2 to 2FM. Coincidentally, Cathal McCabe became head of music programming (all music) in RTE. According to him, the change came about because, after ten

years of broadcasting, the station was facing into a new climate of competition and needed a revised image. The new name also reflected the technical advances which had been made in the decade: in 1979 relatively few listeners used FM receivers, preferring medium-wave sets, but nowadays FM sets are the norm. 2FM's programmes are organised to meet market demand, so because the proportion of twenty-fives listening between 8.30 am and 4 pm is small, the programmes between those hours cater for young adults at home and at work, with more flexibility in the music played. After 4 pm the audience is mostly under twenty fives, so chart music predominates between then and midnight.

2FM has now shifted into top gear to meet all the challenges the competition can throw. Part of the strategy is flexibility. In the old days of Radio 2, changing a schedule was like turning the QE2. The 'new' station is permanently poised for fast action—and reaction.

The new approach has worked in the way the station bosses value most: it has attracted new listeners in droves. And, apart from that, it has proved that the lowest common denominator is not always the most popular option. As Gerry Ryan puts it: 'Taking risks, doing things that are a little bit more dangerous, working closer to the edge, just may be the future of broadcasting. Being bland certainly is not.'

'LIKE POLITICS, RELIGION GENERATES GREAT TALK'

Kevin O'Kelly talks about modern religious broadcasting

If you ring RTE and ask for 'Religion', the operator will have to ask you for more information before she can put you through. The religious output is wide-ranging and the men and women working on religious programmes serve more than one audience: believers and unbelievers, the sick and the well. While the sick and the housebound look to radio and TV for the Sunday morning service, others, especially the young, look to religious programmes because they offer an alternative view of world affairs.

Time was, long ago, when RTE was a youngster with only one channel to its name, and a producer's big ambition was to have a bishop on the screen. And that was a very big deal indeed. To have a cardinal on camera was astonishing. (These were the far-off deferential days when, as we tend to forget, the idea of cross-questioning a politician, much less a government minister, on TV was unthinkable.) But a cardinal? There were conferences about what questions might be asked. But that was before Cardinal Ó Fiaich got used to puffing his pipe contentedly in television studios; before the church (and political parties) realised they could use television for their own ends. It was long before Pope John Paul II canonised the mass media when he went on RTE from Galway and told the hundreds of thousands on TV: 'Young people of Ireland, I love you.' It was also before TV authorities realised that religious programmes, with proper budgets, were high in the

TAMS—up with the best of the rest: the *News* and the *Late Late Show*. The 'God-slots' ceased to be thought of as off-peak fillers. Programme controllers discovered that they would attract audiences because, in a literal sense, they were about matters of life and death!

CURRENT AFFAIRS AND THE SCRIPTURES

Today there is very little religious television centred exclusively around bishops, cardinals or priests of any church, though the pope has become a media star in his own right and, here in Ireland, as well as Cardinal Ó Fiaich, the other Christian churches have produced a crop of accomplished TV and radio performers. Archbishop Robin Eames, the Church of Ireland primate, has proved himself a master of the soft answer that turns away wrath in face even of that most difficult of questions: the ordination of women, which has made world headlines during the past year.

Religious TV, at its best, is essentially about what's happening now. It should be as relevant as the news bulletins; maybe more so. Von Clausewitz, the Prussian military writer, said, 'War is the continuation of politics by other means.' Religious television is a continuation of current affairs by other means: current affairs viewed in the light of the scriptures and traditions of the great

religions: an alternative world view that transcends partisan politics, national and international.

Since the great religions are increasingly outspoken on world affairs, hundreds of TV camerapersons and reporters turn up at assemblies at Rome or Canterbury or, indeed, at gatherings organised by any of the great religions because they know they will have a fresh point of view on the international scene. The Irish Catholic Bishops' Conference, the Church of Ireland Synod, the Presbyterian Assembly or the Methodist Conference all make local news for the same reason.

But religious programmes have an added fascination—for those who make them and those who view them—because, above all else, they are about important ideas; about the reason why things are the way they are; about why we are here and where we are going. And, like politics, religion generates great talk.

NO HALOES, PLEASE!

However, though religious programmes have a useful place in any radio or TV schedule, it would make no sense to engrave a halo on their office door. When the men and women of Religion break for coffee, they leave their cameras, notebooks and word-processors and swop ideas with their colleagues from Sports, Drama and all the other depart-

'WHEN ATHLETES TAKE DRUGS, THEY RAISE A MORAL QUESTION AS WELL AS A RELIGIOUS ONE'

ments that make up RTE. The truth of the matter is that the feel and flavour of the total output of any broadcast organisation is the product of a dedicated community of communicators; people who have a compulsive interest in what's going on.

When athletes take drugs they raise a moral question as well as a question of discipline. The lack of peace and justice is on the *Six-One* news because it produces riots in the streets. But it might also be discussed in a religious context and, even on the *News*, it may have had a religious point of view. Often it is priests and religiously motivated men and especially women who can give the most honest account of the reason for those riots and of the suffering of the oppressed. Because they work in the midst of the people.

'The Nun's Story' is no longer, typically, about life in a secluded convent. She may well be under gunfire caring for the wounded or in the slums of far-off countries living with the poor. And, like our own *Radharc* productions, it is often she and her religious and lay colleagues who themselves help to make some of the most interesting current-affairs programmes because they view world affairs from the bottom up, where it hurts, rather than from the olympian heights of the United Nations or the parliaments of the world.

One striking feature of most European television, as distinct from the American brand, is that when it deals directly with religious belief it is not evangelistic. It does not try to convert anybody; much less raise the millions of dollars so regularly scooped up by the TV spectaculars mounted by the likes of Gerry Falwell. Instead, the mass media in these islands try objectively to report what's happening in the great religious movements and then discuss the implications. Why is one tradition ordaining women and the other not? What has the Gospel to say about the world debt crisis? The theologian Hans Kung says that there can be no world peace until the great religions of the world learn to live together and that this process cannot begin until all Christians live in harmony. This can be achieved only if they talk to one another—and television can help to make their discussion heard as widely as possible. At its best, broadcasting is an agent of peace through understanding.

Kevin O'Kelly presents Addendum *on Mondays at 8.02 p.m. on Radio 1*

Quiztime
a MEGA and very tricky quiz

compiled by Michael Ross

1. Which artist has spent the longest time in the Irish singles chart with one record?

2. What was Kate Bush's first hit single?

3. What was U2's first Irish hit single?

4. What is TR Dallas's real name?

5. Name The Hothouse Flowers' first album.

6. What is Bob Dylan's real name?

7. For whom was Buddy Holly's song *Peggy Sue* written?

8. About whom did Don McLean write his song *Vincent*?

9. About whom did Roberta Flack write *Killing Me Softly With His Song*?

10. Who wrote a song called *Alison*?

11. Who is Paul Hewson better known as?

12. Who wrote a song called *Clair*?

13. What is Elvis Costello's real name?

14. Which of the four Beatles has appeared in the most feature films?

15. What was the name of Blondie's singer?

16. What band did Lou Reed begin his career with?

17. Who released *The Monster Mash*?

18. In which year was Ireland's first singles chart broadcast?

19. Which artist has had the most Irish hit singles?

20. What band had hits with *Ballroom Blitz* and *Teenage Rampage*?

21. What is Madonna's full name?

22. What is Sting's real name?

23. Name the members of The Police, apart from Sting.

24. What US state is Bruce Springsteen from?

25. Name Simple Minds's singer.

26. Name all of U2's albums.

27. Who originally played keyboards with Roxy Music and went on to produce two U2 albums?

28. In what year did The Rolling Stones play at Slane Castle, Co. Meath?

29. Who plays guitar with Queen?

30. What is Johnny Rotten's real name?

31. What was Elvis Presley's middle name?

32. What is the name of Elvis's Memphis home?

33. Which Irish band had a hit this year with *Forget Georgia*?

34. What is the biggest selling 12'' single ever?

35. Who recorded *Give Ireland Back to the Irish*?

36. Who is U2's manager?

37. What group, whose name is just one letter, had a hit with *Pop Muzik*?

38. Which two Irish-born musicians play with The Pogues?

39. What is Prince's full name?

40. Who directed U2's *Rattle and Hum* film?

41. Name the four Furey Brothers.

42. Prior to his death, what was Elvis Presley's last British number 1 hit single?

43. Name the three members of Bros.

44. What Irish band released an album called *High Ace to Heaven* in 1989?

45. What was the title of Michael Jackson's autobiography?

46. Who wrote the U2 biography *Unforgettable Fire*?

47. Who was the shortest Beatle?

48. What professor of English wrote controversial biographies of Lenny Bruce, Elvis Presley and John Lennon?

49. Who was George Michael's partner in Wham!?

50. Which single has remained in the British charts for the longest time?

51. Which member of The Rolling Stones served in the RAF?

52. John Simon Ritchie was better known as who?

53. Who made *Don't Look Back*, the documentary about Bob Dylan?

54. Which composer's work does Woody Allen feature in his film *Manhattan*?

55. Morrissey wrote a book about which dead film star?

56. Whose album did former Smiths guitarist Johnny Marr play on this year?

60. What do Sinéad O'Connor and Ringo Starr have in common?

61. Who is James Newall Osterberg better known as?

62. Who performed alongside Frank Sinatra in his Irish concerts in 1989?

63. About which group did Decca Records say: 'We don't like their sound. Groups of guitars are on the way out.'?

64. Which 1989 album had a musk-scented sleeve?

65. What soul singer is serving six years in an American prison for aggravated assault?

66. Whose 1972 album *Talking Book* contained sleeve notes in braille?

67. Who did Police drummer Stewart Copeland's father work for?

68. Ex-Monkee Mike Nesmith is heir to what business empire?

cut his own hair without using a mirror?

72. What snooker player recorded a song called *147*?

73. What Christian name did Diana Ross give her daughter?

74. After which weed did Keith Richards name his daughter?

57. Mike, Matt and Pete are better known as which pop trio?

58. What photographer do U2 use for their album sleeves?

59. Name the only person whose face has appeared twice on U2 album sleeves but who is not in the band.

69. Dweezil and Moon Unit are the children of what singer?

70. What rock star's autobiography begins: 'The lettuces were not behaving themselves'?

71. Which Rolling Stone used to

75. Name the Pet Shop Boys.

76. What two bands has Paul Weller formed?

(Answers on page 159)

SELINA AND THE MAGIC PURSE

A fairy-tale by Sofia Bury

Illustration by Ger Garland

Once upon a time there was a young fairy called Selina who lived in a seashell at the bottom of the ocean. At the centre of the shell was a deep blue pool, and here Selina would sit, dabbling her toes in its clear waters.

One day Selina heard a strange sound by the pool. Above the rhythm of the waves was a distant murmur. As she listened Selina grew more and more curious, and soon she knew that she must leave her lovely shell to find the source of this magical sound. When her friend Myriad, the silver fish, came to visit her, Selina told him of her plan. And Myriad said, 'Selina, the noise you hear is the sound of the ocean's roar many miles away. If you leave your lovely shell to explore the seas beyond, I shall be frightened for you. Stay here, and I will tell you tales of the ocean, with its tall ships and buried treasures.'

But even as Myriad spoke Selina knew that the lure of the ocean's roar was strong, and she must explore the unknown waters beyond her shell. And so she told Myriad, who said: 'Selina, I understand, and I wish you well on your journey. Take this silver purse to help you on your way. Inside is a headdress of hope, a robe of faith, and a mantle of love, each of which has special powers.'

Selina thanked Myriad for his gift, and bade him farewell. Then she took a deep breath and dived through the tunnel of calm water forming the entrance to her shell, to find herself for the first time in the open seas beyond.

Selina swam many many miles before night began to fall. The once sparkling seas were now dark and foreboding. She began to search for a shell in which she might spend the night. But she could find no such welcoming sight. At last she found a black mussel shell and tapped lightly on its walls to see if it was empty. A hollow sound echoed back, and Selina dived through the open walls. Clamp! The shell slammed closed behind her. And Selina found herself face to face with a huge mustard-coloured mussel who glared down at her.

'The mussel let out such a roar'

'I see I shall have an unexpected guest for dinner tonight,' he roared as he stroked his big black beard. Frantically Selina looked for ways of escape but the shell walls were tightly closed. She began to sob quietly. Then she remembered the silver purse. She reached for the clasp very slowly. A beautiful ray of pink light flowed out which twisted and turned in a graceful dance before finally assuming the shape of a headdress. Selina placed the headdress of hope on her head and immediately her despair lifted. She ran up to the mussel and started to tickle his black beard playfully. And the mussel began to laugh, delighted that his supper should entertain him so well. Selina told him funny stories, and the mussel wiped the tears from his eyes as he laughed and laughed. Slapping his thigh he said, 'Go on. Go on.'

As Selina reached the funniest part of the story, the mussel let out such a roar of laughter that the shell walls opened. Quick as a flash Selina slipped through and the walls slammed shut behind her. The mussel roared. This time in anger.

Tired from her adventure, Selina floated gently down to the seabed where she found a small cowrie shell, and swam inside. The water lapped on the sides of the shell, lulling her gently into a deep sleep. When Selina awoke the next morning she could hear the ocean's roar sound louder in her ears and she dived out of the shell to explore the clear waters beyond. Spider crabs scuttled along the seabed beneath her and starfish sunned themselves lazily on the rocks. Selina swam on through the warm seas, mile after mile, using the sound of the ocean's roar as her guide. Until she came to a bed of coral weed, gently moving in the current. She had heard many tales of this beautiful coral, shaped like a necklace of flowers with a thousand tendrils swaying in unison. Selina swam closer and the coral's soft lacework brushed against her body.

Selina continued on her journey. But as she swam the seaweed tangled around her ankle. She tried to free herself, but became more tangled. And Selina began to panic. Then she remembered the silver purse. It had saved her once, perhaps it would work a second time. She unfastened the clasp, and a shaft of yellow light flowed out of the purse to take the form of a dazzling yellow dress. Selina touched the hem of the robe and it instantly clothed her. Feeling calmer, Selina waited for the robe's magic powers to free

her. But nothing happened. She waited and waited. No fish swam near, and no crabs crawled by. She was completely alone. It was growing dark, and she was tired and weary. At last, unable to keep her eyes open, Selina fell asleep.

With the onset of sleep Selina's body relaxed. The weed's coral tendrils worked themselves free with the motion of the sea. And when Selina awoke the next mor-

ning she was floating freely in the waters once more. With a strong kick of her legs she started swimming once again in the direction of the ocean's roar. After a morning's swimming the mysterious roar sounded louder still, yet she could not tell from which direction it came. She sat on a rock, thinking the matter over.

'May I help you?' came the shrill question from behind. Selina

spun round, only to let out a scream. For there before her was a most frightening creature, grey, with strange scaly fins, an ugly mouth and large pop eyes. Selina shrank back in horror. The poor fish smiled hideously and said: 'Hello, I'm sorry, Miss, I didn't mean to frighten you, but perhaps I could be of help?' 'Thank you,' said Selina haughtily, 'but I don't think I need your help.' And she turned her back on the fish and swam away.

When she turned to look at the ugly creature his head was bowed and he looked miserable. Selina realised she had been rude, yet could not bring herself to apologise. A single tear rolled down the fish's cheek. Yet still her heart was hardened. Then Selina remembered the silver purse and its one last gift, the mantle of love.

DORY

She opened the purse, and a great flood of white light flowed out, rising upwards before settling at Selina's feet in the shape of a fine mantle. Instinctively she wrapped the mantle around the shoulders of the poor fish, and he was transformed. The muddy grey scales changed to silver and peacock blue, and his eyes became deep set and kindly. The fish swam excitedly in circles, admiring his new looks. And Selina smiled happily, sharing in the fish's joy. Then she remembered how badly she had treated the friendly fish and apologised for her rudeness. Selina promised that she would never again shun any living creature because it was not beautiful. The fish nodded in approval.

'My name is Dory,' said the fish, 'perhaps now I can be of help to you?' 'Oh yes,' she said, 'perhaps you can. I am looking for the source of the ocean's roar. I have travelled far, and the roar of the ocean sounds loudly in my ears. But try as I may I cannot find it.' 'In that case I can be of help. Follow me.'

And Dory led Selina to a tunnel in the rocks nearby, and together they swam through the long passageway. They floated up to the water's surface at the far end of the tunnel and a mighty roar greeted them. Selina clasped her hands over her ears and looked around. She was in a cave with soft sandstone walls. At the cave's entrance was a flat rock on which waves pounded hard as they travelled inwards. Foam and spray rose many feet into the air. And when Selina uncovered her ears the sound was deafening. At last she had come to the source of the ocean's roar.

Delighted, she turned to thank Dory for his help. But he had gone—a flash of a fine peacock blue and silver tail was all that remained as he disappeared down the tunnel. Looking around, Selina noticed a deep blue lagoon on the far side of the cave, and she swam towards it. The ocean's roar was quieter here, and she stretched lazily on a rock. The lagoon was so beautiful. A soft light played on the water's surface and reflected on the ceiling of the cave. Selina wished that she could have stayed forever, but it was now time to make her return journey. Diving below the water, something caught her eye on the seabed. It was a large grey shell. And as Selina swam closer, she gasped. For it was her own shell, that she had left many days before. As she swam inside she found everything just as she had left it. But hanging near the shell's entrance were the headdress of hope, the robe of faith, and the mantle of love. And Selina truly

marvelled at such strange happenings.

A few hours later Myriad visited Selina. She greeted him in amazement. 'How did you find me?' she asked. 'And why are you so far from home?'

Myriad pretended to look startled as well. 'But Selina, this is my part of the sea. I have not travelled anywhere. I was just calling in to check on your shell as I have done every day since you left on your journey.'

'You mean, I have travelled all this way, and had so many strange adventures, in order to end up here, right where I started?'

'It would certainly seem that way,' smiled Myriad.

'Sssh,' said Selina, 'let me listen for a moment.'

And sure enough, the faintly audible murmur of the ocean's roar could be heard. That selfsame sound that had so fired Selina's imagination many days before. Selina smiled back at Myriad. Perhaps she would never know the whole story, she thought. But of one thing she was certain. While she was happy to be back in her lovely shell with her dear friend again, she knew now that one day she would set off for further adventures.

'Tell me about your journey,' said Myriad.

Selina unbuckled the silver purse from around her waist and settled back to begin her tale.

LIZZY QUIZZY

A story for children by Kathleen Lambe

Illustration by Ger Garland

Lizzy Quizzy just could not mind her own business. She spent almost all of her time trying to find out what other people were doing and what other people were saying. She was always peering through windows, listening at doors, opening drawers and reading private letters; no wonder she had big ears, a long pointed nose and eyes that stuck out like organ stops.

No one liked her. Doors were slammed in her face, curtains were closed, gates were padlocked and barbed wire was used on fences and walls to keep her out, but somehow Lizzy Quizzy just went on minding other people's business. Nothing cured her. She had fallen off a wall while looking into someone's garden; she had a door banged on her nose while she was peeping through a keyhole, and she had been pushed head first into the river by an angry fisherman who found her nosing about with his picnic basket. Once she had been so busy listening to two ladies talking in the railway station, that she followed them onto a train she had not meant to take and she ended up miles from home! But in spite of all this, she didn't improve one bit.

One day the circus came to the village. The big top was set up on the village green and the caravans parked beside it. Everyone in the village turned out to see it. Most of them were pleased, but some of them were not. Nabber Grabber was pleased and so was Sally Screamer. Mumble Grumble grumbled about the noise and Mona Groaner groaned about the

mess, and Greedy Macready just hoped that there would be some free food after the performance. Lizzy Quizzy was delighted of course because it meant that there would be so many new things to see and a lot of peeping and prying to be done.

NO ONE LIKED HER

To begin with, she went round the caravans looking in the windows and trying the doors. She found one of the caravans unlocked so she went inside. It belonged to one of the clowns and was full of interesting costumes; big baggy trousers, huge black shoes and a set of large red noses. Lizzy had a great time trying everything on. She had just put on a pair of baggy yellow trousers when she heard someone coming to the door. She squeezed behind the rail where the clothes were hanging and tried to keep absolutely still. The clown came into the caravan, whistling a cheerful tune; he took off his jacket and hung it on a hook. Well, he thought it was a hook, but it was actually Lizzy's large nose, sticking through the costumes. Then he made a pot of

tea, took some currant buns out of a tin and sat down for a nice rest before the circus started.

Lizzy Quizzy kept quiet for as long as she could, but the jacket hanging from her nose was heavy and she could hardly breathe. Suddenly, she sneezed, the jacket fell to the floor and the clown jumped up in surprise. Lizzy rushed to the door, the baggy yellow trousers flapping. She tumbled down the caravan steps and ran across the village green with the clown chasing after her, shouting and waving his arms about. The baggy yellow trousers were far too big for her and she tripped and fell. The clown tried to catch her by the foot, but all he got was the trousers, because Lizzy managed to wriggle out of them and rush home.

You would think that would have cured her of being so nosy, at least for a day or two, but no; she was soon back to the village green, crawling under the circus tent, determined to find out how things worked before the show started. She climbed into the ring which was covered in fresh sawdust and looked up to the roof of the big top. There were special spotlights fixed and there were high wires and trapezes. She had the sense not to touch any of the ropes hanging down from these, but turned instead to a table at the side of the ring which was covered with strange musical instruments belonging to the clowns. She picked up a small pipe and tried to play it, but all she managed was a tiny squeak. With some difficulty, she lifted up a huge trumpet that was twisted like a giant corkscrew, and as she blew into it, a whole lot of bubbles came out.

She was really enjoying herself and quite forgot that she shouldn't have been there at all. There was a violin with a floppy bow, a saxophone that shot out a bunch of paper flowers when she blew it, and a trombone that fell to pieces when the slide was moved.

Lizzy Quizzy was by this time making quite a mess, but her big mistake was banging the drum. She meant to give it a gentle tap, but in her excitement she gave it a mighty thump with the

barrel of a cannon standing near by. The voice grew louder. 'Who's there?' There was no time to think, and Lizzy climbed into the cannon just as the clown in the baggy trousers came along. He was very angry when he saw what a mess the musical instruments were in and Lizzy heard him mutter something about getting his own back. She now had no chance of escape before the show started.

From her dark hole, she could hear the band playing, the monkeys chattering and the horses trotting past her on the way to the ring. Now she could

nonball. There was a roll on the drums, and suddenly Lizzy was fired into the roof of the big top and then bounced head first into the safety net. The audience roared with delight, and as she tried to get down from the net the laughter continued. There were lots of people watching who knew Lizzy and were all too familiar with her inquisitive ways. They realised at once that she must have been up to all her old tricks again and was paying the price for it. The more she struggled to get out of the net, the more she stumbled and bounced and the people kept on laughing and laughing.

drumstick and the noise echoed all around the big top most alarmingly.

'Who's there?' someone shouted, 'What's going on?'

Lizzy dropped the drumstick and ran towards the entrance of the ring, which was a silly thing to do as the voice came from that direction. She looked around anxiously for a way out but saw none. Her only chance was to hide down the

hear laughing and clapping, even the gasps from the audience when the tight-rope walkers were performing their dancing tricks; but poor Lizzy Quizzy could see nothing. Instead of sitting in a comfortable seat watching it all, there she was stuck in a dark hole not daring to move.

But things got even worse; the cannon was being moved. The ringmaster was shouting something about a human can-

The clown in the baggy trousers eventually helped her down and he was laughing too. 'That'll teach you to go peeping and prying into other people's business!' he said, 'Next time I'll fire you to the moon.' Poor Lizzy Quizzy said nothing. She staggered across the ring and out of the big top. She felt very shocked and shaky, and swore to herself that she would never be so nosy again.

JEREMY AND THE BARREL WHACKERS

by Pat Ingoldsby

Illustration by Ruth Jennings

Jeremy Thwisk watched the workmen through his window. They dug with their shovels and they drilled with their drills and they picked with their pickaxes. They smoked with their pipes and drank tea from their mugs and laughed with loud 'Ho Ho Hos'. At the end of the day they looked at their watches, locked their tools away in the hut and went home on their bikes. Behind them they left a huge hole in the middle of the road. It was surrounded by flickering red lamps and lots of red and white barrels. Jeremy looked at his own watch and yawned. 'Ho hum,' he said, 'off I go to bed for an early night.' Twenty minutes later he was sound asleep.

'Boom! Boom! Boom!' Jeremy woke up in his dark bedroom and listened. Somebody or something was beating loudly on a drum. The noisy row was coming from outside his house. Jeremy crept over to the window and peeped through the curtains. There was nobody out there. The road was deserted. 'Boom! Boom! Boom!' The noise was coming from the red and white barrels which were all wobbling from side to side. Jeremy scratched his head. Whoever or whatever was drumming on the barrels was doing it from the inside. He looked a little closer. A red alarm clock was peeping over the top of each barrel and jigging up and down.

Whoever or whatever was drumming on the inside of the barrels had alarm clocks perched on top of their heads.

'If I'm going down there to investigate I'd better wear one as well,' he thought, and he dressed himself quickly. Down the stairs and out into the street he went with a yellow alarm clock perched on top of his head.

'Come out of those barrels whoever you are,' commanded Jeremy in a loud voice.

Suddenly the drumming stopped

and a high-pitched squeaky voice answered, 'Not on your life! You come into one of our barrels, whoever you are!'

Lots and lots of squeaky voices joined in and piped together 'Yes

Yes! Perfectly right. You come in if you are so smart!'

'If you don't come out this second, I'm going to pour red hot bubbly porridge in on top of you,' threatened Jeremy Thwisk, which was sort of a lie because he didn't really have any.

'No, No! Not that! Not bubbly porridge. We surrender,' squeaked the voices.

Out of each barrel popped a large spring with arms and legs and drumsticks where their hands should be. Each of the springs wore an alarm clock on top of its head. They hopped and sprang around Jeremy shouting 'Being Boing! Being Boing! Make way for the barrel whackers!'

'You woke me up with all your Boom Boom whacking,' complained Jeremy. 'How am I supposed to sleep with that row going on?'

'How are we supposed to send messages to each other if we can't Boom Boom on our barrels?' squeaked a senior spring. 'God gave us drumsticks so that we can beat out recipes for omelettes and knitting patterns for shaggy jumpers.'

'You'll just have to Boom Boom during the day when I'm not trying to sleep,' said Jeremy.

The barrel whackers shook their heads and hopped and sprang and shouted. 'Not on your life! We are night-time boomers.

Story continued on page 106

THE SECRET OF GOOD TV
by
ZIG ᴬⁿᵈ ZAG

THE PEOPLE INVOLVED.

① THE PRODUCER :
Is the one who gets loads of munso to make programmes, if he thinks they are worthwhile making.

② THE DIRECTOR :
Does a very important job. He presses lots of buttons and shouts a lot !
— it's not easy, you know!

③ THE CAMERAMAN :
There is great skill involved. One must have good eyesight and a keen sense of direction.
...and a camera, I suppose !

④ **THE SOUNDMAN :**
Records the
programme's sound
with great dedication
and concentration.

⑤ **THE DESIGNER :**
Is responsible
for the set and
clothes, so that
they reflect the
type of programme
being made!
– or so they keep
saying!

⑥ **THE PRESENTERS :**
Most important
is to get the
right presenters
for the right
programmes!
Once you have this
you're guaranteed
success!!

TAKEN FROM ZIG AND ZAG'S 'so you wanna be on TV, ya big sissy'.
VOLUME 14.

(left to right) David James,
Elizabeth McNally, Christine
Cooley, Patrick Fitzgerald Mooney,
Catherine Behan, John Tate,
Charles Maguire

THE SWEET STRAINS
OF THE ORCHESTRA

Deirdre Purcell on the exciting things
going on in the pits

The sweetest, most exciting sound in the world to a music-lover is the long sustained tuning-up of an orchestra before a concert, the unison of all those woodwinds and brasses and strings. Well the brilliant news of 1989 for the RTE Symphony Orchestra was that the sound was to become stronger. More players are being hired to bring the orchestra up to the full strength of ninety performers.

And for both professional orchestras—the symphony and the concert—the additional good news of the year was the appointment of the first general manager, Gareth Hudson, who will oversee the performance policy. Mr Hudson, perhaps best known for his introduction of the *Music For Fun* series with the concert orchestra, points out that the number of performances put on by all the RTE performing groups, including the choirs, string quartet and 'support' ensembles for operas and ballets, is staggering. 'In terms of the numbers of the concerts we promote, we would put Jim Aiken and Oliver Barry in the shade. They might have the big show business names coming, but it is only a few times a year...' By the end of 1989, the concert orchestra alone will have given eighty-five concerts, to an average audience of 85 per cent of capacity.

Both moves, the augmentation of the RTESO and Mr Hudson's appointment, are a sign of the times. With the new commercial environment, the orchestras will be marketed more professionally and the new general manager thinks that the market is wide open. 'Any outside orchestra coming here with some very simple marketing ideas could make it.'

For instance, when he introduced his *Music For Fun* series six years ago—a 'fun' series involving audience participation for children—people queued in long lines for tickets before the box office opened. 'RTE had never seen anything like it.' But the organisation had no mechanism to follow through. 'Every time we do one of those concerts we get requests for merchandise—concert orchestra sweatshirts, tee-shirts, badges, cassettes', but no-one was in charge of this side of things. This, you can be assured, is about to change. And Gareth has another idea, a music club, where the public can mix socially with players and other music lovers. 'It's been a great success in the BBC.' He is also a great believer in commercial sponsorship.

PERFORMANCE A NEW PRIORITY

Under Gareth Hudson's leadership there will be more emphasis on the orchestras as a resource—and not simply as an expensive responsibility. And even that emphasis is to change somewhat. In former years the orchestras' primary function was to broadcast. The public performance aspect of their work was coincidental. From now on, the orchestras are to be part of the public face of the station—its performance arm. Its broadcasting will be, not paramount, but parallel. 'Traditionally the orchestras would have been run from a radio perspective. While radio will obviously continue to be a main employer, you can no longer run professional orchestras with radio producers doing administration, marketing and all else. They don't have the right perspective... The guy choosing the programmes is a radio producer. So he says, ''wouldn't that be nice to broadcast?'' The fact that that wouldn't get much in the way of box office or that it would cost a hell of an amount to put on, as the piece needs ten percussion players—that would never enter his head! The idea is that the general manager should primarily be responsible for the RTE Symphony Orchestra, but have around him a staff who are not in any way tied in with the broadcasting service, whether it be radio or television. That's a very new step.'

The question of RTE's stewardship of what are, in essence, Ireland's national orchestras arises all the time in the newspaper columns. 'And there has always been a veiled threat from the government that if RTE were seen to get rid of one of the orchestras, the licence fee would suddenly be snatched back.' Depending on perspective, should RTE have such prestigious stewardship—or be so lumbered? Mr Hudson regards this as a difficult question. 'No other broadcasting station in Europe has this dual role. The BBC don't have that millstone around their neck. They have orchestras but they're not the national orchestras of Britain. There are four other major symphony orchestras in London alone, which operate as national orchestras in that they regularly tour internationally. In Ireland the two RTE orchestras have to do the whole lot.'

The main difference between the two orchestras, apart from size, is not ability, but repertoire and versatility. The RTESO plays (of course) the serious, symphonic, mainly the 'romantic' repertoire, 'Beethovenish to Tchaikovskyish', according to the person who chooses a lot of it, Jerome de Bromhead. And he is not all that

happy about it, but in a sense, he must bow to the inevitable. The repertoire is geared 'very much' to audience tastes. 'We do have an eye on the box office—it's of no advantage to play to an empty hall. We do try to be a bit adventurous, but I'm afraid that Dublin audiences are very conservative indeed.' He does not blame them—'the trend is world-wide, the trend is that the repertoire is getting narrower and narrower'—but he thinks this is something to be fought against and points out that there is a law of diminishing returns. Beethoven's Fifth Symphony will always get a full house. But there is a delicate balance to be maintained. How many times a year will people come to hear it?

In a sense, it is a matter of education. Many people believe that modern music with its dissonance and unusual instrumentation and progressions is unpleasant and inaccessible. 'But these things are relative. In his time, Mozart was accused of dissonance—in fact one of his string quartets is called the Dissonance Quartet. The kind of harmonies used in rock music and in jazz are very dissonant.'

'NO APOLOGIES AT ALL'

While accepting its limitations, Mr de Bromhead is very proud of his symphony orchestra. 'Comparing like with like—the radio symphony orchestras of the smaller German states which would be the top of their league, it stands up very well indeed. We would have no apologies at all.' (And of course with the augmentation and the new performance policy, the future is very exciting).

The diary for the RTESO, as with most orchestras of its type, is normally two years ahead—and this alone would contrast it with the RTECO. The orchestras work on two entirely different schedules. 'If you were to get somebody in Arts Administration to look at the

two orchestras' schedules for an average month,' says Gareth Hudson, 'if you were to take the names off the top, and ask, ''What do you think of those two?'', the administrator would say: ''Well, they can't possibly be working in the same country or belong to the same organisation!'' ' No one week looks the same as any other week for the concert orchestra, whereas if you were a member of the symphony orchestra and you desperately wanted to know about some date in 1990 or 1991, you could, with a reasonable degree of certainty, find out what it was.

VERSATILITY

Another basic difference, of course, is repertoire. The RTECO, according to Mr Hudson, 'plays anything from classical music to film music, TV music, if necessary orchestral rock. It has to be able to go from style to style and be equally good at it all.' One week, the RTECO will be backing the Eurovision Song Contest, the next, playing in the National Concert Hall 'almost as a chamber orchestra where you're dealing with artistry at a very high level, perhaps at an international level. You're then thrown into a TV studio where you are backing Colm Wilkinson as he sings show tunes. And the concert orchestra has never been the political football that the symphony has...'

A third essential difference is one of image. 'A symphony orchestra will always have an image of being the national orchestra and I think within reason that's quite right. It is the flagship.' But this in no way implies that the concert orchestra (full-time staff of thirty-six, frequently augmented to as many as fifty) is in any way a second-class band. 'Certainly not in terms of standard of playing. It has attracted a lot of particularly good young players. It has managed to raid the symphony orchestra for a few of the better players.'

The sound of any orchestra has a lot to do with size and strength. In a full-sized orchestra, the decibel strength should range, according to Mr Hudson, from being almost inaudible 'to an absolutely deafening sound'. Neither of the RTE orchestras spread themselves that wide. 'We would be dealing very much with the middle range. This is partly training and tradition, particularly to do with the brass section. The crowning glory of a big orchestral climax has to be the brass section. In Britain, there is a great brass band tradition. We don't have that tradition; ours tends to be, to an extent, in strings and woodwind.'

And finally, in any orchestra, there is the human factor. At the end of the day, orchestras are composed of human beings—and artistes. However much they may knit or read or feign indifference when they are *tacit* (when the piece the orchestra is playing has no notes for them individually), they are sensitive souls. The advantage of running an orchestra is that if you treat them well, they will play their hearts out for you. The disadvantage is that they can really make trouble for any would-be reformer they do not trust. Embarking on his new, exciting—and terrifying—job, the new general manager, an ex-player himself, is well aware of the potential danger. 'You only need one trouble-maker to put a rumour in an orchestra and it's like lighting a fuse...'

Above (left to right)
Pádraig O'Connor, David James,
Charles Maguire.

IN THE NEWSROOM

Deirdre Purcell revisits her old workplace

Ten minutes to six o'clock in the evening used to be the worst. Anyone with a titter of sense would have avoided the RTE newsroom. To open the door was to be assaulted by a wall of sound. Hammering, old-fashioned typewriters, a furiously rotating copying machine, shouts from the sub-editors looking for copy, the chief sub calling out last-minute changes to the long-suffering production assistant who was typing and answering telephones at the same time—and over all, the clarion calls of the studio director to the newsreader and anyone else who was interested: 'I'm going down to studio *now*!' Whereupon he would rush out the door trailing pieces of paper after him while the production assistant, wresting the last sheets from under the chief sub's pencil, followed in his wake, frantically shuffling more papers into some semblance of order...

These days, before the bulletins, there is merely a plushy hush. Voices murmur over the discreet 'plock-plock' of keyboards and all is organised calm. The newsroom has become computerised.

Not just any computerised. 'Newstar' is the envy of the newsrooms of Europe and indeed a great deal of manager Luke Smith's time is given over to accommodating the groups of executives from other TV stations who come to see it. 'In 1981,' says Luke, 'when we first started to think about computerisation, the newsroom was generating more than a tonne and a half of paper

a year.' (Every item of raw news-copy, whether generated from home or from the wire-services, was circulated to all the services: radio news, television news, Network 2 news, Radio 2 news, Raidió Na Gaeltachta and *Nuacht*. Copies had to be made also for filing and legal purposes. And within each service, each person in charge of an area had to have a copy of each 'finished' item—in television news, director, production assistant, vision mixer, sound person, chief sub, autocue operator, VTR operator, telecine operator and newsreader.)

CAMERAS THAT MOVE BY THEMSELVES

Having made the decision to computerise, the management involved the staff in the selection of the system. Newstar was eventually chosen because it was the most flexible, innovative and cost-effective. 'One of the things we didn't do was to buy fancy gear and try and ram it through. Everybody should see a good reason why it should be there. People want a meaningful job to do and if they get it, there is no great problem with change. With the computer, we were able to release journalists from desk jobs, creating time and space for them where they are now more efficiently used in going out there and getting the stuff.'

As he spoke, Luke Smith was jet-lagged, having been to Newstar

Wesley Boyd, Head of News

headquarters in Madison, Wisconsin, to study the latest developments in the system. The next step is 'touch-screen'—for instance, where a sound engineer in studio is enabled to raise or lower transmission sound by moving his finger in a certain direction on the screen of his terminal. Once codes are entered by the director, the computer can now run cameras, adjust lighting, generate graphics and call up stills photographs. On the floor of a news studio, where there used to be two camerapersons, two stage hands and a floor manager, 'now you need no people at all, just cameras that move by themselves...'

With the coming of Newstar, the staff has been reduced (to 142),

but by natural wastage and voluntary early retirement. And in tandem, newsroom output has been increased by 25 per cent. On television alone, the newsroom puts out 560 hours of TV news each year. Constantly being upgraded and updated, Newstar has now been extended into sport, radio and television programme divisions.

For the technically minded, the Newstar main-frame computer is being upgraded to 300 megabytes, while independently, each desk terminal has 120K of memory. This is important because it means that when the pressure is on, for instance coming up to bulletin time, the entire system does not slow down.

But the real beauty of newsroom computerisation, according to Luke Smith, is that control of the news story is being put back where it belongs. 'It's bringing us back to the last century, when the journalist wrote the story, set it in type, printed it, and went out and flogged it in the street. He had the responsibility that went all the way through the entire product. Then technology came along and specialists started to be implanted between the journalist and the product. Now that's all been swept away and the journalist is being given back the media. I think it's fantastic.' A random sample of journalists agrees.

In the newsroom on the day this photograph was taken were:
(left to right, seated front) Peter O'Driscoll, Mark Kavanagh, Kay Ennis, Eddie Liston, Orla Guerin, Michael Lewis, Donal Kelly; (left to right, standing back) Niall Martin, Bryan Dobson, Andrew Kelly, Tom McCaughren, Vincent Woods, Wesley Boyd, Kieron Wood, Vincent Wall, Jennifer Smith, Kevin McDonald, Shane Kenny, Liam Cahill, Seán O'Rourke; (left to right, seated centre) Orla de Barra, John Ellis, Mary Butler; (left to right, in far distance) Harry Houston, Morgan O'Kelly, Denis Devane

QUIZTIME
CURRENT AFFAIRS
set by Diarmuid de Paor

1. What was the name of the block of flats in Ballsbridge, Dublin, in which two people died in a gas explosion on New Year's Day 1987?

2. Who is 'The Border Fox'?

3. Who did he kidnap?

4. George Bush and Michael Dukakis were the Republican and Democratic candidates in the 1988 US presidential election, but who were their respective vice-presidential candidates?

5. What was the name of the oil rig on which 166 people died in an explosion in July 1988?

6. In December 1987 a UDA leader was killed by an IRA bomb in his car. Who was he?

7. In June 1987 Geraldine Kennedy and Bruce and Mavis Arnold were awarded £50,000 in damages. For what?

8. What does SIPTU stand for?

9. What does SWAPO stand for?

10. What book by Dr Alex Comfort was banned in February 1987?

11. What, after hundreds of years of debate, was finally declared fake in November 1988?

12. In August 1987, whose leaked holiday plans led to Garda embarrassment?

13. Who beat Gilbeys for control of Irish Distillers?

14. What French politician referred to the death of six million Jews in World War II as 'a detail' of history?

15. Name two of the three IRA members shot dead by the SAS in Gibraltar.

16. In October 1988 what senator had an eleven-year campaign vindicated in Strasbourg?

17. What does MRBI stand for?

18. What action did the McGimpsey brothers take in the High Court?

19. Who is the first chairman of the National Heritage Council?

20. Who was expelled for remarks about catching soup with a fork?

21. Why did nobody want to have anything to do with *Karin B*?

22. What former minister for justice was elected to the European Parliament in 1989?

23. Name the Mozambican president who was killed when his plane crashed in South Africa in October 1986.

24. What was the name of the 85,000 tonne iron ore carrier which ran aground off Baltimore on 24 November 1986?

25. Who coined the term GUBU?

26. What does it stand for?

27. Who was caught selling Irish passports in the Irish Embassy in London?

28. Who wrote *Spycatcher*?

29. In May 1987 Rust caused great embarrassment to the Soviet authorities. How?

30. Where did Michael Ryan kill seventeen people?

31. What was the name of the young South African activist whose murder led to much controversy concerning Winnie Mandela and her bodyguards?

32. Who was sent home from Brussels; successfully fought against being sent to London; and unsuccessfully tried to get sent to Strasbourg?

33. Who gave Maureen Haughey the diamonds?

34. Name Ronald Reagan's national security adviser who resigned over the Irangate scandal.

35. What was the name of the car ferry which capsized at Zeebrugge in Holland on 6 March 1987, killing 189 people?

36. In 1988, new directors were appointed to: a) The National Gallery, b) The National Library, c) The National Museum. Name them.

37. Who was Rory O'Hanlon's predecessor as minister for health?

38. What candidate obtained the highest number of first preference votes in the 1989 general election?

39. Who, in 1988, was elected the first woman premier of a Muslim country?

40. What central American leader visited Ireland in May 1989?

41. What portfolio does Ireland's EC commissioner, Ray McSharry, hold?

42. What do they call the parliament in Israel?

43. Who became the 'Father of the house' after the 1987 general election and again in 1989?

44. Who was the oldest deputy elected in the 1989 general election?

45. What former papal secretary is an Irish bishop?

46. He is a stonemason and the leader of an Irish political party. Who is he?

47. How many seats must a party have to obtain full Dáil privileges?

48. Which is the oldest political party represented in Dáil Éireann?

49. What former leader of an Irish political party won a seat in the 1989 European elections for another Irish party?

50. What does OECD stand for?

(Answers on page 159)

NETWORK NETWORK NETWORK NETWOR

THE STORY BEHIND

NETWORK
NETWORK
NETWORK
NETWORK
NETWORK

Clare Duignan

The relaunch of RTE's second channel, previously RTE 2, as Network 2 in 1988 is one of the great success stories of Irish broadcasting in recent years.

When RTE television came on air back in 1961, there was only one channel, with much fewer broadcasting hours than we have today. Gradually the broadcasting day lengthened and as more and more programmes were produced by RTE and acquired from other companies, it became increasingly difficult to accommodate them on just one channel. So, in 1978 RTE launched RTE 2, which was intended to provide an alternative range of programmes to those of the main channel.

Catering largely to minority tastes, RTE 2 was moderately successful, but it was always seen as the 'second' channel and never really attracted a substantial audience. When the then Minister for Communications, Ray Burke, announced his intention to allow for the establishment of a commercial television channel in Ireland, RTE prepared to face the challenge presented by Irish competition, in addition to that already being provided by the four British channels.

One of RTE's responses was to examine the operation of the second channel, RTE 2, and in the spring of 1988 it was decided to relaunch RTE 2 with a new range of programmes, a new image and a new name.

Five people were given the responsibility of organising the relaunch. It was quite a challenge! What was needed on a second channel? What would appeal to the viewers? What style of presentation would appeal to them?

Audience research indicated that while RTE 1 was still attracting a very good share of the available audience, there was still a sizable number of people who, when not watching RTE 1, were watching BBC1 and ITV. It was found that they particularly liked watching the comedy, soap operas and light entertainment shows on those channels.

It was also discovered that RTE was not attracting all that many viewers in the fifteen to thirty-four age group, and yet these were the very people who the advertisers were anxious to gain access to. RTE is dependent for funding on both the licence fee and advertising revenue, and the advertisers

were very keen to see a relaunched RTE 2 which would appeal to that younger segment of the audience.

The working group responsible for the relaunch commissioned extensive market research and analysis to discover the types of programmes which would appeal to the fifteen to thirty-four year olds. Participants were also asked about the image of RTE and their response to it. What attracted them to any particular TV channel? What sort of programmes really turned them off? What sort of programmes did they identify with?

The group did extensive research on what was happening in the television industry world-wide. Television, like any other industry, has to cope with constantly changing consumer/audience demands, and it was important to be aware of how audience tastes were changing in other countries. Members of the group attended TV programme markets, the showcases of new television programmes from all over the world. From the enormous volume of programming available at these markets, they identified the best series and programmes not

ETWORK NETWORK NETWORK NETWORK

previously shown in Ireland or Britain which they felt would appeal to the kind of audience the relaunched second channel hoped to attract.

The new channel needed a new name, and once again market research was used. Out of an original list of several hundred possible names, a short-list of eighteen was drawn up. The names were tried out on members of the public and the clear favourite was 'Network 2'.

Once the name was picked, RTE's graphic artists got to work, choosing colours, lettering, music and animations which, when combined, would provide the channel's visual identity, the 'station logo' which would be used dozens of times a day around commercial breaks, in the newspapers, press releases and so on—the 'look' of Network 2.

But the most important task was to design the programme schedule for Network 2. The programme schedule is the transmission plan for a channel—outlining which programmes should be shown, at what time, and on what night. The schedule eventually agreed on was a mixture of home-produced programmes, soap opera, light entertainment and comedy, with documentaries, sport, nature and music programmes spaced throughout the schedule.

Some things were very new. All children's programmes moved to Network 2, running from 2.30 pm till 6.00 pm every weekday. A brand new soap, *Home and Away*, was to go out daily at 6.30 pm. Comedy was scheduled nightly at 9.00 pm as an alternative to the main evening news on RTE 1, and brought back to the screen such comedy classics as *Mork and Min-*

Part of the great success of Network 2 is Ian Dempsey and Zig and Zag

dy, The Good Life, Spitting Image and so on, as well as many new series.

A new news bulletin, *Network News*, was introduced, and all sports coverage was moved to the new channel. A number of new series were introduced which it was hoped would appeal to younger viewers—*Degrassi Junior High, Jo-Maxi, Home and Away*, and of course one of the real innovations of Network 2 was *Nighthawks*, a visit three times a week to 'Hay' Healy, Tanya, Boris and friends at the Nighthawks Diner.

Network 2 came on the air on 8 October 1988, just five months after the decision was made to relaunch RTE 2. The viewers' response has been excellent. People know Network 2. They watch it. They like the programmes. Viewing figures are well above those for the old RTE 2. Advertising on Network 2 is considerably higher than it was on RTE 2. Many Network 2 programmes now get a TAM rating well above whatever programme is showing

on RTE 1 at the same time, an unheard of happening in the past.

Young people in particular like Network 2. *Home and Away* is the top rated show on Network 2, beating *Coronation Street* into second place, and *Degrassi Junior High* is also in the Network 2 top ten—both programmes with a high proportion of young viewers. *Nighthawks* has of course become cult viewing, and indeed programme makers from abroad have visited the *Nighthawks* studio to see in detail how this original show is produced.

From RTE's viewpoint, its new second channel has a definite identity and a schedule of programmes which satisfies the audience and compliments the range of programming on RTE 1. In preparing to face new competition, RTE has strengthened its position with Irish viewers by introducing a new channel which provides entertaining and stimulating programming.

It looks like Network 2 is here to stay.

2FM 2FM 2FM 2FM 2FM 2FM 2FM 2FM 2FM

LARRY GOGAN

'I wouldn't do it if I didn't enjoy it. I love it.'
by Michael Ross

Larry Gogan is just like he sounds. Warm, enthusiastic and well fed, he comes across as a very laid back man, moving at his own pace, with a good word for everyone. The worst he will say of someone is 'very nice fellow' and scrunch up his face as if sucking a lemon.

The way he tells it, he has risen to the top of his profession in a meandering, unhurried way. Straightforward, open, generous with his time, he is unusual in that, though he has stayed at the top of 2FM's schedules since the station opened, none of his colleagues, even in private, away from preying journalists, have anything but praise for him. Producer Bill O'Donovan sums him up like this: 'Larry Gogan is a superb man at his craft. There's nobody in the world like him, there just isn't, who retains the same enthusiasm for his job as he did when he started. A fellow like him, he's the base, he's the foundation. If we moved Larry anywhere in the schedule he'd bring his listeners with him. There are few people you can say that about.'

Larry speaks quietly and drinks Diet 7-Up, part of a successful effort to tighten up his waistline. We met on a Saturday afternoon. Larry had spent the earlier part of the day picking records for the following week's programmes. That evening he drove to Abbeyfeale to open a shop. He used to do a lot of personal appearances, but does only a few nowadays, and never in the winter.

He smiles and furrows his brow at the idea of him as ambitious, as if it was totally foreign to him. 'No, I don't think so. People probably think I'm ruthless. I certainly keep up to date with the pop world, and I could have moved to Radio 1, where things are more prepared for a presenter.'

Was he ever a hustler? 'Mmm. No... I suppose I must have been at the beginning. I was lucky, too, I suppose, to come along when new voices were needed, much as happened again when Radio 2 started. I'd like to do more television, maybe a game show, nothing too serious. But they've never asked me, and they're so busy that you have to be going to them all the time saying you have a great idea for a show.'

He was born in Rathgar into a family of shopkeepers. His grandfather ran a chain of fourteen sweet shops, but by the time Larry was growing up, this number had dwindled to two. Larry's seven sisters and brothers all opted for more secure jobs than spinning

records and recording radio advertisements. He left St Mary's school in Rathmines after getting his Inter Cert, and took the only full-time job he has ever held, inking bus conductors' ticket machines in the CIE garage in Ringsend. Larry's first taste of broadcasting was a verse recital on Radio Éireann, and it hooked him on radio. There were few full-time openings in radio, so he started off reading scripts on sponsored programmes. 'I always wanted to be a DJ. That's all I ever wanted to be, for some reason. I used to listen to Luxemburg as a young fellow, and I used to think, "That's what I want to be". And that's what I did become. I didn't know anybody or anything. People always say that you know people, and people get you into things, but that's rubbish.'

'THEY USED TO CALL ME ONE TAKE GOGAN'

The Gogans had a newsagent's shop in Fairview. One of their customers was Maura Fox, who worked for an advertising agency. 'I hounded the woman until she gave me an audition. She put me on a show called *The District Nurse*, sponsored by Cussen's soap. I played a young lover. My mother used to say that I never had a proper job,' says Larry. 'I used to worry about it when I was just married. But now, twenty-five years later, I wonder why, because I've been working all the time. But is anything secure anymore? Years ago people went into the civil service or Guinness's. But now there's a different

2FM 2FM 2FM 2FM 2FM 2FM 2FM 2FM 2FM

Larry Gogan

environment.' Which only highlights how, in his youth, Larry differed from his peers who opted for secure employment. 'Oh, yes, all my friends were in insurance or the bank. Still are.'

At one point he did fourteen sponsored programmes each week. 'I made most of my living from sponsored programmes for the first fifteen years. There were no DJs at the time, really. Most of the people who did sponsored programmes were actors. They read scripts, and wouldn't necessarily know the records in the programmes. My big battle was to work without scripts.'

His first pop programme was *Discs-a-Gogan*, a weekly show seventy-five minutes long. 'When I went on that programme first they said that an hour and a quarter was far too much for one man to do, so they gave me two other disc jockeys, Ken Stewart and Val Joyce. It's extraordinary when you look back on it now, when you do three or four hours, no bother.'

'I had an extraordinary image in RTE. They never let me on on Holy Thursday, even up to thirteen or fourteen years ago. *Discs-a-Gogan* was on Thursdays. They just would not let me on because they said, "He might say wowee or something." '

Larry has a reputation for doing his homework and working fast with little rehearsal. 'Oh, yeah, they used to call me One Take Gogan. They still do in the commercials studios.' Similarly, he is

known for being able, when recording commercials, to read a script in exactly the required time, adding or shaving a fraction of a second when asked. 'Peter Hunt, who had a recording studio in St Stephen's Green, used to say that I had a stopwatch in my head. It was good fun doing commercials, and you learn a craft as well.'

'I thought the Sex Pistols were really weird'

When Radio 2 started, Larry and the late Vincent Hanley were the only presenters from Radio 1 to be given daily programmes. 'Vincent Hanley and myself were always agitating for an all-music station. He was the biggest success when Radio 2 started. And he fought them tooth and nail. The Stations of the Cross, he used to call it. The thing about being obliged to play ballads, that used to drive him around the bend.' Larry spent seven years doing the lunchtime

programme. It was a peak time for listenership, and when he moved to the mid-afternoon slot the peak moved with him.

He is genuinely enthusiastic about his work. 'I wouldn't do it if I didn't enjoy it. I love it. There's always new things coming along, new sounds, new bands.' Larry has always moved with the times, even times like the glam rock of the mid-seventies, when artists like Marc Bolan and Gary Glitter wore stack heels and stardust. 'I used to wear high boots then—you had to—it was the in thing,' he says. 'But I stayed away from the glitter. The only music I didn't enjoy was punk. It wasn't very melodic. I thought the Sex Pistols were really weird.' He finds a lot of current chart music merely—he spits the word—pleasant. 'The Stock Aitken Waterman stuff is desperate. It's real kids' music. I don't know how long it can last.' He plays the music which either he likes or is demanded by listeners. He says there have been only a few efforts to corrupt him:

2FM 2FM 2FM 2FM 2FM 2FM

'Years ago there used to be, from some of the Irish fellows. I was sent a tenner once. I was sent twenty pounds on another occasion. Each time I sent it back with a letter. That's the only payola I was ever sent.'

'You have to present stuff that suits the listener, not just stuff you might like yourself. You do play records you don't like, though you can't say bad things about them because it sounds stupid to the listener. And if you're stuck in a top forty groove then you have to play chart music. I suppose the charts could be manipulated. But I don't think anyone would bother. There are these stories alright, like that the lake in Mullingar is full of showband records from the sixties. Maybe at one time it would have paid a band to do it, when a hit was important and would put up their fee for playing the ballrooms, but I can't see anyone doing that now.'

The young pretenders to his throne generally seek his advice, he says with a sigh:'You get a lot of them alright. Every day of the week you get fellows who want to be DJs.' And what advice does he give them? He clears his throat, then coughs, then clears his throat again. 'They should be themselves, as individualistic as they can. And they should know their music.'

When it started, the programme was full of spots—the factory spot, the sentimental spot. The only survivor was the Just a Minute quiz, which has the virtues of brevity and occasional howlers. What do the letters COD stand for? Fish. What part of your body are your vertebrae in? Your head. Where is the Great Wall? Crumlin. Where is the Taj Mahal? Opposite the Dental Hospital. What business is associated with Fleet Street? The ESB. What do you keep in a quiver? Jelly.

No matter how outlandish the answers, Larry always treats the contestants courteously and respectfully. 'You do feel like laughing at some of them, but I don't think you can be rude to people. If you make more of a laugh of them it only pinpoints them wherever they live, and people might be laughing at them.'

Never an RTE employee, Larry, like all RTE presenters, is retained on contract, but he says he seldom worried about the future: 'There were periods alright when I wasn't that busy. But when things improve you forget about those times.' He is fortunate in that he has never been laid up through illness: 'I think I've missed only two days since Radio 2 started. I got laryngitis. Good health is a great asset: no work, no money.' Unlike some of his colleagues, he does not find broadcasting strenuous: 'I enjoy the work, so it doesn't affect me at all. If tomorrow it finished I'd have to do something else, but I'd be happy broadcasting for a long time more.' Buying a country pub to retire to holds no appeal for him: 'Oh, no, no, I wouldn't like that at all. I'd hate to run my own pub. I'd hate to be stuck running my own business. No freedom.'

A design, Pleass!

Deirdre Purcell met RTE's head of design, Alan Pleass

RTE TV's design department runs all along the front of the glass and steel TV building in Montrose. On the inside, it is tucked away behind a staid line of portable green area dividers beloved of open-plan office designers, but what goes on behind those barriers is anything but staid—and always vital to the look and 'feel' of every single television programme, from *Nightlight* to *Glenroe*, from the *Late Late Show* to *The Whole Shebang.*

The head of design is Alan Pleass. Born in Cardiff and living in Ireland since 1963, he was appointed head of design in 1968: 'Essentially, what television design is all about is a corporate picture. Every programme wants its own identity, it wants to be different from the next one—yet they are all being done very much in the same studios...' For instance, out of Studio 4 comes, each week, *Live At Three*, *Cúrsaí*, *Kenny Live* and *Nighthawks*. And the summer project for that studio, while those programmes went on holiday, was RTE's new urban drama serial, *Fair City*, the sets of which were 'shoe-horned' onto the studio floor from April onwards.

Fair City was and is a great challenge. The set is based on a particular area of Dublin and the challenge is to make the settings look real, without causing distraction. 'You have to deal with what we call simulated reality, or contrived realism,' says Mr Pleass.

'Sometimes things look too real and they get in the way. This is the great art of the designer; it's not so much what to put in, but what to leave out. If the set gets overly fussy, if it intrudes onto the performance of an artist, then it is not doing its job...'

If the designer and producer/ director are working well together, he says, the designer becomes in many ways the eyes of the producer/director. He instances a case, in a period drama, where there were a huge number of characters based around two families. 'The only way the designer could help the viewer cope was to dress one family in brown and the other family in green...' In the case of *Fair City*, RTE will build, for the very first time, on its own grounds, an actual studio lot, just like in the major studios in Hollywood. 'We'll start quite small as these things can be very expensive. But by bringing it onto the premises here, we can obviously cut the cost tremendously...' (And there are other advantages. Should they shoot on actual location in Dublin, the real occupants of the real houses shown in the series might well be upset by being implicated in a particular storyline...)

The design plans are very tight, with no allowances for luxuries, like tiny inaccuracies in the camera work. 'You see scenery built for drama production in other countries where 10 per cent of it is never seen in case a cameraman might shoot 'off' or a character would stray off a mark. We can't afford that luxury. Every inch will be used. We have very accurate cameramen!'

The greatest challenge faced by the design department in its 29-year existence was the Eurovision Song Contest of 1987. 'Without blowing trumpets, we did it better than anyone else has done it ever! The BBC's chief of engineering stood open-mouthed when he saw the set and said, ''I

hope we don't win because we can't better this.'' He wasn't joking.'

When recruiting designers (the numbers fluctuate, but hover around seventeen) Mr Pleass can immediately recognise those who are suitable. 'I look for an innate ability, like riding a bike—there are people here I spotted in art college in the seventies. Suddenly you see that they can think in terms of sequences of pictures. A lot of designers can see things only in a theatrical sense, in a box. TV designers have to think in terms of 360 degrees, in three dimensions. We give them elaborate tests to see if they think as a camera sees, that's the important thing. If a camera had a mind you would have to be able to get into the mind of that camera. On the screen everything looks that

little bit different. It's this transition between what the eye actually sees and what the camera will actually transmit which is the important factor for training a TV designer.'

In other stations, designers are recruited for specific areas—some design only for light entertainment, some only for talk-shows, some for drama. RTE's designers must be capable of doing all of these.

Mr Pleass remembers an American film director he met: ' ''Alan,'' he said, ''we're really very privileged...'' I said, ''What do you mean?'' and he replied, ''We're allowed to play games and we're paid to do it!'' He was right. It's all cowboys and Indians...'

On the set as it was being built for the new urban series Fair City *were producers Paul Cusack and Margaret Gleeson.*

QUIZTIME

KNOW YOUR SPORT

set by George Hamilton

'Origin obscure' says my dictionary, regarding the root of the word 'quiz'. There is, though, a glorious tale of enterprise told about just how the word came into being. But whether or not you choose to believe it—and it concerns an Irishman who won a bet that he couldn't create a new word that would be generally understood—the fact is that the quiz remains, without question, generally popular.

Everyone loves a challenge. And what could be more simple than answering a challenge to pit your wits against another's. Add the common currency of sport, and the challenge, in my experience, is irresistible.

How about this one for starters? What do the former World Snooker Champion, Dennis Taylor, and the boxing promoter, Barney Eastwood, have in common? That question, I've found, guarantees instant participation in the quiz. And, most likely, you'll be round the houses once or twice at least before the correct answer emerges. Quite simply: they both played minor football for Tyrone.

Warming to the footballing theme, you might like to try this one. Ronnie Whelan, in accepting the FA Cup at Wembley after Liverpool had beaten Everton in the 1989 final, became the fifth Irishman to receive the trophy as the winning captain. Who were the others?

The answer to that poser, and the others that I'll set before I've finished, you'll find elsewhere. To insert it here would be to snuff out the challenge—and it's on the challenge that the quiz will flourish.

For how else could you explain the fact that we are inundated with applications to compete each time we announce a new series of *Know Your Sport*? Those who actually get on the air are the top 80—the very best—so the winner has to possess a powerful memory bank of sporting knowledge.

Jimmy Magee's questions are quite capable of catching out even the champions of *Know Your Sport*; I'm quite sure mine wouldn't. But, anyway, here's another: one of Ireland's most popular rugby captains of recent times was Willie John McBride. Willie John? Well, no, as a matter of fact. So, for what does that initial 'J' really stand? And while you're at it: where, when, and against whom did Willie J score his only try in an Irish shirt?

I'm beginning to enjoy this; have a go at these: at the start of *Know Your Sport* each week, we see Ronnie Delany coming home to win the 1500-metre gold at the Melbourne Olympics. But who's taking silver and bronze behind him? The same title sequence featured a European Championship goal from the finals in Germany in 1988. Ronnie Whelan is volleying Ireland into a 10 lead over the Soviet Union in Hanover. Who took the throw that set it up? And a third Ronnie Whelan question: where, when, and against whom did he make his senior international debut?

Some questions on venues: Where is Ballymore, and what would you play there? Who is at home at Love Street? In which city would you find the Letzigrund?

If those have set you thinking, it proves another point about the quiz; quite simply, that it's the straightforward question that can be the most effective. Certainly, in terms of *Know Your Sport*, this has proved to be the case. Even when visual clues are involved, the questions tend to be straight to the point. No tricks; either you know, or you don't. And when it comes to tension in our quiz, simplicity holds the key.

The True or False round increases the pace; the final round of straightforward questions on specialist sporting knowledge builds up to the climax. But it's the simplicity of it all—direct answer to a direct question—that brings you to the edge of your seat.

Of course, when it's finger-on-the-buzzer time, and answers are sometimes being offered before the question has even begun to be read, the screw is turned still further, and the tension mounts.

But, always, it's the challenge of the simple question that is the key. Do you know the answer? For that is all that matters. And that is where we come in.

Everyone loves a challenge; and the quiz presents that challenge in its purest form. As for the origin of the word: it is reported that our Irishman went around Dublin painting every available gable wall with his newly invented word, and that by the next day, the whole town was quizzing itself about this new phenomenon.

Be that as it may, I can with absolute assurance stand over the answers to the questions I posed above.

(Answers on page 159)

BRUSH SHIELS

Medical thoughts of a television panellist

And speaking of *Kenny Live*, they had people in the audience; they had one guy with a sacroiliac joint out; they'd one guy, Paddy, who I knew meself, who had osteo-arthritis, which is different from rheumatoid arthritis; they'd one lady who was after being in a car accident and one lady who had a trapped nerve. Now in a million years, no matter how much praying you do, the trapped nerve's not going to go! There are only about three people in Ireland who can actually untrap the nerves. Tony Quinn was on the programme too and there's this thing called spiritual healing that Tony Quinn does and I understand how that works because there was another person on *Live At Three* who explained it. The whole thing is, if you really don't hold any grudges, really not hold any grudges, or bear any resent-ment, there's a really good chance that the body will heal itself of certain illnesses. Holding grudges tends to create certain chemicals, it's been proved through the years that negative thoughts create negative chemicals. I read a story once about a guy who had a thing called ankylosis spondylitis which is like arthritis of the spine. But he

WATCHED FUNNY FILMS FOR TWO YEARS

reckoned that he brought it on himself. And the best thing to do was to laugh it away, so he watched all these funny films for two years and it disappeared...

But I know three guys who got rheumatoid arthritis on Christmas Eve. In actual fact, rheumatoid arthritis is one of those things that can disappear overnight and nobody knows why it comes. But one of the reasons is if you have a lot of stress. And people tend to get down on Christmas Eve. Maybe it's because they never got any presents or something like that...

I started looking into that and I was talking to Seán Boylan about it and the way he does it is with herbs, so I went out and I bought this book on herbs and I read that there is a different herb for every illness...and they all look like the illness except the one for rheumatoid arthritis because that's caused by uric acid... The difference between rheumatoid arthritis and osteo-arthritis is that the osteo-arthritis is in the joints, mainly in the hips, and the rheumatoid is mainly in the outer areas like the shoulders and the hands... The herbs are basically to try and get the uric acid out of the areas it's in, and there's a lot of manipulation that goes on as well, to open up what's commonly called the meridians in the body, all the energy channels that's in everybody's body that get blocked by the acid. The acid is sort of like cement and when you take the herb drink that sort of softens it up, and the right person, if they know what they are doing, they can push it and manipulate it into the blood stream so it can be carried away.

So I got interested in that. And then I got interested in trapped nerves. Doctors do their best for you but they don't really know how to deal with trapped nerves. I find that a very interesting area. As far as I can see, from the letters I got after *Kenny Live*, half the country seems to have trapped nerves and nobody can do anything about them. The side effects of the trapped nerve is that you can have complete disorien-

Brush Sheils—Cont. from page 103

tation in the body. It can be very frightening, you can easily believe that your hearing is going. Your eyesight goes as well.

So I came across a very interesting nerve called the trigenital nerve which goes up through the jaw and behind the eye and this guy's mother rang me after the show and told me that they were going to operate on him through the ear to try and get at this nerve and there wasn't even a 50/50 chance of them getting it right. An Indian doctor had told them that they might be better off trying to get it fixed some other way. The effects of this trigenital nerve being trapped, which is very interesting, is severe neuralgia, so you go along to the dentist and he might take out one of your teeth. I came across this lady—we were actually going for a drive to Kilmore Quay and Seán Boylan was with me and this person and her husband—and she was after getting a lovely tooth taken out that she didn't want taken out but she thought that was causing the pain. But the pain didn't go. So we got out of the car and Seán Boylan actually untrapped this trigenital nerve for this lady. That was the first time I'd ever seen him do this particular thing....

The sciatic nerve is another one. A well-known ballad-singer around town, he sings through his nose so everyone will know who he is, he rings me up. It happens to a lot of guitar-players. You appear to go one-sided and you get this pain in the strangest places, like the ball of your foot...and it comes up through the shoulder blades...'

QUIZTIME

THE RTE QUIZ

set by

Clare Duignan

1. What was RTE's first radio station called?

2. Who presents *Play the Game*?

3. For what Olympic Games did RTE first provide television coverage?

4. Name the family who were the central characters in *Tolka Row*

5. What time does *Morning Ireland* start at?

6. Complete the programme title _____ *Junior High*

7. Who presents *The Arts Show* on Radio 1?

8. Who played Mrs Kennedy in *The Kennedys of Castleross*?

9. Who presented *Quicksilver*?

10. Name either of the actresses who star in *Cagney and Lacey*.

11. Who presents *Questions and Answers*?

14. Who was Battie Brennan's wife in *The Riordans*?

15. Who presents *The Sunday Game*?

16. What was the first home-produced programme transmitted in colour on RTE?

17. How many times has Ireland won the Eurovision Song Contest?

18. What was the name of Miss Ellie's first husband in *Dallas*?

19. Who became famous for his expression 'If you feel like singing, do sing an Irish song', on the Waltons' radio programme?

20. What was the name of the oldest son in *The Waltons* television programme?

21. The first chairman of the RTE authority was a very well-known Irish broadcaster who

12. What is the name of the title music of *The Gay Byrne Show*?

13. In what country is *Home and Away* set?

died recently. Who was he?

22. Who are Ian Dempsey's two co-stars on *Dempsey's Den*?

23. Name the actress who played the part of Pam, Bobby's wife, in *Dallas*?

24. When did *Dallas* first appear on RTE?

25. Who is the cookery expert on *Live at Three*?

26. Name the actress who plays Roseanne in the Network 2 series *Roseanne*

27. Who presents *Know Your Sport*?

28. Name the pub in *Coronation Street*.

29. Who plays MacGyver in the TV series of the same name?

30. What foundation does MacGyver work for?

31. Name RTE's four women news casters.

32. What is the name of Biddy and Miley's daughter in *Glenroe*?

33. Name the two main characters in *Miami Vice*.

34. During the past year RTE screened a weekly average of how many hours of television sport? a) 3 hours, b) 9 hours, c) 15 hours

35. Who presented the cookery series *Simply Delicious*?

36. Name the Cork hairdresser who is the agony uncle on Radio 2's *Gerry Ryan Show*.

37. Which regular panellist on *Play the Game* had a baby daughter this year?

38. Who is the RTE News' western correspondent?

39. Who plays Father Deveraux in *Glenroe*?

40. What television programme did Bibi Baskin present before hosting her own chat show *Bibi*?

41. Who presents *Check Up*?

42. Who played the part of Alexis in *Dynasty*?

43. If the Springboks are playing the Wallabies, what sport and which countries are involved?

44. Which well-known British naturalist and TV personality wants to save Irish bogs?

45. Aside from the *Late Late Show*, name two other television programmes presented by Gay Byrne.

46. Who presented the *1988 Eurovision Song Contest*?

47. What country won the *1988 Eurovision Song Contest*?
(Answers on page 159)

CLASSICAL MUSIC QUIZ ANSWERS

1. *Funiculì-Funiculà* by Luigi Denza
2. False. Joyce entered the Feis Cheoil in 1904 when he came second
3. Jacques Offenbach, who signed himself on a hotel register as O. de Cologne
4. *Sheep may safely graze*
5. Jeremiah Clarke, Roman Hofstetter, and Leopold Mozart respectively
6. *Der Tapfere Soldat* (*The Chocolate Soldier*) by Oscar Straus
7. John Field
8. Farinelli, the male soprano—he sang the same four songs for Philip V every night after that for twenty-five years
9. *The Blue Danube* by Johann Strauss II
10. Andrea Amati c. 1520-1611 of Cremona
11. Small drums made from skin tied over a bowl of clay, leather, wood or copper. First used by the Saracens, they were adapted as military drums by the Crusaders
12. William Vincent Wallace, born in Waterford, composer of *Maritana*
13. Michael Balfe, born in Dublin—later composer of *The Bohemian Girl*
14. Eric Coates. The tune is *By a Sleepy Lagoon* and the programme *Desert Island Discs*, which began on 29 January 1942
15. Cork Symphony Orchestra has performed under the baton of Aloys Fleischmann for more than fifty seasons since 1935. (Classified as Most Durable)
16. Joseph Haydn who wrote 107 symphonies. There were earlier composers of the eighteenth century 4-movement symphony, especially those of the Mannheim school, but Haydn brought the form to a new peak
17. *Plaisir d'amour*. Martini's real name was Johann Paul Aegidius Schwart-zendorf, born in Freistadt in 1741
18. Jenny Lind, born in Stockholm in 1820. Her voice was remarkable for its purity and agility in cadenzas and ornamentation and she caused a sensation wherever she appeared
19. John O'Sullivan, born in Cork 1878, died in Paris 1955. He was much admired and championed by James Joyce. Joseph O'Mara, born in Limerick 1866, died in Dublin 1927. Founded the O'Mara Co., 1912
20. Piano, violin and cello
21. Franz himself
22. Neither—they are identical in pitch
23. *The Dolly Suite* by Fauré

JEREMY AND THE BARREL WHACKERS
(cont. from page 87)

by Pat Ingoldsby

That's when we do it. That's why we wear alarm clocks on top of our heads.'

'What happens when your clocks start to ring?' asked Jeremy Thwisk.

'We all stop whacking and get to sleep,' answered Senior Spring.

'Aha...I see,' thought Jeremy, but he didn't say it. 'Aha.....Aha...I see....'

Late next night it happened again while Jeremy was sound asleep. 'Boom! Boom! Boom!' The walls of his bedroom shook with the noise. The floor under the bed vibrated. Down on the roadway the red and white barrels shook and wobbled. Inside each one the springs were bashing out messages to one another. They whacked and clattered and banged with their drumsticks.

'Oh dear me,' yawned Jeremy as he sat up in his bed. 'There's only one way to deal with this.' And he reached for his yellow alarm clock. 'BRRRRINNNNNGGG!' Jeremy leaned out of his bedroom window with the clock in his hand. The shrill ringing echoed on the night air. 'BRRRINNNGGG!' It rang noisily around the barrels until one by one the springs pricked up their ears and listened.

'My goodness,' one of them squeaked, 'doesn't time fly. That was a very short night.' And he stopped whacking. Then another...and another, until one by one the red and white barrels stopped wobbling and were very very still.

'Time for bed,' squeaked the very senior spring.

'Time for bed is right,' laughed Jeremy Thwisk. And that's exactly where he went!

Marian Finucane

MARIAN FINUCANE

Deirdre met Marian: 'her strength is her own personality'

Marian became a radio announcer in 1974. 'I wasn't a very good radio announcer.' (Probably because radio announcing is a very formal art. Marian's strength is her own personality.) She moved to television as a continuity announcer and her first television appearance, her first night ever, ever, went like this:

8.00 pm she introduced *Cannon*. There was vision and no sound...

9.15 pm, after *The Nine O'Clock News*, there was a delay of seven minutes before *Seven Days* 'and I filled for two minutes in vision, unprepared'. ('Filling' is where the continuity announcer comes on, in theory totally unflustered, totally in charge. Two minutes is an awfully long time on live television. Especially when you are unprepared. Even more so when it is your first night ever, ever.)

10.00 pm, after *Seven Days*, there was a problem with the film *Sweet Charity*. 'Part of the country was off the air—and I was in and out of the film apologising...'

11.30 pm (approximately) 'I left RTE like a spot of perspiration.'

Small wonder that Marian is grateful for radio. Don't get her wrong, she loves 'the buzz' of television, *The Women's Programme*, *Down The Tube*, but nothing can beat her beloved radio. 'I think it's less superficial. I think that the technology actually does come between the person interviewing and the person being interviewed. People listening to radio listen in ones, and that is more personal as well. Long-term love, it would be radio...'

All the ratings show that the long-term love is returned on *Liveline*. The programme has tapped in to the Irish people's love of sounding off. Although the topics are carefully chosen and researched by the programme's production team, there is no guaranteeing what people will have on their minds. Everyone who rings in gets the same courteous attention, no matter how way-out, unpopular or unjustified their stances or rantings. In the programme's history, Marian remembers losing her temper with only one caller, a man who rang in with an attitude of unrepentant racism. That man stepped over her limits. 'I actually buy the philosophy of the programme—in the desirability of people being allowed to air their point of view.

AIRING PREJUDICE

When people come on airing prejudice, I believe it is a useful thing to tease it through and to highlight it for what it is. That is how I handle things. If someone comes on and says all unmarried mothers should be shot, I would talk them through without compromising my own principles. I would allow them their say.'

Marian was born and reared in Glasnevin in northside Dublin. 'At one stage, a group of us were going to establish the Dublin 9 or the Dublin 11 Club to counteract the Dublin 4 image ...!' She and John, a farmer, have two small children, Sinéad and Jack. She counts herself lucky in the career/job juggling stakes 'because John is around the house most of the time. Therefore, I wouldn't have the same kind of pressures that most women who were working full-time outside the home would have. He's there an awful lot of the time. Also, I wouldn't have to leave the house at eight in the morning and I would rarely be home later than five o'clock in the evening.' So she doesn't get bogged down by 'arrangements': 'John might get bogged down by arrangements, I tend not to.'

Neither does she tend to notice her outside image. She shops in the chainstores like the rest of the human race and is not conscious that people gawk. 'We lived in a small community (near Delvin in County Westmeath) for eight years and we're in another small community now (Punchestown) and you're a four-day wonder and then people don't pay you any more attention.' She does pay great attention to her appearance: 'I find it's good for me. In a very peculiar way, I take much more care of my appearance working in radio than I ever did in television. It's to do with the fact that I believe that the people coming in to be interviewed deserve the courtesy of one attempting to look half-decent... Funnily enough, when I worked in television on *The Women's Programme*, I used to trollop in to work in my jeans every day of the week...' And as for continuity announcing: 'I remember Maurice O'Doherty surveying us one time and saying: ''If the public could just see you lot from the waist down!'' '

GERRY RYAN

Deirdre Purcell met this 'quiet, calm individual'

You may hate him, you may love him, but there is no ignoring him. Ponytailed lout or macho sex-symbol, loud-mouthed idiot (his words) or sympathetic guru, he is there and there to stay, and 2FM will never be the same.

The Gerry Ryan Show has become much more structured of late. 'Preparation has become more formal. The execution of that preparation is also more formal, yet the programme seems to be looser on air. And I'm now beginning to believe the old maxim that the more preparation you put in, the luckier you get the next day. Reports, prepared scripts, interviews, all these things are now becoming part of it. In the beginning we just weren't able to cope with them and we would make up for lack of serious conversation or reporting by more madness.' The fear was that by becoming more professional, the show would also sound stale or boring. 'But no, not at all. In fact it just makes you more relaxed at what you're doing.'

The show is, according to its presenter, 'only in its infancy. If you look across the house to *The Gay Byrne Show*, that's been there for twenty-five years, still very successful, on its good days it can be brilliant. I see no reason why we shouldn't have a crack.'

Mr Ryan's was not an overnight arrival. Trained as a solicitor, he is the son of a dentist from Clontarf in Dublin and a former 'pirate' deejay who once thought of being an actor. He has been with 2FM since its beginning, as Radio 2, in 1979. He says he has identified what is exciting in all broadcasting, including current affairs. It is the What was that? factor: 'What was she saying there? What was he doing there?'

Another factor is originality. The broadcasters to whom the public respond, no matter in what field they broadcast, are the 'originals', the people whose own personalities are indelibly stamped on their material. 'But how do you define originality? Is it genetic, hereditary, environmental, circumstantial—an aberration?

Probably at the end of the day, originality is something which is actually awry with a person's personality. When you think about it, all the most fascinating people have been loonies!'

Loonies, of course, are not that easy to live with and he is the first to admit that his wife, Maura, a graphic artist (possessed, he says, of 'serious talent', unlike his own, which he classes as of the 'buffoon' variety), has a lot to bear. 'I know my family find me very difficult to live with. My career is such a loud, dominating type of career...' Like many people in the public eye, to survive, he splits himself into two distinct personalities: 'Me at work is Gerry Ryan-The-Personality and Gerry-The-Sort-Of-Spontaneous-Exploding-Creature. I can see it like an 'out-of-body' experience. I'm floating up in the air looking down at Ryan. But at home, I'm pretty much a quiet, calm individual, washing the dishes like the rest of us.' To help him preserve the distinction, he has no home telephone and he spends a great deal of time with his four-year-old daughter, Charlotte.

He defends himself against charges of being big-headed: 'I think the big-headed thing is more of an illusion. In Ireland, if you have a larger vocabulary than ten words and you talk very fast, people think you are big-headed...'

The show, which hits highspots of Monty Pythonesque humour, draws heavily on the inner resources of RTE. (It has been said that half of the members of the staff in the Radio Centre are working on it anonymously, as a hobby.) 'We do have a repertory company which is drawn from the most extraordinary parts of the organisation. It's a unique experience for people who might be working in slightly duller, though very worthy areas, to come on board and preserve their anonymity and get a chance to live out their fantasies. A lot of these people are the Monty Python generation, they're the people who came into school on Monday and were able to do the Parrot Sketch from beginning to end...'

Although basking in his success, Mr Ryan recognises that the public and the press are fickle and that while today he is their darling, he can be tomorrow's man in the stocks. He had a flavour of it during the 'Lambo' experience (the infamous survival course where he and the rest of the survivalists were supposed to have killed a lamb with a rock in a sock—but didn't) and he now believes that the episode was instrumental in his maturity. Part of the maturing process was the recognition that throughout the episode, RTE treated him very well, like an adult. Up to then, he had blithely felt himself invincible, that all was fair in the bubble that was broadcasting, but he had to face the fact that this time he might actually have been wrong.

The Gerry Ryan Show was the beneficiary.

In June 1989 we photographed The Gerry Ryan Show *team. They were (left to right): Siobhán Hough, Joan Torsney, Brenda Donohue, Barbara Jordan, Willie O'Reilly, Gerry Ryan (seated front)*

FOR PAT KENNY
1990 SHOULD BE FUN

Deirdre Purcell talked to the workaholic who did, this year, take a month off!

If Pat Kenny had been asked in 1988 what he saw in store for himself in RTE in 1989, what he would have said was *Today At Five* on radio and *Today Tonight* on television. But 1989 saw him on television with *Kenny Live* and on radio with *The Pat Kenny Show*. 'Two events changed everything. One was the Eurovision Song Contest, the other was standing in for Stephen Roche on *Saturday Live*. The Eurovision and that appearance on *Saturday Live* sowed seeds in people's minds that I could change...'

It is hardly surprising, therefore, that Mr Kenny is cautious about committing himself to any predictions about 1990. All he will say, gingerly, is that he does not want to go back solely to current affairs broadcasting in the foreseeable future. 'It's not a very interesting time in current affairs... a lot of the time is spent dealing with subjects in which I have no interest.' However, even if he does find himself in those barren fields, Mr Kenny applies his considerable energy to ploughing them. 'I do believe it's the broadcaster's job to try and sell every single item as hard as every other. I believe that is one characteristic that I have. I try to sell everything as hard as I can, whether it is women's knitting patterns in the *RTE Guide* or an outbreak of AIDS in Bantry. That's my job.'

Pat's private life as a bachelor-around-town is always a subject for the gossip columnists. Eligible, interesting, intelligent men of forty-one are quite a rarity in Dublin. His upbringing was conservative, even if his father had a

very unusual job—elephant-keeper in Dublin Zoo. It is not surprising, perhaps, that Pat, despite the squash and the pints with the mates and the clubbing, is quite a conservative person too. 'I'm conscious of the fact that I'm getting older. I'll never see grandchildren, for instance—that's a reality.' Marriage is a thought he retrieves every so often from the back of his mind (although to be accurate, he usually dusts it off and puts it back again: 'I've gone past the point of being a youthful parent!').

Age, or perhaps maturity, has also caught up with his workaholic habits. For the first time ever since he joined RTE, he took an entire month's holidays in 1989. He had

A GAME OF SQUASH IS THE BALANCE

begun to feel that he was never out of RTE, or more particularly that RTE radio and television were never out of him. Even reading the Sunday newspapers was a professional chore for the week ahead. 'I began to see that it was a bit much and that I would have to work out a different way of handling my life and work.' When he is completely physically and mentally jaded, the remedy, he finds, is a really hard game of squash. 'Squash is the balance. You go out and play for an hour and a half and suddenly you're up

How many young RTE hopefuls do you recognise in this photograph with Pat Kenny?

joining the management 'side'. 'I found a lot of my colleagues backed off. People with whom I would drink in Madigan's (the watering-hole in Donnybrook favoured by many RTE people) suddenly weren't drinking with me any more. But that's calmed down now.' He enjoys the work of the Authority 'because I understand business, I'm a broadcaster and also I'm a technical person, so I understand a lot of the technical stuff.'

The knowledge of the 'technical stuff' is a consequence of his early training. He won a Master's degree in chemical engineering from Georgia Tech, in Georgia, USA, and was actually a lecturer in Bolton Street College of Technology when he read the advertisement in *The Irish Times* seeking part-time radio announcers for Radio Éireann, as it was in 1972. He answered the advertisement 'absolutely on a whim, a total whim...'

His first view of the old studios in Henry Street 'fitted in very nicely with my idea of what radio studios were like. A lot of institutional green, loads of it, and big speakers that looked like they were built in World War II, big microphones, clocks with lights on them, a very civil servicey place, long corridors... You would never see the controller of programmes from one end of the day to the next.'

But Pat believes that the modern RTE is a very different place. 'The personnel now running television and radio are very tuned in to the modern climate of broadcasting. Unlike in the past, there's a great willingness to change now and to change fast.'

1990 should be *fun*.

and running, completely energised.'

Professional to the last hair on his well-groomed head, Pat does his homework. 'Generally, if you don't feel briefed, you do feel intimidated. That's why the homework is so essential. If you're at a summit and you want to put a question to Mrs Thatcher—and you are not fully briefed—she can wither you with a phrase.' By and large, however, at this stage, interviews are challenges more than anything

else! 'I'm older than some government ministers now!'

Pat is a member of the nine-person RTE Authority, an experience he finds fascinating 'although I found the proceedings to be a lot more formal than I expected'. He says he thought long and hard before accepting the offer to become a member of the Authority, 'but then I thought, if I turn this down and they put someone in whom I think is a waster, I'd never forgive myself!' There was a penalty to be paid for

BRENDA COSTIGAN
COME AND GET IT AT THREE!

The *Live at Three* cook tells us what it's like to be a TV cook,
and a family one, too

The counter top is all ready—my tablecloth, my flowers, all my finished dishes laid out. The dishes I will feature are at various stages of preparation—one is ready in the oven, one half prepared, with a display of all the ingredients required. Have I forgotten anything? Have I placed the wooden spoon beside the bowl? Are my oven gloves in position? The seconds tick away, and the three big cameras move silently over to stand in front of the kitchen counter, like huge big friendly aliens, staring patiently. The floor manager gives the signal and we're on live—on *Live at Three*!

Anyone looking into my car that morning and indeed every Friday morning as I drive in to Telefís Éireann would be amused—bowls, dishes, served out food, flowers, cutlery, you name it—all delicately balanced on the seats and floors. It's the ramps that kill me—three of them in the grounds of the Montrose complex. My heart is in my mouth as I ease over them. I do all my preparation at home. The reason is not only because the studio kitchen is too small, and that I'd be in everyone's way on the studio floor, but simply because there are hours and hours of preparation.

The main hazard of preparing food at home is the passing 'nibblers'. My family is well used to seeing food on the kitchen counter, with a big notice attached saying 'Don't touch TV Food!' They have given up wistfully asking will I be bringing it home because the answer is always no! When the show is over the food is either given away to a charity or, if too perishable to travel, it is eaten by the crew. One way or another it means that the food must not only look good for the camera, but taste good too. The wonderful thing about the TV camera is that it shows the food up in such a lifelike way that there is no need to have recourse to any tricks. I only wish that it could transmit the lovely aroma of the dishes. Maybe some day they'll have a 'smell button'!

The choice of subject for any Friday is arrived at by mutual discussion between myself and charming Catherine Cahill, the researcher in charge of food—with the imprimatur of Noel Smyth, the series producer. Noel has a particular interest in 'family type' on Fridays, which is 'right up my alley'. So many of us have so much family food to prepare whether we like it or not. This format has proved very successful and the postbags requesting my recipes are tremendous. Voices can be heard from between the sacks saying 'Brenda, please choose recipes that no one wants for a change!' A meatloaf recipe

Opposite:
Live at Three *cook*
Brenda Costigan

baked in pastry was a great favourite, as were ideas for stewing steak, pot-roasts and weekend puddings. Easy Saturday cooking ideas got great response and the demand for the wedding cake seemed like half the country was getting married!

It's hard work, but it's great fun and the whole *Live at Three* team, with the wonderfully professional Thelma Mansfield and Derek Davis as presenters, are lovely to work with.

One might not associate actual cooking with radio but the Gay Byrne hour had a 'first' this year with a pancake-tossing competition. The large studio had gas cookers specially installed. The 'tossers' were Bishop Walton Empey, Aonghus McAnally and Brendan Shine. I had to show them how to make the batter and how to flick the wrist to toss them, because two of them had never made a pancake before. Hilarious! Gay kept a close eye on proceedings, checking the progress and passing on to me various queries from listeners. The competition itself finally got underway with the marvellously distinctive voice of Micheál Ó Muircheartaigh giving a witty commentary. He knew, he said, that Aonghus wouldn't win because of his size 14 shoes! I ask you! Normally radio is more restrained, sitting comfortably at a table talking to Gay Byrne about the subject in hand, be it fish on Good Friday or cakes for Christmas or whatever.

Then I go home to cook the family meal!

'And come into the studios and tell Gay all about it'

SIOBHÁN CLEARY did tell—well, nearly all

'Will you go off on the boat to Holyhead tomorrow and see what this new duty-free lark is all about?'...Yeah! Yeah! Sure!

'And come in to studio, the next morning, and tell Gay all about it?'...(Gulp!) Yeah! Sure!!!

So there I was the following afternoon, shopping for toys and a new kettle, in Wales, and loading up with dirt-cheap booze on the way back. And there I was the next morning, a total Nervous Nelly, sitting opposite The Man Himself in studio 5. It was during the commercial break and Gay was trying to calm me down, and wind me up at the same time, and getting nowhere. I was petrified.

Then he suddenly exploded across the table. 'You know what! YOU'RE A GORGEOUS LOOKING WOMAN!' I burst out laughing, the red light flashed on, and we were away. It was the best diversionary tactic I've ever seen.

After that it became a regular date, and during my years on *The Gay Byrne Show* I found myself in some tight spots. Like the time I went to the Amateur Snooker Championship in the Pioneer Club in Mountjoy Square. There was nobody on the door selling tickets, so I just went on in and sat down. There were six of us in the room—the two finalists, their two pals, the referee and me...Mrs Woman, Mammy-of-Two, Everyday Housewife. Nobody spoke to me, they just looked, and I just sat

(cont. from page 113)

and waited for the rest of the spectators to arrive. But no one else came in. I was the audience, and I was dying of embarrassment.

When the snooker table had been examined minutely by everyone, including me, the Championship began, and I tried to make myself as small as possible, so as not to get in the way of the amateur champs. No easy thing when you're five foot ten in high heels.

You could have cut the atmosphere with a blunt knife. When one of the contenders would come around to my side of the table, I was afraid even to breathe in case I would trip him up. When they were on the other side of the table, opposite me, they were in my direct eyeline, and no matter where I looked, I could feel they were blaming me whenever they missed. And they missed a fair few.

The final straw came when the fellow who was doing a bit better than the other fellow, came round the table to take a tricky little shot right in front of me. He leaned over the green baize, and his shiny backside landed just inches from my face. That was it! I shot out of the chair, out of the door, down the stairs, and I didn't stop running until I reached O'Connell Street.

Well I didn't see too much of that particular match, but I made up for it about a year later when I had a ringside seat at Goffs to watch Alex Higgins in action. At the interval I was brought 'backstage' to meet the dreaded Hurricane, who turned out to be so nice and charming I could hardly think of anything to say to him. But I obviously made a big impression, because during the second half of the match he kept winking at me and cracking jokes. And of course he won hands down. It could have been my big night if I'd hung around afterwards!

I gave up snooker then and went on to try karate, horse riding, cricket, set dancing and tea dancing. I checked out endless Santas, much to my children's delight, and I saw a dog show, a cat show, a horse show, a pigeon show, a tropical fish show and walked the feet off myself at the Chelsea Flower Show. I spent a day in the *Irish Times*, a day in the Four Courts, a day at the races, a day delivering singing telegrams, and a day passing myself off as a tourist from somewhere in 'mittel Europe', to see if I'd be ripped off by the natives (and I wasn't, not once, even though I was practically throwing the money around). And I spent a day with the taoiseach of the time, Dr Garret Fitzgerald.

That was an amazing day, seeing government work, at close quarters. But there was one small incident I'll never forget. It was when Dr Fitzgerald brought me home to have lunch with himself and Mrs Fitzgerald. Just before we left to go back to Leinster House, Mrs Fitzgerald looked at the taoiseach's blue tie and decided that he needed a brighter one because he was going to a social function in the evening. Dr Fitzgerald went straight to the bedroom and came back with two coat hangers full of almost identical blue ties and started rummaging through them. He held one up for my approval. 'What do you think?...Is this a bit more cheerful?...Yes, yes this will do!...Yes indeed!'

I nearly died when he started to put it on because there were soup stains all down it. I wondered if it would be more a breach of etiquette to tell the Leader of the Country that his tie was dirty, or to say nothing and be responsible for letting him make appearances in a grotty tie.

I don't know if it was telepathy or what but he suddenly said, 'Oh dear, this won't do!' and took it off again. Another dilemma solved for Mrs Woman, Mammy-of-Two, Everyday Housewife. But that was one story I didn't tell Gay!

BIRDIE O'HANLON MEETS MRS DOYLE

by John P Kelly

OK, let's begin with a straight question. Which drama series has had the longest run on radio? Alright, don't all shout together! *The Kennedys of Castleross*! Ah yes, we remember it well. Birdie O'Hanlon and Peadar Mahony enriched all of our lives. Those as young as myself will remember running home from school to be a part of the exciting world of Castleross.

Well, you were wrong. *The Kennedys of Castleross* ran for approximately 2000 episodes. In June of this year, *Harbour Hotel* celebrated its 3675th edition. And it's still going strong. 375,000 listeners can't be wrong. Mrs Doyle and Charlie Conway became an extra course on the RTE radio lunchtime menu. A couple of years ago, shortly after a beloved character had suffered a heart attack, I was approached by a lady who had been told that I was the producer of *Harbour Hotel*. 'If Gabriel Murphy dies,' she said, 'I'll never listen to RTE again!' But this was her follow-up: 'That's the second time I've made that promise. The last time was when you got rid of John Corrigan!' Ah yes, you must remember John Corrigan. No? You mean you're younger than I am?

We in Radio 1 are very proud of our drama. Each week throughout the year we provide 210 hours of entertainment. From soap to classical plays, from *Only Slaggin*

to serialised books, from children's theatre to Dramaí Gaeilge, all of it comes from just one studio—Studio 9.

To watch a radio play in production is to enter a magical world. Who, when listening to the cooing of an intimate duo as 'he' tries to pop the question to 'her' before the moon sets, can possibly imagine the reality? Studio 9 is a large square box, lit by glaring white light and devoid of any atmosphere. Thanks only to the skill of the actors, sound personnel, production staff and writers, we are transported through time and space, or often into the deepest thoughts of characters we have only just met. Radio drama can be more expansive than any film epic and more intimate than any published book.

The cast of Harbour Hotel *at work*

Every day you can listen to the work of our repertoire and freelance actors. Last year, the Radio Éireann Players celebrated their fortieth birthday. Their numbers may be fewer now than in earlier years, but they are no less talented, with the co-operation of a large pool of freelance colleagues. There is, however, another unsung bunch of people who deserve some credit here. Much of the magic I spoke of earlier is due to the input of our 'spot' people.

Radio actors, unlike their counterparts in the theatre, never handle a cup and saucer or tear a page or do any of the million little actions of everyday life recreated on the stage. The actors concentrate on the script and on the characters. I remember with pleasure Daniel Reardon playing a soldier talking as he mounted five flights of stairs. I remember also Peter O'Connor (Mr Spot) playing Daniel Reardon's legs up and down three wooden steps. But mostly, I remember a sympathy between both performances which together created one real radio person.

What is the reality? I recently spoke to someone who had listened to a radio play I had directed. We compared the setting from his imagination with my own dream. Even the wallpaper matched. That, of course, was the exception and nothing more than a coincidence. We in radio drama can collate many realities. If we have 100,000 listeners, we have 100,000 sets. What colour is Katherine O'Connell's hair? How does Marie dress? Yes, you are right—red and blonde and dark and minis and jeans etc etc etc. We give you freedom to create your own realities. We are proud to be a part of your world, and through the magic of radio we will continue to welcome you into ours.

Oh, by the way, before I leave, here's a little question. Between the ending of *The Kennedys of Castleross* and the beginning of *Harbour Hotel*, a series graced our lunchtimes. Can you name it?

Answers please on the back of a £50 note to:

Jack McCann
The Dubliner
Kilmanon
Ennismore
Everywhere

Or contact our solicitor, Aidan Belton, directly. 'Birdie Must Fly!'

Credits:

Birdie O'Hanlon	—	Pauline Delanee
Peadar Mahoney	—	Philip O'Flynn
Mrs Doyle	—	Daphne Carroll
John Corrigan	—	Norman Rodway
Charlie Conway	—	Kevin McHugh
Gabriel Murphy	—	Chris Curran
Willie Bracken	—	Daniel Reardon
Katherine O'Connell	—	Barbara McCaughey
Marie Belton	—	Colette Proctor

The Kennedys of Castleross produced by William Styles

Harbour Hotel edited by Laurence Foster

THE SUN ALWAYS SEEMS TO SHINE ON
ROOM OUTSIDE

Gerry Daly

Gerry Daly is forever being quizzed about his gardening programmes: 'How is it that the sun is always shining in your programmes and the soil is so fine and crumbly?' The reactions to his programmes are many and varied: 'I get all fired up with enthusiasm watching you but when I go out to my own garden and the ground is like concrete, it wears off again!' And the listeners are not always gardeners: 'I have no interest at all in gardening but I often listen to your programme on Saturday morning because I find it entertaining; you get some great ones on.' So what does Gerry himself have to say?

GREATLY FLATTERED

'Before colour television became the norm, gardening was not featured very much, varied shades of grey not being terribly interesting. Colour was its making. Plants look so well on the small screen, their shape accentuated by contrast with the flat rectangle; their roundness compressed by the trickery of the lenses; the colour of the flowers highlighted as we watch in a darkened room. And close-ups; the camera's close-in view of the flowers or leaves of a plant is unlike any inspection of the same plant with the naked eye. The end result of putting pictures of plants on TV is that the plants are greatly flattered.

'A plant we featured on *Room Outside*, called Daisybush for its profusion of white daisy-type flowers, looked so much better in close-up than its everyday reality that one garden-centre owner reported dozens of enquiries about the plant until we showed it to them and their faces dropped. Very disappointing for the nursery man too, no doubt!

'Anyway, this flattery of plants is no bad thing if it brings them to people's notice for the first time and perhaps opens their eyes to the beauty of plants. Even experienced gardeners sometimes see new value in a familiar plant when the camera gives its version.

After all, that is what gardening programmes are for; to give an introduction to the world of plants, their beauty and the satisfaction to be gained from dabbling in growing them.'

'Gardening generates a real sense of achievement. When you spend a couple of hours in the garden at the weekend, even mowing the grass, you can see what you have done. This sense of satisfaction is all the more real for the physical tiredness or slight ache when finished. People run the roads and go to gymnasiums to achieve the same feeling, with little to show at the end of it except some worn-out runners!'

MADE FOR EVERYBODY

'It is always nice to hear that somebody, despite having no great interest in the subject, finds a programme entertaining. Programmes are made for everybody, not just those with an existing interest. Nor are they made to promote gardening, but if they do so, that is an admirable bonus. Their real purpose is to give pleasure to the viewer and the listener; an end in itself. Half the nation must be in bed at ten o'clock on Saturday morning if I am to judge by the number of times I have been informed that the radio gardening phone-in is listened to in the ''scratcher''.

'The gardening phone-in is unique among radio programmes in depending entirely on calls from the public for its material. The calls are taken straight on air without the pre-selection and calling back that is the norm with other phone-in programmes. This allows the listening public to set its own agenda, neither too lofty nor too basic. It also affords the disinterested listener a slice-of-life glimpse of, or more correctly 'listen' to, the Irish public. Listeners, I think, enjoy putting a 'character' on the programme callers just by their speech—callers are so natural and matter-of-fact about the whole thing. I find fascinating the reaction of listeners to some of our callers; one person's ''narky ould so-and-so'' is another's admired ''fellow that really put it up to you''.'

'The parallel feature in the television programme Room Outside— the visits to viewers' gardens— evokes great interest too, and interest of a similar nature. People love to see other people's gardens and the person who created the garden. There are lots of ideas to be picked up from seeing other gardens, and on a very simple level, there is the enjoyment that comes from seeing nice pictures of a pretty garden. Not by any means everybody enjoys gardening, but I have never met anyone who does not enjoy a nice garden.

CONCRETE GARDEN

'The only one to come close was a caller to the radio programme who was, on reflection, probably trying to put one over on us, suggesting he was so completely fed up with the garden that he wanted information about concreting it over. He became totally flummoxed when he was taken seriously by the panellists and offered sound advice about concrete, but entreated to leave some little pockets of space for plants in odd corners. In nine years, that was the only time a caller was not genuinely seeking information, and even then maybe he was!

'The sun always seems to shine in Room Outside—only because we do outdoor jobs when it is not raining, otherwise we repair to the greenhouse. Simple, isn't it?'

THE EDUCATION DEPARTMENT OF RTE RADIO

by Teri Garvey

If somebody in your house was doing the Leaving Certificate this year, you may have been aware that *King Lear* was serialised in six half-hour programmes. Bought in by RTE from Thames television, it was introduced by Professor Augustine Martin, who analysed the production specifically for Leaving Certificate students. You and the exam candidate may also have been tuning in to *Education Forum's* 'Examline' phone-in advice programmes on Leaving and Intermediate Certificate subjects. These programmes came from the Education Department in RTE, which covers radio and television. While it caters for exam students, its entire range of programmes covers a much broader area than the exam system or indeed the formal school system.

On television, there were bought-in programmes on cookery (from the ancient art of cookery, to Mediterranean cookery, to a taste of China, to cooking for celebrations); the planets and the stars; art in Italy; the history of portraiture; interior design; colour in knitting with Kaffe Fasset; the craft of the weaver; maths; micros and the electronic office, and continental languages. Home-produced programmes included *Hard Times*, a series about communities and individuals who are tackling poverty and unemployment in Ireland today; *Give Us a Chance,* the series that gave us a chance to see young, secondary school students and hear their views on the Irish education system; and *God's Houses*, a series on Irish Church architecture.

The range of educational programmes on radio is, if anything, even broader, and home-produced to boot! Although often slotted away in the recesses of the night or FM 3, where one has to be a dedicated radio fan to find them, regular listeners are rewarded by the educational variety being produced. The range includes *Monday at Nine*, an hour-long digest of ideas and information, covering philosophy, literature, music and science; *The Open Mind*, a weekly magazine, airing ideas, experiences and news from the world of education, and those famous live phone-ins on exam subjects or on entry requirements for third-level colleges. *Not so Different* looks at the realities of being labelled 'disabled' in Ireland today. This realistic, non-patronising programme has been so successful that it has attracted broadcasting teams from other countries to come and look at what RTE is doing in this area.

Hard Times was a series complimenting the TV series of the same name, dealing with unemployment. *Ways of Knowing* was an intriguing series in which Dr Mike Cooley reflected on how we come to a knowledge of the world around us. *Cogar* and *Abair Abab* were lively, up-to-date programmes in Irish for beginners and for those whose Irish was a little rusty. *Women and Poverty* ex-amined some of the key issues affecting women who are poor in Ireland. *Beyond the Cloisters* also looked at women—nuns who work in the community. *Child Minding* explored the growing interest in the whole question of child day-care outside the home. *Cities and Changing Villages* looked at how and where we live. In *Passions* enthusiasts talked about their particular hobby or craft or way of life. *The Developing World* went outside Ireland to look at some of the causes of the problems in the Third World.

And to entertain and educate you on those warm summer evenings, there were those vignettes, *The Way of all Flesh, The Music of Sound, Looking at Pictures*, and *Coaches and Milestones*.

And there is more, much more. The complete spectrum of education in its fullest sense, from infancy to old age, in all sections of the community, at home and abroad, is covered; and it is made possible by a hard-working group of producers. These are the people who conceive the ideas, draft out the plans, draw up the panels, trek off to interviews with tape recorders under their arms, spend hours closeted in booths listening to tapes, timing them, editing them, organising music to suit, etc, and finally the programme goes on the air. If they're lucky, they get a brief mention at the 'back' of the programme . . . 'that programme was produced by Tim Lehane, John Quinn, Bill Meek, Liz Sweeney, Peter Mooney, Martha McCarron'. They don't look for recognition. As craftspeople their satisfaction comes from a good finished product. One producer has likened it to the bottom of the Ardagh Chalice. As he said, the craftsman who made the intricate, exquisite design on the base knew it would only rarely be seen, but his dedication to it was no less. And so it is with them.

So on television or radio, turn up the chalice and look at the bottom. You'll never be better educated!

'THEY HAVE GOT USED TO THE SOUND OF THEIR OWN ACCENTS . . .'

Donna O'Sullivan

'It'll do alright as soon as the Cork people get used to the sound of their own accents', producer in charge, Breandáin Ó Ciobháin prophesied, and it did. Ireland's first local radio service began as a thirty-minute programme, five days a week, in the summer of 1974. It wasn't long before *Corkabout* established itself in the minds and hearts of Cork people—as the programme about Cork, made in Cork and broadcast throughout Cork.

Local radio was an entirely new idea at the time. What could the people of Cork possibly have to say that would be worth listening to—every day? What would the programmes be about and who would make them? Jim Sherwin and John O'Donoghue were the first two professional presenters of the programme, but the other contributors were all 'freshers'— charmingly fresh in some cases, as when a CIE official, giving his daily traffic report, said that the whole of Cork city was 'banjaxed'. It didn't take the people of Cork long to realise that this local radio

was theirs whether they wished to use it to locate straying ferrets, return lost pigeons to their lofts, voice their anger at city-based joyriders or replace a caravan for a travelling family in need. Over the years Cork local radio has been used for all of these causes— sometimes as trite as looking for a costume for a local dramatic production, sometimes as deeply touching as the massive response to the Ethiopian Famine Appeal Fund which in a matter of a few weeks raised over £½ million from Cork purses.

For radio to be truly local it must be accessible. Listeners must feel they can talk directly to the pro- gramme makers. Thousands of people have trooped into the RTE studios, sometimes with a story to tell, sometimes just looking for tea and sympathy—and our tea is tops! A recent contributor to the programme arrived at the recep- tion desk only to find receptionist Tom Creedon with the telephone balanced on his shoulder and a six-week-old baby cradled in his arms—all part of the service.

While local radio is obviously much smaller in scale than the national service, its obligation to listeners covers quite a broad spec- trum. Top priority is given to local news, which is the busiest and most demanding programme area, and while it does not cover world affairs, local politics and in- dustry provide a constant flow of material and stories—many of which are of national significance.

Then there are the endless con- troversies that most communities engage in; whether it's modern street sculpture in Kinsale or the speed limit in Kanturk—if it's a local talking point, it's local radio.

CORK PEOPLE LOVE TO TALK

Current affairs is the real meat of any radio service and local radio in Cork has discovered that social and political issues find a ready and avid audience, who are anx- ious not just to participate as listeners, but in the 'on air' broad- casts too.

Ó DISCOS I LONDAIN
GO
RAIDIÓ NA GAELTACHTA

Seán Bán Breathnach

Cork Local Radio
(cont. from page 120)

Certainly, you can't fill five and a half hours of programming every day with purely local material but you can give more general items a local slant. Listeners' favourites focus on the gardening advice, given weekly to dozens of callers, with Billy Browne's earthy chuckle; and there's environmentalist Tom O'Byrne, known as the 'wildlife' man with the gentle voice; and owners of cats and dogs would be lost without the homespun animal wisdom dispensed by John Clifford.

It was a great help to discover that Cork people love to talk, whether it's when approached on the street by a reporter or invited in to the studios for a live debate—and very lively some of those have proved to be. Cork people almost always have something to say, and are not shy to say it!

The staff at Cork local radio are a closely knit bunch, and deeply committed to the idea of public service broadcasting at the local level—but they'd like longer broadcasting hours of course, to deliver a fuller service to their audience. They feel they have their finger on the pulse of the people of the area, and have over the years translated it into lively and vigorous local radio programmes.

And there are lots more programme ideas for Cork, a loyal audience there to listen and able and willing to join in. And yes, they have got used to the sound of their own accents.

Oíche Dé Máirt, an chéad lá de Aibreán 1969, a rinne mise mo *début* craoltóireachta in Éirinn ar seó beo ar Radio Éireann; an chéad phopchlár as Gaeilge ariamh, *Pop Seó na Máirte*. B'é an t-iarGreenbeat, John Keogh, a bhí i mbun a léirithe. Bhí Liam Devalley ina cheannasaí ar chláracha ag an am agus ba eisean a d'iarr orm an clár a chur i láthair. Bhíos féin i Sasana

ag an am agus gan mé fós ach i mo dhéagóir i 1969. Marach an glaoch gutháin sin a fuaireas ó Liam Devalley, seans gur i dtalamh Sheáin Bhuí a bhéinn go fóill. Rugadh mé dhá mhíle siar ó bhaile beag an Spidéil i nGaeltacht Chonamara i 1949, agus cosúil le beagneach chuile dhuine eile san gceantar, is ag smaoineamh ar an mbád bán a bhí mé ó caitheadh ar an sop mé.

Is cuimhneach liom go maith an chéad uair ariamh a chuaigh mé ar stáitse i gColáiste Chonnachta ag geamaireacht mhór a d'eagraigh Cumann na Réadoirí. Amach i lár na hoíche, bhí ceoltóirí nár tháinig in am, agus an lucht eagraithe 'stuck' mar a dearfá. Tharla cúpla seachtain roimhe go bhfaca Pól Ó Foighil mé i seomra ranga ag aithris ar Mhicheál Ó hEithir. Níor rinne sé tada ach breith orm idir chorp, chleite agus sciathán agus mé a leagan suas ar an stáitse. Thosaigh mé ag caint agus níor stop mé ariamh ó shoin.

Ní raibh mé ach beagáinín le cois sé bliana déag nuair a chuaigh mé go Sasana. Trí mhí a bhíos ansin nuair a bhuail mé le col cúigir le Alan Freeman, an deejay ón Astráil. Fear é seo a bhí ag plé le Mobile Discotheque i dtuaisceart London, ie discos, bainiseachaí, srl; thairg sé post dom, ag casadh ceirníní le linn na deire seachtaine, agus ní gá a rá gur ghlac mé go fonnmhar leis.

Bhí go leor stáisiúin bhradacha ag craoladh go mí-dhleathach ar chósta Shasana ag an am. Ina measc Radio London agus Caroline, agus bhí ainmneacha aisteacha ar na deejays. Daoine cosúil le Spangles Muldoon, Vauxhall Harry, Jesus Christ me srl. Chaith Doug Freeman cúpla seachtain ag lorg ainm dhomsa-faoi dheire, DJ B. A., Benny Arnold, a thug sé orm.

Ní morán disco i London nár chas mé ceirníní i 1967 agus 1968. Sin iad na blianta a raibh na Hippies agus Flower Power i mbarr a réime agus bhaineas féin ard spraoi as an rud go léir. Bhí an t-ádh liom nach raibh aon bhaint agam le druganna, mar bhí siad go fliúrseach an t-am sin. Is cuimhneach liom go maith gur péire pyjamas psychedelic a bhíodh mé chaitheamh ag na discos. Bhí deartháir liom ag fanacht sna digs liom, agus níor labhair sé fhéin ná an landlady liom ar feadh bliana. Deire na bliana 1967, rinne mé sraith cláracha seachtainiúil do Radio City. D'iarr siad orm dul ar bord loinge leo go lán-aimseartha, ach dhiúltaigh mé mar bhí job maith agam i rith an lae ag obair ar an mbuildeáil agus £25 sa tseachtain. Rinne mé cúrsa craoltóireachta san Hertfordshire School of Broadcasting agus is iontach a sheas sé dom go dtí an lá inniu.

D'éirigh thar barr leis an gcéad sraith clárach sin a rinne mé ar Radio Éireann i 1969. Is dóigh liom fós go chuir an saghas ceoil a bhí mé ag casadh iontas ar go leor san eagraíocht fhéin, mar i ndeire na seactúdaí is beag cuir amach bhí ag daoine óga ar Reggae, Bluebeat, Soul agus Motown. B'é *Pop Seó na Máirte* an chéad chlár i Radio Éireann go raibh cead ag an deejay ad-libeáil. Roimhe sin bhíodh ort an scriopt a bheith i lámha an léiritheóra cúpla lá roimh ré. Fuair mé an t-uafás litreacha ó chuile áit san tír. Is féidir liom a rá freisin nach raibh na litreacha ar fad moltach. Bhí roinnt daoine ag iarraidh a rá liom go gcuirfinn deire leis an nGaeilge. Dúirt Máirtín O Cadhain liom oíche amháin gur 'cac' agus nach 'pop' a bhí mé a chasadh. Bhí muintir RTE an-tsásta leis an sraith, ach ní bhfuair mé amach ariamh ó shin cén fáth nár lean siad leis an bpolasaí nua-aimseartha a bhí acu.

Thosaigh mé ar an teilifís i 1970 le sraith cláracha dár teideal *Imeall*; méascán de cheol traidisiúnta agus amhráin folk. Ní dóigh liom fhéin gur éirigh leis an gclár, mar nár thuig mé fhéin an teilifís ag an am, agus nach raibh focal Gaeilge ag an léiritheoir. Bhí Tadhg de Brún ag obair liom ar an gclár sin agus thug sé an-mhisneach agus cúnamh dhom.

I 1973 roghnaigh Bob Quinn mé leis an bpríomhpháirt a ghlacadh sa scannán 'Caoineadh Airt Uí Laoghaire', agus is mó scileanna a d'fhoghlaim mise ón dá bhliain a chaith mé ag scannánaíocht le Bob ná ó rud ar bith eile. S'é Bob Quinn a chuir ar mo shúile dom an chéad uair ariamh céard is proifisiúntacht ann. Is mar gheall ar seo agus an craoladh go léir a bhí déanta agam ar Raidió na Gaeltachta ó 1972, a bhí an oiread sin fuinnimh, misnigh agus muiníne agam asam fhéin nuair a thosaigh *SBB Ina Shuí*.

Liam Ó Murchú agus Joe (Uasal) O'Donnell ba chúis leis an gclár a thosaigh i 1977 agus a mhair go 1983. Ag breathnú siar anois ar chúrsaí, is dóigh nár thuig mé fhéin ná Gráinne Ghleoite ná an fhoireann chomh maith agus a bhí ag éirí linn. Is ar éigin a bhí an clár amuigh as an Tam rating, agus shroich muid uimhir 2 le hathchraoladh i samhradh 1978. Is dóigh liom go bhfuil áit dá leithéid de chlár i gcónaí agus ní gá a rá go bhfuilim ar fáil. Níor tháinig aon chlár ó shoin a thug seans do ghrúpaí nua. Thosaigh go leor grupaí linn, ina measc Foster and Allen.

Is iomaí uisce imithe le fána ó thosaigh Raidió na Gaeltachta, Domhnach Cásca 1972. Tá gach cineál cláir déanta agam ó shoin, ach is dóigh go bhfuil trí ócáid a sheasann amach i mo intinn: troid Sheáin Uí Mhainnín a chraol muid beo ó Madison Square Gardens, bua na Gaillimhe san All Ireland i 1980, agus agallamh a rinne mé leis na Hothouse Flowers i studio *Top of the Pops* nuair a chas siad 'Don't Go' ar an gclár. Is iontach an t-omós a thaispeáin siad dhomsa agus do Raidió na Gaeltachta, mar dhiúltaigh siad glan labhairt le haon iriseóir eile.

Tá mé an-sásta le mo chuid oibre i Raidió na Gaeltachta, agus is

cinnte gur mór an dul amú a bhí ar go leor daoine a thug breith báis orainn i dtús ama, agus a dúirt nach mairfeadh sé ach cúpla bliain.

'Aon duine a cheapann gur pop ar fad atá uaimse, tá dul amú mór orthu'

Cosúil le chuile shórt eile níl muid gan locht agus níl ort ach ceist a chur ar na daoine óga le sin a fháil amach. Mise ceann do na daoine a mhol ag an tús gur cheart amhráin as Béarla a bheith againn. Táim fós ag troid na cúise th' éis ocht mbliana déag agus creidim fós go bhfuil an ceart agam. Ach cosúil le *Pop Seó na Máirte* fiche bliain ó shoin, ceapann daoine fós go gcuirfeadh sé deire leis an nGaeilge. Sin deargsheafóid, tar éis an tsaoil níl ar dhuine ach cnaipe a bhrú ar an raidió nó teilifís agus is féidir leo a rogha ceoil a fháil. Tá an iomarca daoine meánaosta gan mórán cur amach acu ar an óige ag déanamh cinnidh an-tabhachtach.

Tá beirt pháiste againn, seacht mbliana agus cheithre bliana, agus is minic a thugaim liom ag discos iad. Níor labhair siad focal Béarla ariamh. Tá Teilifís na Gaeltachta ar na bacáin againn anois, agus tá súil agam ón tús go mbeidh polasaithe deimhne cinnte acu, agus gurb é an chéad rud a chuirfidh siad rompa ná cartoons do pháistí óga. An lá a bhéas Pop-Eye agus a leithéid i nGaeilge tá leath an chath gnóite. Aon duine a cheapann gur pop ar fad atá uaimse, tá dul amú mór orthu. Tá ardmheas agam ar cheol, cultúr agus amhráin na tíre, agus is dóigh liom go bhfuil an oiread céanna cur amach agam ar chúrsaí sean-nóis agus a leithéid, agus atá ag daoine a ligeann scil orthu fhéin.

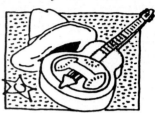

QUIZTIME
COUNTRY MUSIC

set by Niall Toner

(cont. from page 15)

13. What famous country singer recently came out of retirement and had a number one hit with Dwight Yoakam?

14. Apart from the obvious, what have Emmylou Harris, Linda Ronstadt and Dolly Parton got in common?

15. Who composed the song *Paradise* (sometimes called *Mullenburg County*)?

16. From what building was the *Grand Ole Opry* first broadcast?

17. Who composed *Forty shades of green*?

18. Two Irish singers modelled their style during the seventies on the style of George Jones and Tammy Wynette. Who were they?

19. Name two instruments prominent in bluegrass music.

20. Name the theme music used in the films 'Deliverance' and/or 'Bonnie and Clyde'.

21. Who had a world-wide hit with the song *Blanket on the ground*?

22. Name Bob Dylan's 'Country Album'.

23. The Rolling Stones recorded a straight country number in Los Angeles in the late sixties which later became one of their best-known songs. What was it called?

(Answers on page 158)

AG ÉISTEACHT LE RAIDIÓ NA GAELTACHTA

Nollaig Ó Gadhra

Is iomaí scéal éadóchasach agus ábhar bróin atá luaite maidir le scéal na Gaeltachta le fiche bliain anuas. Agus maidir le dáiríreacht an stáit Éireannaigh féin do chothú ár n-oidhreachta teanga, nó go deimhin maidir le cosaint bhunchearta an mhionlaigh theanga atá againn sa tír seo, ní mór an t-ábhar gaisce atá le maíomh againn ach an oiread. Rud mór amháin a baineadh amach, áfach, sa bhliain chéanna nuair a chinn muid mar phobal ar dhul isteach i gcorcán leáite an Chomhphobail Eorpaigh ná bunú Raidió na Gaeltachta. Seirbhís raidió a bheadh lonnaithe sa Ghaeltacht féin agus a thabharfadh tús áite ina cuid oibre go léir do phobal na Gaeltachta cibé áit ina raibh cónaí orthu.

Raidió áitiúil a bhí i gceist mar sin i gcás na dtrí phríomhphobal Gaeltachta, i dTír Chonaill, i gConamara agus i gCorca Dhuibhne, a fuair bunstruchtúr nua craoltóireachta. Ach bhí níos mó ná sin i gceist. B'é dualgas na seirbhíse freastal ar an nGaeltacht uilig, idir bheag is mhór, idir theaghlaigh agus dhaoine aonair. Mar, faoi mar a dúirt an Corcaíoch ó shin nuair a cuireadh ceist air, is ionann ballraíocht i bpobal na Gaeltachta san lá atá inniu ann agus 'state of mind'.

Príomhbhua Raidió na Gaeltachta ná an ceangail aeir úd atá déanta aige idir na pobail éagsúla Ghaeltachta ar fud na tíre. Agus i mBaile Átha Cliath ar ndóigh. Ní fhéadfaí a bheith ag súil leis an tionchar deimhnitheach atá aige ar shaol na Gaeltachta go léir ó shin i leith, gan an ceangal sin a bheith ann. Tá tábhacht leis an gceangal sin do lucht canúnachais, dóibh siúd atá buartha faoi fhorbairt na teanga nua-aimseartha, dóibh siúd ar fud na tíre ar mhaith leo a cheapadh go bhfuil soláthar breá dea-Ghaeilge le fáil acu in aghaidh an lae, ach an tseirbhís a chasadh air ar a gcuid mionraidiónna faiseanta—raidió láimhe mar a thugann muintir Chorcha Dhuibhne ar a leithéid, deirtear liom. Ach thar rud ar bith eile, tá tábhacht le Raidió na Gaeltachta i ngeall ar an gcaidreamh agus an chomhthuiscint atá cothaithe aige idir pobail éagsúla na Gaeltachta. Dream a bhí scartha óna chéile le fada ag paistí móra Béarla agus Galldachais agus ar beag an aithne a bhí acu ar a chéile—seachas an dream a théadh go dtí an tOireachtas nó Comórtas Peile na Gaeltachta. Nó a chasadh ar a chéile cois Life, i Londain nó i mBoston.

Níor dearnadh an fhorbairt chothrom chéanna ar an gcaidreamh seo sna pobail Ghaeltachta éagsúla ná go deimhin i ngach gné den saol a bhfuil tábhacht chumarsáide ag baint leis san lá atá inniu ann. Go deimhin tá éisteoirí rialta leis an tseirbhís, cosúil liom féin, a dhéarfadh nach i bhfeabhas atá an scéal ag dul le blianta beaga anuas nuair is lú líon na gclár caidrimh agus díospóireachta idir lucht comhspéise sna Gaeltachtaí éagsúla, le hais an ruda a bhíodh ann sna '70aí abair. Tá cúiseanna éagsúla leis sin gan amhras. Agus ní fhágann sé nach dtugann an chuid againn atá lonnaithe i gceantar Gaeltachta amháin cluas don méid a bhíonn le rá ag Tír Chonaill agus ag Ciarraí i mo chás-sa, gan trácht ar Bhaile Átha Cliath mar a bhfuil an pobal éisteachta is mó ar domhan do chláir Ghaeltachta, is cosúil.

Cúrsaí nuachta agus cúrsaí reatha an rud is tábhachtaí ar Raidió na Gaeltachta de réir dealraimh. Fágann an leagan amach atá curtha le fada ar an tseirbhís go bhfuil ní amháin nuacht náisiúnta agus idirnáisiúnta le fáil go rialta, ach go bhfuil ag pobal na Gaeltachta freisin, an tseirbhís nuachta áitiúil is fónta in Éirinn uilig. Arís, bíonn an tseirbhís seo spotach go minic. Bíonn éagothromaíocht idir an bhéim a leagtar ar ábhair éagsúla agus go deimhin ar phobail éagsúla, ar bhealach a thabarfadh le tuiscint b'fhéidir gur cheart duit do scéal féin a sheoladh isteach más mian leat é a chloisteáil, in áit a bheith ag fanacht ar fhoireann atá sách crúógach, is cosúil, le dul amach á bhailiú. Ach seo gné eile de Raidió na Gaeltachta atá thar a bheith tábhachtach—páirtíocht. Breathnaíonn pobal na Gaeltachta ar fad agus go deimhin mórchuid de phobal Gaeilge na tíre ó Bhéal Feirste go Cléire, ar Raidió na Gaeltachta mar a ngléas cumarsáide féin. Níl le déanamh agat ach éisteacht le clár na bhfógraí gach tráthnóna. Nó smaoineamh ar an tábhacht atá leis na fógraí báis. Tá fógraí báis an raidió chomh tábhachtach céanna sa Ghaeltacht le fada agus atá na fógraí cáiliúla a dhíolann an oiread sin de nuachtáin laethúla na hÉireann. Seán Ó Ríordáin, sílim, a dúirt nach bhfuil aon duine básaithe i gceart, in intinn oifigiúil na muintire i nDún Chaoin, a thuilleadh, mura bhfuil sin fógar-

Nollaig Ó Gadhra

tha ar an raidió. Agus is fíor. Ní amháin sin, ach is cosúil gur mó an tábhacht atá leis na scéalta seo ón bhaile sna pobail bheaga Ghaeltachta atá scaipthe ar fud na Mí agus Chill Dara ná sa bhaile.

Tá pobal mór 'cúl-éisteachta' ag Raidió na Gaeltachta ar fud na tíre a bhaineann taitneamh agus leas, eolas agus pléisiúr as cláir an stáisiúin. Agus tá sé mar pholasaí ag Raidió na Gaeltachta deis a thabhairt don lucht cúl-éisteachta seo páirtíocht áirithe a ghlacadh sa tseirbhís iad féin, de réir mar a oireann. Is beag Gaeilgeoir ar fud na tíre le 15 bliana anuas nach bhfuair deis a chuid saineolais ná a scéal féin, nó a shainspéis a roinnt leis an gcuid eile againn ar Raidió na Gaeltachta. Sin é an rud a shaibhríonn an tráthchlár agus a fhágann go mbíonn rud éigin úr le cloisteáil ar an tseirbhís go rialta. Ní amháin sin, ach tá éirithe leis an bhfoireann gréasán lucht

teagmhála a bhfuil Gaeilge acu, a chur le chéile ar fud an domhain ar bhealach a fhágann gur minic Raidió na Gaeltachta chun tosaigh ar RTE féin maidir le léargas dúchasach Éireannach a sholáthar dúinn ar mhór-imeachtaí na cruinne. Is fánach an áit nach bhfaighfeá gliomach, a deirtear. Mar an gcéanna i gcás lucht Gaeltachta.

Tá bearnaí agus easnaimh ar an seirbhís i gcónaí gan amhras. Bearna an tráthnóna an ceann is measa faoi láthair, dar liom, ag am nuair atá stáisiúin thráchtála áitiúla ag teacht ar an aer agus nuair a bheas ar Raidió na Gaeltachta an fód a sheasamh, ar lic a dhorais féin. Agus tá gnéithe d'iompar na foirne féin a chuireann olc ar éisteoirí ó am go chéile. Ceann acu is ea caighdeán na Gaeilge féin. Ceann eile is ea an leisciúlacht a bhaineann le roghnú ceoil agus an t-ardán a

thugtar go minic do dhroch-cheirníní agus go deimhin d'amhránaithe áitiúla nach bhfuil thar mholadh beirte, díreach toisc go mbaineann siad leis an áit. Tá dóthain lucht ceoil den scoth ar fáil sa Ghaeltacht agus dóthain ar téipeanna agus ar cheirníní den scoth le stop a chur leis an gcineál seo ruda. Nó, ar a laghad, lucht na grágaíle a theorannú do chláir ar leith atá dírithe ar thalann nua na háite.

Tá gá freisin le comhordú níos fearr le RTE féin, go háirithe i ré seo an tráchtálachais nuair atá cláir mhaithe sách gann agus nuair nach acmhainn do RTE go mbeadh dhá chlár fhiúntacha ag trasnáil ar a chéile. Maidir leis an bpointe deireanach seo, ní mór cuimhneamh ar ndóigh go bhfuil dualgais mhorálta agus reachtúla ar RTE i gcónaí maidir le soláthar ábhar i nGaeilge dá lucht éisteachta ar Raidió 1 agus Raidió 2—dualgais atá sách deacair a chomhlíonadh sa ré nua, agus nár mhiste a phlé agus a chomhordú le Raidió na Gaeltachta.

Ach thar rud ar bith eile, sí teist an fhiúntais a bhaineann le Raidió na Gaeltachta ná líon na ndaoine ar fud na hÉireann atá sásta cluas a thabhairt di go rialta agus sin go minic i gcás daoine nach mór é a gcleachtadh ar Ghaeilge a chloisteáil ar an raidió. Déanann siad an iarracht mar is fiú é. Tá mise i measc na ndaoine sin. Cuireann Raidió na Gaeltachta go mór le saibhreas teanga agus cultúir na craoltóireachta in Éirinn. Pobal na Gaeltachta is mó a bhaineann leas as an tseirbhís sin. Ach ba thrua í a theorannú, ar bhealach ar bith. An duine atá in ann an méid seo a léamh, agus nach dtugann cluas do Raidió na Gaeltachta go tráthrialta, mhol-fainn dó a intinn a athrú. Ní fada go dtuigfidh sé nach muintir na Gaeltachta amháin a chuireann spéis sna cláir a bhíonn le fáil. Tá mé cinnte nach mbeidh aon chathú air, má bhrúann sé an cnaipe nua. Féach an t-eolas teic-niúil atá i dteannta na haiste seo, de réir mar a thuigim.

Cúrsaí Cúrsaí Cúrsaí Cúrsaí Cúrsaí Cúrsaí Cúrsaí Cúrsaí

CÚRSAÍ

Michael Davitt, one of a new batch of producers/directors, gives some impressions of his first season with *Cúrsaí* (five nights a week, Network 2)

'Fáilte go *Cúrsaí* etc, boy. We've already put out eighteen editions, we've been grossly understaffed, I haven't had a holiday in years, I have a bit of a *tinneas cinn* so I'll be brief,' arsa an t-eagarthóir. 'I want you to do comedy. Keep it simple and straightforward. One plus one mock interviews—Cynthia can do a brilliant nun and Charlie Bird type pieces to camera, with buses and jack hammers in the background. Tadhg does a great character, Tadhg-an-Dá-Thaobh, and interviews himself in studio!'

'When do you want the first programme?' a d'fhiafraíos-sa, ag iarraidh mo sceimhle a cheilt agus a fhios agam go maith má bhí spota dubh amháin i sceidil RTE ó thús, gurb é cúrsaí grinn é.

'Friday week.'

'Friday week?'

'All right, Friday fortnight. And I don't care how many mistakes you make as long as you give it a good lash!'

Lá Samhna 1988, mo chúrsa traenála díreach curtha díom agam, mé ar dhuine de sheachtar léiritheoirí ar an gclár *Cúrsaí*—breis is fiche duine san iomlán ar an bhfoireann, idir thaighdeoirí, chúntóirí léirithe, agus rúnaithe. 'Sea, murach go bhfuairis an

chéad súnc beag sin, seans nach mbeadh aon bhuille snámha go deo agat! Bhuel, níor báthadh éinne uaidh sin go Nollaig cé gur chuathas gairid go maith dhó ar uairibh.

PRÍOMHBHUA

Leathdhosaen clár grinn a d'éirigh linn a chraoladh ar deireadh, Pilib (Tadhg Mac Dhonnagáin) agus Yvonne (Cynthia Ní Mhurchú) á gcur i láthair: Yvonne den scairdghlúin, fíochmhar Bleá Cliath Theas; Pilib arna fháisceadh as síltheagasc na hathbheochana, fear cúise ó bhonn a bhuataise leathair go muineál a gheansaí Árainn. B'iad na glaonna 'speisiúla' gutháin is mó a raibh rath orthu: Pilib ag glaoch ar an gComhdháil ag moladh dóibh fáinne triantánach a sholáthar do na homaighnéasaigh; Yvonne ag glaoch ar Chomhaltas féachaint an molfaidis ceol Gaelach a bheadh oiriúnach do radharc i scannán ina raibh fear, bean agus súp allais leo—moladh di dul go Peadar Ó Riada nó Paddy Moloney. D'éirigh le Pilib teidil na dtrí leabhar ba theo sa Ghaeilge a mhealladh ó bhainisteoir Áis...

Rud trialach, rud a bhfuil géarghá leis i saol na Gaeilge (ar eagla go dtachtfaí le sollúntacht sinn), ach rud é a éilíonn go leor acmhainní agus réamhphleanála. San athbhliain leagadh cláracha ceoil agus spóirt mar chúram orm.

Thugamar cuairt ar chliamhán rugbaí, Terenure College, mar a bhfuil Árainneach, Caomhán Ó Conghaile, gafa go mór leis an 'thugs' game played by gentlemen'. Ó dheas go Cathair Chorcaí agus an gomh ar Éamon Young chuig 'sharks' nua Chumann Lúthchleas Gael. Le teacht Michael Jackson go Páirc Uí Chaoimh, dob fheidir a rá gur tháinig deireadh le Ré na nDíograiseoirí agus tús le Ré na gCuntasóirí!

Ó thaobh an cheoil de chuireamar na fadcheirníní ba dhéanaí á meas ag painéal léirmheastóirí. Meán an phopcheoil gualainn le gualainn le meán ársa na Gaeilge, foirmle a fheictear agus a chloistear go seachtainiúil i *Scléip na hÓige* ar Raidió na Gaeltachta agus leathanach Ruaidhrí Uí Bháille in *Anois*. Foirmle a n-éiríonn léi ach í bheith inchreidte, dírithe ar phobal cinnte seachas pobal samhailteach. An dream is mó a bhfuiltear tar éis faillí a dhéanamh iontu le fada ná déagóirí a bhfuil labhairt agus tuiscint na teanga acu. Braithim go bhfuil an clár 'guiz' *Eureka* ag treabhadh cuid den ghort sin go héachtach, ach gort fairsing é agus seo am an ghátair.

Ansin, go hobann, bhí na toghcháin orainn. Ar dtús Údarás na Gaeltachta agus Párlaimint na hEorpa agus ansin thug Charlie a léim. B'é mo chéad bhlas den pholaitíocht agam é mar

Cúrsaí Cúrsaí Cúrsaí Cúrsaí Cúrsaí Cúrsaí Cúrsaí Cúrsaí

léiritheoir, marab ionann is láithreoir an chláir, Seán Ó Tuairisg, a bhíonn ag comhaireamh vótaí sa leaba istoíche agus an chuid eile againn ag comhaireamh caorach. Léiríomar (má bhí gá le léiriú) a bhuailte is atá na ceantair Ghaeltachta ag dífhostaíocht agus a leathbhádóir, an imirce. Thugamar painéal polaiteoirí isteach chun aghaidh a thabhairt ar scata mac léinn ar lú a muinín sa chóras polaitiúil ná muinín an phainéil.

Lá an chomhairimh bhí mír timpeall deich nóiméad ag *Cúrsaí* gach uair a' chloig go leith. Measaim gur éirigh linn é a choimeád bríomhar, gonta agus gur chuir sé leis an iomlán seachas é a bhearnú. Ó thaobh na teanga, tá roinnt rudaí suntasacha a sheasann amach im chuimhne: (1) gur thug triúr ceannairí páirtí agallamh substaintiúil i nGaeilge líofa, 'beo' ar an aer, lá an chomhairimh, (2) gur labhair cúigear TD nua linn i nGaeilge lá athoscailt na Dála, 25 Meitheamh, agus go raibh triúr eile nua a dhéanfadh amhlaidh ach an glaoch a fháil, (3) gur gheall Ó hEochaidh go gcuirfí Teilifís na Gaeltachta sa tsiúl laistigh de thrí mhí nó mar sin dá ndéanfaí a pháirtí a ath-thoghadh. Beifear ag faire gan dabht.

Cuimhním, leis, ar an ngeábh a thugas féin agus an Méalóideach siar go Rath Chairn ar thóir 'vox pops' faoi cad a tharlódh sa Dáil 25 Meitheamh 1989. Mar seo a d'fhreagair Máirtín Mac Donncha nuair a d'fhiafraigh Seán de ar cheart do Fianna Fáil agus na PDs dul in aon leaba amháin: 'Nach cuide dhen muic a drioball!' a deir sé. Nár thréige an saibhreas sin sinn.

Agus mé á scríobh seo, braithim an giar síceach sin ar tí athrú (síos nó suas?) im cheann. Tá *Cúrsaí* curtha a chodladh don samhradh agus mé ag dul i mbun dualgas nua leis an gclár *Off Mike*, tír nua le triall uirthi i 'Where in the World?' seo na teilifíse.

Pilib agus Yvonne (Tadhg agus Cynthia)

Seán Ó Méalóid

Michael Davitt

Seán Ó Tuairisg

Mary Fitzgerald back on the screen with How Do You Do

Candle making

You can make a selection of candles for yourself or to give as presents to family or friends at Christmas or any time of year. When you make candles, always have an adult with you. Cover your work area with newspaper and have all your supplies ready before you start to melt the wax.

For all candles, you will need paraffin wax (available at hardware shops) and pieces of crayon (which add colour to the wax.) Hot wax can catch fire so it should never be melted directly over a flame.

To melt it, put three or four pieces of paraffin wax and crayon in an empty can (a bean or pea can). Set them in a large pot of water and clip them to the pot with clothes pegs. Put the pot of water on the cooker. Turn the heat on, the water will boil and the wax will melt. To use the melted wax, remove the clothes pegs and hold the can with a pot holder or oven gloves.

1.   Moulded striped candles

All sorts of containers can be used to make moulded candles. Disposable moulds such as paper cups or fruit juice containers are best because you simply tear away the mould when the candle is made.

You will need
2-3 moulds (cream or yogurt cartons, paper cups or fruit juice containers)
Candle wick (available in craft shops)
Scissors
1 pencil or stick
Masking tape
1 pot holder
A bowl of ice
Paraffin wax
Wax crayons in different colours

How to make

1. Melt the paraffin wax as described already. Then gently drop several pieces of crayon into each tin can (only one colour per can). As the wax crayons melt, gently stir them with a stick or the end of a paint brush. Melt as many colours of wax as you want to use in your candle. When the wax has melted, turn off the heat.

2. To prepare the mould for the wax, cut a piece of wick that is 75mm longer than the mould.

3. Put a piece of masking tape on the end of the wick. Tape it to the bottom of the mould, placing it in the centre.

4. Roll the top end of the wick around a holder, such as a pencil, and rest the holder on top of the mould.

5. With a pencil, mark the side of the mould, dividing it into as many stripes as you want in your candle.

6. Once you have prepared the mould, you are ready to make the candle itself. Using a pot

holder, take a can of melted wax from the pot. Pour wax into the mould, up to the first mark you made. This will be the first stripe. If you are going to use that colour again, put the can of wax back into the pot of hot water.

7. Put the mould into a bowl of ice and hold it there for a few minutes. The ice will harden the wax. Each layer must be hard before you pour in the next, otherwise the colours will run together. When the wax is hard, take the mould out of the bowl of ice.

8. Choose the colour of wax for the second stripe. Pour it into the mould up to the second mark. Put the mould into the bowl of ice to harden the wax. Repeat these procedures to make the rest of the stripes.

9. When the last layer of wax has hardened, peel the paper cup or fruit juice container from the candle.

10. Remove the pencil. With scissors, cut the wick so that only 12mm sticks out from the top of the finished candle.

2. Ice-cube candles

Ice cubes and melted wax do not mix. By mixing ice cubes and melted wax you can create a candle with unexpected holes and crevices.

You will need
Melted wax (see introduction)
A fruit juice or milk container, cut to 150mm high.
100-125mm candle, 12mm thick.
A bucket of ice cubes.

How to make

1. Holding the can of melted wax with a pot holder, pour a 12mm layer of wax on the bottom of a mould.

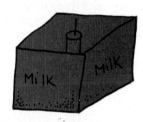

2. Put the candle in the centre of the container. The wax in the bottom will help to hold the candle in place.

3. Carefully put ice cubes all around the candle. Made sure it remains upright and in the centre of the container.

4. Using a pot holder to protect your hand, pour melted wax into the container—all the way to the top of the candle. Set the container aside for about an hour until the ice cubes melt.

5. When the ice has melted, pour out the water.

6. To extract the candle, gently tear the carton away from it.

Gift wrapping

For Christmas or birthdays, wrap up your presents in unusual gift wraps. Simply select a box to suit your gift and create a crazy creature.

1. Cheeky chicken

You will need
1 box 15 x 13cm and 8cm deep approximately (a small cereal or biscuit box)
1 sheet yellow card
1 sheet white card
2 pipe cleaners
sticky tape
1 sheet gift wrapping paper
11-12 coloured feathers
Glue
Scissors
Pencil

How to make
1. Cover the box with wrapping paper.

Foot · Cut 2   Beak Cut 1

2. From yellow card, cut two feet and one beak as in diagram.

3. Make a hole in each foot marked with a black dot. Push a pipe cleaner through the foot and stick to the back of the foot. Bend pipe cleaner to make knees and then stick centrally underneath the box.

4. Fold along dotted lines of beak and bend under tabs. Stick them to box front close to top edges.

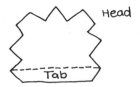
Head
Tab

5. Cut a 15cm square of white card. Stick wrapping paper to both sides of the card. Cut out one head as in diagram. Fold along dotted line and bend back tab.

6. For eyes, cut two big white eyes and two small black eyes. Cut one big yellow lid and cut it in half. Stick a black eye on a white eye and a lid on top. Stick eyes on head and stick head on top of the box.

7. Stick three coloured feathers to the top of the head in a fan shape. Then add three to either side of the box for wings and two to the back of the box for a tail.

2. Poppy pig

You will need
A cylindrical box approximately 8cm long and 12cm wide (a washing-up-liquid box or a dishwasher-powder box)
1 sheet gift wrapping paper
1 sheet pink card
1 sheet black card
1 sheet white card
1 roll gift wrapping ribbon
Glue
Scissors

How to make
1. Cover the box with wrapping paper.

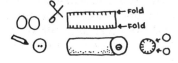
Fold
Fold

2. From pink card, cut two oval snouts 4 x 5cm and a 16 x 3cm strip. Fold over both long edges of the strip by 1cm and cut at intervals. Bend strip round and stick to snout ovals. Draw black dots on it for nostrils. Stick snout to front of box.

Eyes Lashes

3. Cut two black paper eyes and two black lashes. Fringe the lashes and stick eyes to the front of the box.

Leg

4. Cut four legs from white card as in diagram. Stick wrapping paper to the outside of each leg. Curve round and stick. Stick legs to pig.

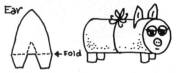
Ear
Fold

5. Stick two 15cm squares of gift wrapping paper back to back and cut out two ears. Fold along the dotted lines forming a dart and tabs. Stick to pig, bending tips of ears forward.

6. Decorate the pig by tying gift wrapping ribbon around his neck. Also stick ribbon to the back of the box for a tail.

4. Percy pony

You will need
A rectangular box 21 x 15cm and 8cm deep approximately (a tea bag box or small cereal box)
4 small matchboxes
1 small box approximately 5cm square
1 sheet gift wrapping paper
1 small ball wool
1 small sheet black paper
1 small sheet white paper
1 ribbon 12cm long
Needle and thread
Glue
Scissors

How to make
1. Cover the rectangular and the square boxes with wrapping paper.

2. Stick the square box to one end of the other box for a muzzle.

3. Cover the four matchboxes with wrapping paper and stick underneath the box for legs.

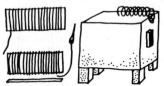

4. Cut a piece of white card 10 x 5cm and bind widthways with wool. Cut a 12cm length of ribbon and neaten ends. Sew the wool loops from card centrally to ribbon for mane. Stick mane to the top of the pony's head and neck.

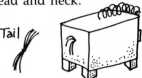
Tail

5. Cut 18cm of wool for tail and tie together in the centre with thread. Stick centre of tail to back of box.

Eyes

6. Cut two big white eyes and two small black eyes. Stick one on top of the other and stick one on either side of the box. Cut out two pink eyelashes and stick over eyes.

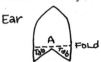
Ear
A
Tab Tab Fold

7. Stick two 15cm squares of wrapping paper back to back and cut out two ears. With point A. on box edge, stick top tabs to box top and side tabs to side. Leave to set.

THE DEVELOPMENT OF IRISH BROADCASTING

Kieran Sheedy

On the evening of 1 January 1926 large crowds gathered outside the Marconi Company in South William Street where a loudspeaker public-address system had been installed to relay the official opening of 2RN, the new Dublin Broadcasting Service. An equally large crowd also gathered outside the premises of W D Hogan, Radio House, Henry Street, which was providing a similar service, while the enterprising firm of McHugh Himself, Talbot Street, was offering a Brownie Crystal receiver, complete with headphones, at the specially reduced rate of 17s 6p. At 7.45 pm a hush descended and the voice of station announcer Séamus Hughes was heard introducing Douglas Hyde, the founder of the Gaelic League: 'Sé seo Raidió Bhaile Átha Cliath ag glaodhach; this is 2RN, the Dublin Broadcasting Station, calling.'

Broadcasting in the Irish free state began relatively late owing to the outbreak of the civil war. In 1923 negotiations were initiated with companies such as the Marconi Wireless Telegraphy Company, the Daily Express Newspaper Group and the Irish Broadcasting Company, but conflict between the various business and political interests resulted in a government decision that broadcasting in Ireland would be run by the state as a public service medium and would be financed by a combination of licence fees and the broadcasting of advertisements. There was already a lively interest in radio throughout the country,

with good-quality broadcasts coming both from the BBC and continental stations. In September 1924 the BBC opened a station in Belfast and the Post Office issued licences at a cost of one pound per annum, even though the fee in the UK was just ten shillings.

By November 1925 plans for the opening of the Dublin Broadcasting Stations were far advanced: a 1-kilowatt Marconi transmitter had been installed in a wooden hut in McKee Military Barracks and a single studio and office accommodation had been allocated in Little Denmark Street, off Henry Street. T J Monaghan, an engineer, formerly with the British Post Office, was put in charge of technical facilities; Dr Vincent O'Brien, conductor of the Palestrina Choir, was chosen as musical director; Séamus Hughes was made station announcer, and Séamus Clandillon, the Galway-born civil servant and well-known ballad singer, was appointed station director.

OPENING NIGHT

The official opening on 1 January was relayed to the UK courtesy of the BBC. The night's schedule consisted mostly of music and included the No. 1 army band, violin and harp solos, traditional music on the Irish pipes, solo singers and a choir. Séamus Clandillon had the temerity to include songs from both himself and his wife, Mairéad Ní Annagáin, thereby giving rise to the first broadcasting joke—her frequent

subsequent appearances resulted in her being christened Mairéad Ní On-Again! Apart from Douglas Hyde's opening speech there were no other speech items included. It was suggested that the absence of such items was due to the fact that many well-known people were away on holidays; the truth was that the new radio service at the time did not quite know how to handle speech items. However, within a year a basic news service had been set up, with talks on farming and literary matters, as well as daily weather forecasts and stock reports.

LIVE COMMENTARY

But it was the first broadcast of a sports event—the All-Ireland hurling semi-final between Galway and Kilkenny in August of that year which indicated the possibilities of a mass radio audience and helped to popularise the medium, particularly in rural Ireland. The live commentary was given by P D Mehigan, a sports journalist. His lively account of the game proved to be very successful, although he was subsequently banished from the press area to the sidelines by his colleagues who were upset by his shouting. But even on the sideline, P D Mehigan was not always safe, as he later recalled: 'I remember one day in Cork broadcasting a hurling final from the sidelines. The crowd around me got out of hand. I could see nothing. Stewards were helpless. I stood on a chair and tried to keep the commentary going. I was hit on the poll, in the ear and on the shoulders with clods and grass sods. Some were hard enough. The crowd swarmed round me and swept the phones away. The match was abandoned and the broadcast broke down.' Soon whole villages were crowding round the best radio sets in their localities to enjoy and enter into the spirit of this new broadcasting occasion. And before long, other sports events were being covered live, including the boxing championships at the Tailteann games, the final of the Free State Soccer Cup and rugby internationals.

In April 1927 the Cork Broadcasting Station—Cork 6CK—was opened. Its studios were somewhat incongruously situated in the women's jail in Sunday's Well, and the station director was Belfast-born Seán Neeson, who had settled in the city. Initially it was planned that the new station, whose broadcasts were also to be relayed on 2RN in Dublin, would provide a third of the entire output. However, owing to the opposition of the Department of

Finance, the output from Cork was limited to two and a half hours every Sunday night. Again music formed the greater part of the station's material, but it also tried to promote radio drama. Owing to the lack of ongoing financial backing, Cork 6CK was closed down in 1930.

There was some expansion in the area of classical music. The original Station Trio had now been heavily augmented and had become the Station Orchestra under the leadership of Terry O'Connor. In 1927 it began broadcasting symphony concerts from the Metropolitan Hall in Dublin.

The growing popularity of radio was not, however, reflected in the number of licence fees being taken—by 1930 there were less than 30,000 licence holders; this situation was largely due to the lack of countrywide reception from the McKee Barracks and Cork transmitters. To ameliorate this deficiency, a high-power ter, with an initial power output of sixty kilowatts, was erected in Athlone.

Éamon de Valera was the first Irish politician to make use of the medium's propaganda power. In 1920 he made a radio broadcast from the United States and when his Fianna Fáil party came to power he made yearly St Patrick's Day broadcasts to Irish-Americans, consisting of fraternal greetings and political comment.

But the 1930s in Ireland was also a period of economic stagnation and rigid censorship. In 1934 when Fr Conefrey, a Leitrim-based priest, began his anti-jazz campaign, he called for the banning of popular music from the airwaves. Certain sponsored programmes were singled out for special reprobation, but because of the badly needed revenue which they brought to the hard-pressed service they were allowed to continue. The anti-jazz campaign fizzled out rather quickly, having made the grave tactical error of castigating Seán McEntee, a government minister, accusing him of having 'a soul steeped in jazz'. However, the government, behind the scenes, applied some pressure with the result that during the next decade popular music to a large degree was not broadcast.

In 1935 Dr T J Kiernan was appointed the new director—his wife was Delia Murphy, the well-known singer of Irish ballads—and he attempted to revitalise the service. A disc recording machine was purchased in 1936, making it possible to record material and to store it for deferred or repeat broadcasts. It was to prove invaluable in the setting up of a

Sunday's Well Radio Éireann studios, Co. Cork, 1930 (Photo courtesy Cork Examiner)

radio archive, though the outbreak of the second world war brought a virtual stop to its activities, particularly in the area of traditional music and lore.

During this period, however, the radio service became a great national asset. On 3 September, the day the war commenced, Éamon de Valera went to the Henry Street studios to reassure an apprehensive nation about the government's position of neutrality. Throughout the course of the war, subsequent broadcasts by de Valera and various ministers of the government helped to sustain the nation's morale as it awaited possible violations of its neutrality; and when the war ended in 1945 de Valera's statesmanlike and restrained on-air reply to Churchill's victory speech was probably both his and radio's finest hour.

In the immediate post-war years there was an unexpected financial boost as the proposed setting up of a short-wave service led to increased staffing in the news service areas; script writers were also appointed, a full-time drama company was set up, the symphony orchestra expanded and a 22-member light orchestra was formed. Ironically, the short-wave service never got off the ground but the radio service naturally made use of its unexpected windfall and in the following dozen or so years, until the advent of television, it enjoyed a period of great popularity among listeners. In the sixties, initial fears that radio would revert to a minority audience following the introduction of the national television service proved to be groundless. High-quality radio reception became available in virtually all parts of the country when the VHF radio network was set up; and the first stereophonic broadcast took place in February 1969 from the Kippure VHF transmitter.

The seventies saw a great change in emphasis for the radio service. In addition to consolidating its traditional role in the fields of music, drama and literature, the revitalised service, reflecting the general trends of liberalisation in Western society, began to capture a very large audience with daily programmes probing issues such as social deprivation, injustice, consumerism, women's rights, the legal system, human sexuality and others. Radio had begun to shed its traditional cosy image but this was seen, particularly among

Vincent O'Brien at studio piano in Little Denmark Street, Dublin, 1926

Michael O'Hehir, sports commentator, aged eighteen

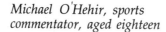

some of the older generation, as an unfortunate development and it gave rise to the eternal question of whether society leads the broadcasters or whether, on occasions, broadcasters could lead society. Further expansions in the radio service included the setting up of Raidió Na Gaeltachta in 1972, daily programming from the Cork Studios in 1973, the provision of a new 55-kilowatt transmitter in Tullamore, the launch of RTE Radio 2 in 1979 and the introduction of a series of RTE community radio broadcasts from mobile studios.

So the medium of radio, described in the thirties by one detractor as 'the child which refuses to grow up', bravely strides towards the third millennium with all frequencies blazing. Its place in the great communications industry is assured.

(cont. from page 65)
Ned Brennan (pol)
Alice Glynn (pol)
Paul Brady Band (ent)
Dr Rob Buckman (pg)
Clarence Rolman (pg)
Drops of Brandy Group (ent)
Derek Daley (pg)
Jackie Stewart (sp)

25 October 1980
Tim Pat Coogan (med)
Bernadette McAlliskey (pol)
Peter Taylor (pg)
David Attenborough (med)
Des Harris (pg)
Peggy Kennedy (pg)
Lorna Kennedy (pg)
Muriel Kerr (ent)
Nicola Kerr (ent)
Kay Toal (pg)
Sharon Crowley (pg)
Harold McCusker (pol)
Robert Bradford (pg)

2 November 1980
John Mulcahy (med)
Judge K Bradford (pg)
John Jimenez (pg)
Tommy Swarbrigg & Band (ent)
Margaret Ring (pg)
Michelle Rocca (pg)
McNamara's Band (ent)
Mr and Mrs Zorza (pg)
Harvey Smith (sp)

8 November 1980
Army Special

15 November 1980
Special on Women in the Media

22 November 1980
Margaret Heffernan (ent)
Gay and Colette Proctor (pg)
Sam McAughtry (pg)
The Roches (ent)
Clive Dunne (pg)
Geraldine Brannigan (pg)

Robert Kee (wr)
Frank McCaffrey (ent)

29 November 1980
Dr Tony Clare (pg)
Gabriel Kiely (pg)
Gobnatt O'Grádaigh (pg)
Anne Cooney (pg)
Geraldine O'Grady (pg)
Lena Zavaroni (ent)
Clannad (ent)
Fifth Avenue (ent)
Dermot James (pg)
Housewives of the Year (pg)

6 December 1980
Red Hurley (ent)
David Soul (pg)
Tommy Makem (ent)

Liam Clancy (ent)
Marie Keane (pg)
John Kavanagh (pg)
Jim Culliton (pg)
Brendan Cauldwell (pg)
Charlie Nash (ent)
Shay McGarry (pg)
McNamara's Band (ent)
Dr Jenny Seery (pg)

13 December 1980
Toy Show
Frank McNamara (ent)
Pat Quinn (pg)
Michael O'Leary (pol)
Dana (ent)
Adele King (Twink) (ent)
Fr Brian D'Arcy (pg)
Paul Venetti (pg)
Seán Smith (pg)
Lilian Maguire (pg)
Sharon Rowantree (pg)
Emma Mulligan (pg)
Enniscorthy Dancers (ent)
The Hillstreet Choir (ent)
Mary Finan (pg)

20 December 1980
Brendan Shine (ent)
Peter Gilmore (pg)
Glen Curtain & Little Girl (ent)
Shay Healy (ent)
Jimmy James (pg)
Dr Joseph Braysich (pg)
Frank McNamara & Band
Noelle Campbell-Sharp (med)
Ita Hynes (pg)
Joan Tighe (pg)
Carolyn Donnelly (pg)
Gabrielle Williams (pg)
Ruth Kelly (med)
Micheline McCormack (med)
Gladys Smith (pg)
Teddy O'Neill (pg)

27 December 1980
Compilation Show—Best of 10 Years

EXTRA:
The following guests appeared on the show in 1980 but no date is given:

Lene Lovitch (pg)
Rabbi David Rosen (pg)
The Concert Party (ent)
Pierce Maloney (pg)
Kevin O'Hara (ent)
Tom and Paschal (ent)
Terence Gray (pg)
Lee Dunne (wr)
Betty Redmond (pg)
Ted Redmond (pg)

1981

3 January 1981
Leo Maguire (pg)

Frank Purcell (pg)
Ray Croft (pg)
Beryl Fagan (pg)
Cecil Barron (pg)
Frankie Byrne (pg)
Dickie Rock (ent)
Brendan O'Brien (pg)
Mary Hegarty (ent)
Prof Louis Smith (pg)
Austin Kennan (pg)
Eoin de Buitléar (pg)
Paddy Keenan (pg)
Fergus Whelan (pg)
Frank Kelly (pg)

10 January 1981
Dusty (ent)
Don Cameron (pg)
Peter Bohannon (pg)
Rosalind Maguire (pg)
Eddie McShorthall (ent)
Ailish Kerrigan (pg)
John Proud (pg)
Philomena Clandillon (pg)
Catherine Donoghue (pg)

17 January 1981
Parapsychology
Kit Pedler
Brian Snellgrove
Russell Grant
Doris Stokes

24 January 1981
Scullion (ent)
George Colley (pol)
Tom Quinn (pg)
Denis Byrne (pg)
Don McLean (ent)
The O'Reillys (ent)
Cassandra Harris (ent)
Patrick Kinsella (med)
Tom McGurk (med)
Noel Mulcahy (pg)
John Kelly (pg)

31 January 1981
David Hayes/Eithne Lynch (ent)
Emmy Lou Harris (ent)
Warren Zievaughan (ent)
Garret Fitzgerald (pol)
Denis Waterman (pg)
Dr John Roche (pg)

7 February 1981
The Blades (ent)
Pam Collins (pg)
Flann Ó Riain (med)
June Levine (med)
Ted Bonner (pg)
Clifford T Ward (ent)
Nigel Collis (pg)
Barry Brogan (sp)
Dr Michael Woods (pol)
Dr Dolan (pol)
Ivor Browne (pg)
Jim Behan (pg)

14 February 1981
No Show

21 February 1981
Rod Hull and Emu (ent)
Horizon (ent)
Tom Waites (ent)
Fachta O'Kelly and Boomtown Rats (ent)
Deirdre Montagne (pg)

25 February 1981
Special on being handicapped in Ireland

7 March 1981
Gina, Dale Hayes and the Champions (ent)

Brendan Grace (ent)
The Yvette Tracey Dancers (ent)
Anne Ziegler and Webster Booth (ent)
Tony Sadar (ent)
Brendan Quinn (ent)
Declan Langan and Pat Flanagan (ent)
William Higgins (wr)
(John Lennon VTR night he died)

14 March 1981
Irish Youth Orchestra (ent)
Sr Joan (pg)
Gloria Swanson (pg)
Zandra Rhodes (pg)
Maria Cassidy (pg)
Jill Crowley (pg)
Mary Foley (pg)

21 March 81
John Wilson (pol)
Mary Martin (pg)
Na Casaide (ent)
Antiques

28 March 1981
Sheeba (ent)
Brush Shiels (ent)
Birr Musical Society (ent)
Sheila Kitzinger (pg)
Dr Robert Harris (pg)
T P Linehan (pg)
Jacinta Kenny (ent)

4 April 1981
No Show

11 April 1981
Veronica McSweeney (ent)
Barry Cowan (med)
Paddy Leahy (pg)
Joe Ambrose (pg)
Tom McGurk (med)
John Feeney (med)
Paddy Monaghan (pg)
Margaret Ryan (pg)
Monica Carr (med)
Peggy Kennedy (pg)
Lynn Geldof (med)
Nuala Ó Faoláin (med)
Anthony Clare (pg)
Al Bannon (ent)
Bad Manners (ent)
Box Car Willy (ent)

18 April 1981
Na Casaide (ent)
Phil Lynott—Thin Lizzy VTR
Roger Gillen (pg)
Jimmy Cricket (pg)
Larry Ryan (pg)
Michael and Mary Burke (pg)
Bagatelle (ent)
Bucking Bronco: 4 DJs on Radio 2:
   Ronan Collins
   Dave Fanning
   Dave Heffernan
   Gerry Ryan
Cormack O'Duffy (pg)
Peter Brabazon (pg)

25 April 1981
Earl Okin (pg)
Matt Meleady Dancers (ent)
Michele Molese (ent)
Maria Klausova (pg)
Morris West (wr)
Des Keogh (ent)
Rosaleen Linehan (ent)

John Bristol (pg)
Bob Clarke (pg)
Norren Green (pg)
Joe Harrington (pg)

2 May 1981
Alma Carroll (ent)
Arthur Ashe (sp)
Tony Stevens (ent)
Stocktons Wing (ent)
Naomi James (wr)
Cathal Dunne (ent)
Kieran Keating (ent)
Mary Rose Doorly (pg)
Gill Bowler (pg)

9 May 1981
Special on Young People

16 May 1981
Mary Sheridan (ent)
The Apaches (ent)
The Wolfe Tones (ent)
Tony Kenny (ent)
Kevin O'Connor (pg)
Rosaleen Linehan (ent)
Des Keogh (ent)
John Kelly (pg)
Ian Withers (pg)
Frank Doherty (pg)
The Brothers Karamasov (ent)
The Bachelors (ent)
Hal Roche (ent)
Johnny Williams (pg)

23 May 1981
The Duskey Sisters (ent)
Terry Wogan (pg)
The Conquerors (ent)
Robert White (ent)
Desmond Kyne (pg)
Firebird (ent)
Mr Pussy (ent)
Paul Wynter (ent)

30 May 81
Winters Rain (ent)
Kevin Lenihan (med)
Jacinta Kenny (ent)
Roger Gillen (pg)
Mary Hegarty (ent)
Drops of Brandy (ent)
Frank McNamara (ent)
Margaret Ring (pg)
Siobhán Henry (pg)
Angela Clarke (pg)
Tommy Doran (pg)
Delia Roche-Kelly (pg)
Geraldine Lynch (pg)
Maureen Potter (pg)
Philomena Kerr (pg)
Carmel Kelly (pg)
Margaret Irvine (pg)
Doreen Nolan (pg)
Fred Goulding (pg)
Ronnie King (pg)

3 October 81
Jim Fitzpatrick (pg)
Randy Crawford (ent)
George and Angela Best (pg)
Michael and Sarah Sellers (pg)
Moving Hearts (ent)

10 October 81
Joe Clarke (pg)
Desmond Morris (wr)
Eamon Dunphy (med)
Hazel O'Connor (ent)
Kirsty McCall (ent)
King Creole Band (ent)

17 October 1981
Frank Hession (pg)
Bagatelle (ent)

Kathleen Behan (Brian Behan, Rory) (pg)
John Prine (pg)
Pat O'Sullivan (pg)
Fr Andrew Greely (wr)
Michael Weston (pg)
Colum Johnston (pg)

24 October 1981
Dr Robert Harrison (pg)
Anne Connolly (pg)
Fr Kevin Doran (pg)
Seán Keegan (pg)
Frank Patterson (ent)
Jonathan Ryan (ent)
Kevin Linehan (pg)
Geraldine Lynch (pg)
Eric Murphy (pg)
Noel Henry (pg)
Rory O'Connor (pg)
Albert Healy (ent)
George Sheering (ent)
Carlene Carter (pg)
Vincent Smith (pg)

31 October 1981
Diana Dors (wr)
George McCaffrey (pg)
Countess de Frenary (pg)
Seán McCabe (pg)
Janet and Stewart Farrar (pg)
The Lookalikes (ent)
The Brothers Karamazov (ent)

7 November 1981
Brendan O'Dowda (ent)
Jane Ewart Biggs (pg)
Gordon Winter (wr)
Des Hickey (pg)
Mike and Mary Cullinane (pg)
Lady Elena Duran (pg)
Catherine McCoy (pg)
The Tweets (ent)

14 November 1981
Ralph McTell (ent)
Jim McCann (ent)
Ile Nastase (sp)
Rod Taylor/Karen Black (pg)
Christine Coleman (pg)
Alan Fanagan (pg)
Felix O'Regan (pg)
Brendan Quinn (pg)
Kenneth Williams (pg)
James Burke (pg)

21 November 1981
Glasnevin Octet (ent)
William Shannon (pg)
Max Boyce (ent)
Mary O'Hara (pg)
David Lyndley (ent)
Dr Hugh Jolly (pg)

28 November 1981
De Dannan (ent)
Paddy Crosbie (pg)
Jimmy Mac (pg)
Elkie Brooks (ent)
Esther Rantzen (med)
Des Wilson (pg)
Jim Martin (pg)
Joe Duffy (pg)
Niall Kavanagh (pg)

5 December 1981
Donacha Ó Dúlaing (med)
Danny Doyle (ent)
Frank Delaney (wr)
Pat McCool (pg)
Andy Somers (pg)
Jim Doherty (ent)
Louis Stewart (ent)
Des and Ita Fitzsimons (pg)

Fergus and Margaret Kennedy (pg)
Tom and Margaret Denihy (pg)
Noel and Ann Gibney (pg)

12 December 1981
Toy Show

19 December 1981
Eivis O'Toole (pg)
Bill McMahon (pg)
Mr and Mrs Frank Keely (pg)
Mr and Mrs George Colley (pg)
Mr and Mrs Mick O'Hara (pg)
Tadgh Ó Croidáin (pg)

1982

2 January 1982
Special on 20 Years of TV

9 January 1982
Kay Toal (pg)
Sharon Bacon (pg)
Angela Lemass (pg)
Marie Sodan (pg)
Annette Cleary (pg)
Barbara Connolly (pg)
Fr Brian D'Arcy (pg)
Jimmy Vaughan (ent)

16 January 1982
Col John Barry (pg)
Paul Doyle (pg)
Anthony Burgess (wr)

22 January 1982
Cilla Black (ent)
Stephen Roche/Seán Kelly (sp)
Mrs Collins-O'Mahony (pg)
Breda Driscoll (pg)
Margaret Spence (pg)
Catherine Walsh (pg)
Carol Moffat (pg)

30 January 1982
Arklow Silver Band (ent)
Susan Hampshire (pg)
Ken Hamilton (pg)
Freddie White (ent)
Robert Ballagh (pg)
Dana (ent)
Mena Bean Uí Chribín (pg)
French Foreign Legion (pg)
Hugh Leonard (wr)

6 February 1982
Garda Choir (ent)
Geoff Hughes (pg)
Ann Kirkebride ((pg)
Eddie Yates/Deirdre Badon (pg)
Diarmuid O'Neill (pg)
John Doyle (pg)
Jim Motherway (pg)
Tom Roche (pg)
Benny Cauldwell (ent)

Dr David Doyle (pg)
Dr Jim Thompson (pg)

13 February 1982
Valentine's Day Special

20 February 1982
No Show

27 February 1982
Elaine Paige (ent)
Russell Harty (pg)
Lorraine Chase (pg)
E P Thompson (pg)

6 March 1982
Barry Devlin (pg)
Virginia Kerr/Jenny Reddin (ent)

Kim Newport (pg)
Paul Costelloe (pg)

13 March 1982
The Furey Brothers and Davy Arthur (ent)
Bob Champion (pg)
Charles Lynch (ent)
Al Banim (ent)
Boomtown Rats (ent)
Bob Geldof (ent)
Paula Yates (pg)

20 March 1982
Rathmines & Rathgar Musical Society (ent)
Maeve Binchey (wr)
Judy Mazel (wr)
Dr John Keaveney (pg)
David Holland (pg)

27 March 1982
Thurles Musical Society (ent)
Jackie Kyle (sp)
Joan Merrigan (ent)
Alma Carroll (ent)
Terry Griffiths (pg)
Brass Quartet (ent)
Fr Michael Keane (pg)
Fr Des Wilson (pg)
Fr Tom Stack (pg)
Fr Michael Cleary (pg)

3 April 1982
Tokyo Olympics Band (ent)
Brendan Devlin (pg)
Anne Weldon (pg)
Nick O'Sullivan (pg)
Maureen Bassett (pg)
DGOS (ent)
Brian McMahon (pg)
Veronica Dunne Trio
Alan Wicker (wr)

10 April 1982
Kenny Ball Band (ent)
Rita McGarry (pg)
Patrick Glynn (pg)
Stella Harte (pg)
Mary Bolger (pg)
Michael Forte (pg)

Séamus Oates (pg)
Joe Dolan (ent)
Memories (ent)
Louis Kenny (pg)
Mary Doyle (pg)
Angela Melvin (pg)
Joan Daly (pg)
Peg McGurk (pg)
Joy Stone (pg)
Marjorie Kavanagh (pg)

17 April 1982
Special from Co. Cork

24 April 1982
No Show

1 May 1982
Stocktons Wing (ent)
Graham Alexander (pg)
Sligo Choir (ent)
Mike McCartney (pg)
Dickie Rock (ent)
Wynn Roberts (pg)
April Ashley (wr)

8 May 1982
PLJ Band (ent)
Máire Geoghegan Quinn (pol)
James Brewster (pg)
Justin Keating (pol)
Eoghan Harris (med)
Biddy White-Lennon (pg)
Shade Band (ent)
Douglas Gunn Ensemble (ent)
Paul Dolye/James O'Halloran/Colin Hamilton (pg)
Walter and Beverley Figgis (pg)
Patrick Dawson (ent)
Catherine Brennan (ent)

15 May 1982
Suzuki Group (ent)
Karen Armstrong (wr)
Colette Doherty (pg)
Auto Da Fé (ent)
Conor Brady (med)
Derek Nally (pg)
Gareth Sheehan (pg)
Gerry Keogh (pg)

22 May 1982
Ezeke (ent)
Deirdre Van Winkle (wr)
John Redehan (pg)
Michael Daly (pg)
Hazel Plunkett (pg)
Kay McMonagle (pg)
Jane Collins (pg)
Mary Roche (pg)
Britt Ekland (pg)
Jim McCann (ent)
Una Keogh (pg)
Eamonn O'Connor (pg)

2 October 1982
Barrie Cooke (pg)
Lynn Geldof/Terry Terry (pg)
Barry Sinclair (pg)
Paul Goldin (ent)
Dr John Kelly (pg)
Jack Gibson (pg)
Brian Dunning (ent)
Maeve Binchey (wr)
Tim Severn (pg)

9 October 1982
Patsy Dunne (pg)
Patrick D Conroy (pg)
Hot Gossip (ent)
Peter Feeney (med)
Sheila de Valera (pol)

Liam Óg Ó Floinn (ent)
Peter O'Sullivan (pg)
Aileen Pringle (pg)
Fr Andrew Greely (wr)
Joyce Weirman (pg)

16 October 1982
Jude Murphy (pg)
Ken McBride (ent)
Gene Fitzpatrick (pol)
Isla St Clair (pg)
Donnie Cassidy (pg)
Foster & Allen (ent)
T R Dallas (ent)

23 October 1982
Ray Lynam (ent)
Terry Prone (med)
Caroline Woods (pg)
Brian Gillavan (pg)
Patrick Gallagher (med)
Michael Parkinson (med)
Jonathan Gregg (pg)
Thomas Verney (pg)

30 October 1982
Special on Fashion

6 November 1982
Barbara Cluskey (pg)
Ulick O'Connor (pg)
Roly Daniels/Anne Williamson (ent)
Anna Raeburn (pg)
Pierre Ben Susan (pg)
Cynthia Payne (wr)
Loreto Musical Society (ent)
John Colgan (pg)
Sgt Michael Murray (pg)
Garda David Martin (pg)
Séamus Breathnach (pg)

13 November 1982
Declan Collinge (pg)
Chris de Burgh (ent)
Jessie and the James Boys (ent)
Rodericka Knowles (wr)
Leona Carney (pg)
Betina Lourcan (wr)
Monk Gibbon (wr)
Kevin Myers (med)
Jimmy O'Brien (pg)

20 November 1982
R D Laing (wr)
Emmy-Lou Harris (ent)
Viv Nicholson (wr)
George McGovern (pg)

27 November 1982
Chris de Burgh (ent)
Jimmy Carey (pg)
John O'Conor (ent)
Dublin Grand Opera Society (ent)
Lord Henry Mountcharles (pg)
Clannad (ent)
Liam Nolan (med)
Barry McGuigan (sp)
Dr Seán Murphy (ent)
Angela Walder (pg)
Dr Michael Coualty (pg)

4 December 1982
Brian and Veronica Cleeve (wr)
Denis Allen (ent)
Freddie White (ent)
Ann Dinnigan (pg)
Eithne O'Sullivan (pg)
Fran Dempsey/Frank McNamara (pg)
Dr Gerard Seery (pg)

(cont. on page 137)

GAY BYRNE

talks with Deirdre Purcell

But Mr Byrne is a modest man, who lives in a modest house and drives himself to work each morning and home each evening in his modest family saloon. He could have a driver, like his famous friend and colleague across the water, Terry, but the self-chauffeuring is by choice. 'It's the only time of the day I can get to myself...'

The man of whom more has been written and said in Ireland than taoiseach, president or pope, is at once impossible to define and all too easy. There he is, in your ear every morning, in your eye on Friday nights. Everyone knows Gay...

Everyone? Hardly anyone...

KISSING HIS BIN

Because Mr Byrne, the most public of Irish public figures, carries an unbreachable wall of privacy inside the house of his public persona. He is a private person who has chosen to live in the fishbowl of public life but who guards his private and home lives jealously. (Sometimes it is not all that easy. Word has spread that Gay lives in Howth and each Saturday and Sunday sees the cars cruising by his gateposts, while people ogle out the windows. He was once told by a woman he met while walking on his beloved hill of Howth, that the woman's friend just could not resist leaping out of her car to kiss his bin!)

Ireland knows, of course, that Gay is married to Kathleen Watkins, and is beginning also to recognise the name Crona Byrne. Crona is Gay's elder daughter, now making a life of her own in public relations. The youngest member of the family, *chez* Byrne, is Suzy, just coming up to Leaving Cert and no slouch when it comes to organising all the rest of them. It was Suzy who initiated and coordinated a recent family holiday to Disney World, filling every second with activity, so that they all came home exhausted.

But that is really all that most people know. And anyone who has ever spent a wet day in the RTE complex knows that when he or she goes home, the very first question from the friends and relatives will be: 'Did you see Gay Byrne? What's he *really* like?'

To Gay it is genuinely, perhaps ingenuously, a mystery why people will keep wittering on about him. 'I'm constantly amazed and astonished at the Irish obsession with Gaybo and I am constantly being made to appear more complex than I am. There is a plethora of analysts and super-analysts who write and speak reams about my supposed ''influence'' and all the rest of it... I know that there is no such thing as a truly simple person, but in my view, I am, actually, quite a simple man. I have built a little wall around the small pieces of myself that I want to keep to myself. It's a great challenge to people, that wall, and

I really believe that it is the reason that they think I have this mysterious other persona behind it. I don't. I love my walks in Howth and my car and my bicycle and my cottage in Donegal and my time off in the summer and a few drinks with a few old pals—and that's the sum total to the private Gaybo. I know that this analysis happens all over the world to people like me, but that does not stop me being amazed at it.'

Even abroad there is no escape. There is now hardly anywhere on earth that has not been colonised by Irish people. Once, when the team from the *Late Late Show* was in New York to beam the programme to Ireland via satellite, Gay went to Mass in St Patrick's Cathedral on Fifth Avenue. After Mass, when he came out onto the steps, there they were, all the smiling faces, all lined up to shake his hand and to get autographs. And they were not all Irish people either. He discovered that day that there are tapes of the *Late Late Show* in circulation all over the Bronx, Queens and Manhattan, twenty-four hours after transmission at home. They are played largely in pubs.

On the other hand, Gay admits to enjoying the positive side of being recognised: 'people are generally very very pleasant.' And whenever he feels bad-tempered about it, for instance when he is accosted by someone looking for something from him just as he is hurrying in to do a programme, he remembers, or tries to, that it is the public on whom he depends. 'I try to remind myself that it is *because* of the public profile that I can lead such a very pleasant life. When I think of all the junior and senior managers, who work all the hours God sends, morning, noon and night, and who certainly have not got as pleasant a lifestyle as I have, it restores my patience!'

Sharpish!

(cont. from page 135)

11 December 1982
Toy Show

18 December 1982
Christie O'Connor (sp)
Johnny Logan (ent)
Frank McNamara (ent)
Noel Kelehan (ent)
Anne O'Briain (pg)
Doris Keogh (pg)
Tony Kenny (ent)
Dr John Fleetwood (pg)
Vonnie Goulding group (pg)
Choir Dublin Boy Singers
  (ent)

25 December 1982
No Show

1983

1 January 1983
No Show

8 January 1983
Autobob (ent)
Ronnie Mortell (pg)
Rita Harpur (ent)
Noel Dorr (pg)
Aileen Pringle (ent)
Roberta Browne (pg)

15 January 1983
Dublin City Ramblers (ent)
Aidan McKenna (pg)
Pierce Mee (pg)
Red Hurley (ent)
Milo O'Shea (pg)
John Bowman (med)
Michael Farrell (pg)
Kevin Boland (pg)
Dr Conor Cruise O'Brien
  (pg)

22 January 1983
Bagatelle (ent)
Ferdia McAnna (pg)
Terry Prone (med)
Gunther Shulty (pg)
Ulysses Quartet (ent)
Hoffman's American Circus
  (ent)
Debbie Alden (pg)
Marise Roblés (pg)
Bono & U2 VTR (ent)
Tom McGurk (med)
Alan Dukes (pol)

29 January 1983
Terry Prone/Ferdia McAnna
  (med)
Nigel Rolf (pg)
Ralf Parkes (pg)
Larry Cunningham (ent)
Dr Edward de Bono (wr)
Auto Da Fé (ent)
Donnacha McDonagh (pg)
Siobhán Corrigan (pg)
John Fiddler (pg)
Gerard Quinn (pg)
Paul Clery (pg)
Robert Swaides (pg)

5 February 1983
Betty Seery (pg)
Mary Fitzgerald (pg)
Ferdia McAnna/Terry Prone
  (med)
Myrtle Allen (wr)
Jimmy Crowley (ent)
Michael Corbett & the
  Detectives (ent)
Tess Daly/Esther Hyland (pg)
Frank O'Connor (pg)
Louis Hegney (pg)
Tony Grant (pg)

12 February 1983
Terry Prone (med)
Gina, Dale Hayes & The
  Champions (ent)
Ferdia McAnna (med)
Brendan Dowling (pg)
Little John Nee (pg)
Colette McGahon (pg)
Brendan O'Neill (pg)
Pat Meade (pg)
Dr John Nolan, MD (pg)

19 February 1983
Marie Cole Dancers (ent)
Don Conroy (pg)
Malcolm Proud (pg)
Kevin O'Doherty (pg)
Eric Gennings (pg)
John Rocca (pg)
Ib Jorgenson (pg)
Michaeline Stackepoole (pg)

Wolfangel (pg)
Paul Costello (pg)
Henry White (pg)
Michael Mortell (pg)
Richard Lewis (pg)
Liam Campbell (pg)
Fr Michael Paul Gallagher
  (wr)
Patrick Moriarty (pg)

26 February 1983
Des Keogh/Phillip Martin
  (ent)
Brendan Grace (ent)
Van Morrisson (ent)
Vincent O'Neill (ent)
Robert White (ent)
Timothy Barrett (ent)
Polly Devlin (pg)
Brian Murray (pg)

5 March 1983
Special on Dublin

12 March 1983
Charles Harris (pg)
Prison Officers Choir (ent)
Kenneth Williams (ent)
The Bards (ent)
Fr George Gabelka (pg)

19 March 1983
Dick O'Riordan (ent)
Ulick O'Connor (med)
Nuala Ó Faoláin (med)
Sheeba (ent)
Fr Brendan Forde (pg)
Ned Sherwin (pg)
Tommy Steele (ent)

26 March 1983
Susan McCann (ent)
Ulick O'Connor (med)
Nuala Ó Faoláin (med)
Dubliners (ent)
Wayne Dickenson (pg)
Young Dublin Singers (ent)

Jean St Clair (pg)
Louden Wainright (ent)

2 April 1983
Colman Pearce (ent)
Michael Deniffe (pg)
Michael O'Kane (pg)
Billy Barry School (ent)
Mary Orr (pg)
Derek Gleeson (pg)
Hugh de Garis (pg)

9 April 1983
Ulick O'Connor (med)
Nuala Ó Faoláin (med)
Phil Lynott (ent)
Frank McDougall (pg)
Monica Barnes (pol)
Maura O'Connell (ent)
De Danann (ent)
Mark McPherson (pg)

Robert Ballagh (pg)
Jim Cumberton (pg)

16 April 1983
Elaine Kelly (pg)
Joan Tighe (pg)
Denise Sweeney (pg)
Frank Kelly (ent)
Christopher Cross (ent)
Paul Malone (pg)
Bernard Cornwell (pg)
Kitty O'Shea (pg)
Niall Woods (pg)
Trudy Abel Peterson (pg)

23 April 1983
No Show

30 April 1983
Lilian Young (wr)
Fr Hugh Garriston (pg)
John Gibson (pg)
The Furey Brothers and Davy
  Arthur (ent)
Take 4 (ent)
Dr Miriam Hederman (pg)

7 May 1983
Des Keogh (ent)
Rosaleen Linehan (ent)
Brendan Dowling (pg)
Fiona Ross (pg)
Ciaran Hennessey (pg)
Lilian O'Sullivan-Greene (pg)
David Nolan (pg)
Little John Nee (pg)
Con O'Leary (pg)

14 May 1983
Mary Harrison (pg)
Rocky de Valera and Rhythm
  Kings (ent)
Wolfe Tones (ent)
Billy McElwaine (pg)
Mary Smith (pg)
Harry McCann (pg)
Roy McGarry (pg)

21 May 1983
Dublin City Ballet (ent)
The Morrisseys (ent)
Philomena Begley (ent)
Barry McGuigan (sp)
Sammy Meck (pg)
B P Fallon (med)
Tony Stevens (ent)
David Jacobs (pg)

28 May 1983
Noel Kelehan Quintet Jazz
  (ent)
Helen Morrissey (ent)
Raheny Band (ent)
David Frost (pg)
Philip Agee (pg)

3 September 1983
(?)

10 September 1983
Barney Curley (pg)
Mary Downes (pg)
Dermot Walsh (pg)
Robert Freeman (wr)
King Singers (ent)
Basil Brushe (ent)
Red Lemonade (ent)

17 September 1983
Mike Wynters (pg)
Angelo Dundee (pg)
Scullion (ent)
Christy Moore (ent)
Sebastian Coe (sp)
Claire Rayner (pg)
Ann Breen (pg)

24 September 1983
Chris Rea (ent)
Fr Tom Stack (pg)
Freddie White (ent)
Red Hurley (ent)
Karen Armstrong (wr)
Brian McKeown (pg)
Peter Scarle (pg)

1 October 1983
Special on Fashion

8 October 1983
Terry Prone (med)
David Nolan (med)
Liz Shannon (wr)
Niall Murray (pg)
Colm C T Wilkinson (ent)
John Cassidy (pg)
Joan Ruddock (pg)
Bishop Eamon Casey (pg)

15 October 1983
Joe Dolan (ent)
Carmel Quinn (pg)
Gina, Dale Hayes & the
  Champions (ent)
Lindsay de Paul (pg)
Paddy Reilly (ent)
Robin Skinner (pg)
John Cleese (pg)

22 October 1983
German choir (ent)
Fr Brian D'Arcy (pg)
Mary Black (ent)
Vincent Manning (pg)
Des Peelo (pg)
Frank Masterson (pg)
Aeolian Quintet (ent)
Robert Cranny (wr)
The Fureys Brothers VTR
  (ent)
Dr Fielding (pg)

29 October 1983
Special from New York

5 November 1983
Maura O'Connell (ent)
Twink (ent)
Vincent Keaveney (pg)
Karen Hess (pg)
Patrick Moore (wr)
Courtney Kenny (pg)
Ann Hatton (pg)
Gordona Leonard (wr)

12 November 1983
Rathmines & Rathgar
  Musical Society (ent)
Desmond Morris (wr)
Johnny Durham (ent)
Monsignor James Horan (pg)
Vincent Browne (med)
John Bruton (pol)
Michael O'Kennedy (pol)
Charlie McGreevey (pol)
Pronsias de Rossa (pol)
Tom Enright (pol)
Frank Prendergast (pol)

19 November 1983
Los Paraguayos (ent)
Tim Booth (pg)
Barry Devlin (pg)
John Feeley (ent)
Suzanne Murphy (ent)
Frank O'Brien (ent)
Paula Yates (pg)
Toddy Lovergan-Kennedy
  (pg)
Patrick Cosgrave (pg)

26 November 1983
Hal Roach Special

3 December 1983
Century Steel Band (ent)
Paddy O'Toole (pol)
Ambrose McInerney (pg)
Jim Duggan (pg)
Siobhan Cuffe (pg)
Russell Harty (pg)
Brendan Shine (ent)
Phil Coulter (ent)
Baron Brian de Breffny (pg)
Pat Corcoran (pg)
Jim Kelly (pg)

10 December 1983
Toy Show

17 December 1983
The Conquerors (ent)
Joe Ambrose (pg)
Eamonn Carr (pg)
Changling Album (pg)
Brigid O'Leary (pg)
Seán O'Dowd (ent)
Anne Fitzgerald (wr)
Brendan Kennelly (wr)

1984

14 January 1984
Jacinta White (ent)
Cathal Dunne (ent)
Taste of Galway (ent)
Raymond & Margaret
  McBride (ent)
Dr David Bellamy (pg)
Calendar of Music—Seán Ó
  Riada
Walter Pfeiffer (pg)
Síoda (ent)
J J Wall (ent)
Ann Bushnell (ent)
Mick Lally (ent)
Mary McEvoy (ent)

21 January 1984
Honor Heffernan (ent)
Louis Stewart (ent)
Seán McBride (pg)

(cont. on page 145)

IN THE LIBRARY

Ann O'Donnell visited the television library

The primary purpose of RTE's TV library is to store videotape and film productions and to select material for retention for future programming or broadcasting. John McMahon is the chief librarian and he, with twenty others, works in the TV library. There is also a second library or archive in the radio division of the station. A vast quantity of material is stored in the TV library: videotape, video cassettes, slides, photos, film, books, periodicals, journals, magazines, newspapers, research files, data bases, as well as a complete index to the *Irish Times*. Over the last few years the work of running the library has become a more efficient task as computerisation and the change-over from film to video as a means of recording is far less labour intensive.

RTE set up its central library in 1968—up to that time the records are relatively sketchy. In 1987 the central library was divided into two sections, one for TV and one for radio. In the early years of RTE about a dozen items of news per year were kept on record. In 1988 RTE stored approximately three and a half thousand news items. All film produced by RTE is deposited with the library, as are all videotaped programmes. The library staff then select what is to be retained in stock.

All home-produced drama, all documentaries made by RTE, the bulk of current affairs material and some aspects of all news bulletins are retained. John illustrates the way in which the library is used by giving an example of a news bulletin which includes a shot of a certain factory. The chances are that that shot will have come from the library, having been stored from a previous programme and logged in the library computer. There is only one programme which is automatically recorded and stored. 'There was a time,' says John, 'when the *Late Late Show* was only a programme— now it's a national institution.' Unfortunately the library does not have a vast quantity of material from old *Late Late Shows* in the pre-library days—nobody knew then that it would be such a success.

VALUABLE HISTORICAL RECORD

John has a personal interest in the historical aspects of the material he stores. He is fascinated by the old copies of *Hall's Pictorial Weekly*, which he believes contain a valuable historical record of the main streets of many Irish towns. He outlines the importance of keeping all interview programmes such as *Hanly's People*, as such copies are 'very handy when a person dies'. This sounds a bit morbid, but from a broadcasting point of view you can see how valuable such material would be in preparing an obituary programme or a news item. In the library they store sample copies of every TV series, so that no matter what current programme may be to the taste of future TV viewers, the library will have some records.

The library is used by researchers, producers and production assistants to seek out material. During the past year the main users were the news programmes, followed by *Today Tonight*, *Cúrsaí*, *Face of the Earth*, documentaries and quiz programmes. For obvious reasons those involved in compiling news broadcasts are heavily dependent on library material. On every bulletin, a considerable number of shots and pieces of film would be from library stock. *Today Tonight* has a special arrangement with the library, in that it has a resource person who is specifically designated to liaise with the library on a full-time basis. At the moment this arrangement is experimental, but it is, according to John McMahon, 'extremely successful'.

While its primary function is to serve RTE, the library is also used by academics, researchers and journalists. In the absence of a national film archive, the RTE library is a comprehensive record of national events. It has very valuable collections of newsreel, *Pathé* news photo collections and other archival material. John mentions two particularly interesting collections of stills: one is a collection by Joe Cashman, a photographer who lived in the early part of the century; the other is a collection of photos of Dublin by Neville Johnston.

The library also has a commercial aspect to its work. There are twelve videos available at the moment, among them the *Dubliners' Late Late Show* and the *Best of '88 Football*, all of which are produced in the RTE library. John and his staff are moving increasingly into the area of merchandising programmes. Commercial companies and advertising agencies frequently buy sections of programmes or footage from the library; political parties purchase footage of *ard fheiseanna*, TV debates and other relevant material which they have been unable to video themselves; and the public are also prepared to pay for material which they badly want.

John expressed some concern about how long the material on video and film will last. 'We have no guarantees of the long-term stability of what we are storing. Video (magnetic tape) has lasted reasonably well so far but we don't know how long more it will last, as it has only been in existence since the early seventies.' He pointed out that black and white film has stored well, but that colour film fades over the years. Storage conditions, especially in relation to temperature and humidity, are very important to ensure long-term quality. John believes that eventually digital storage will be possible, which will transform everything, but 'it's a long while away'.

Meanwhile, look out for the library pictures on your screens—you will see them credited on almost every news bulletin.

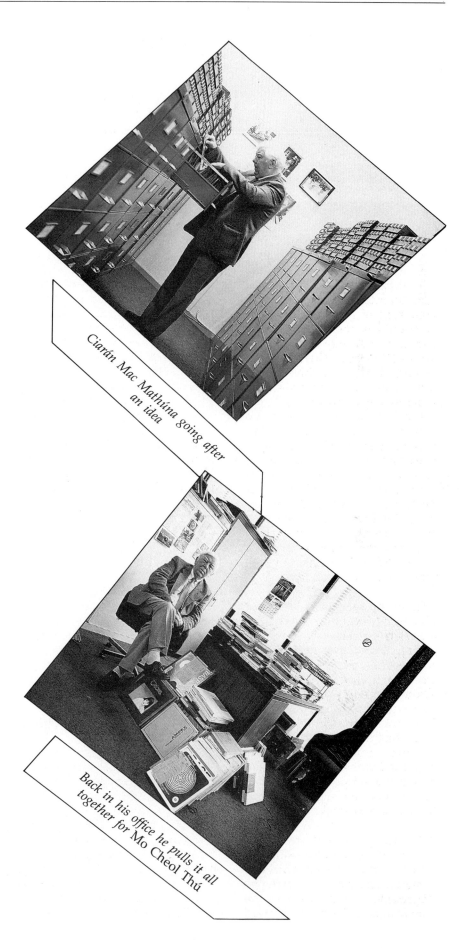

Ciarán Mac Mathúna going after an idea

Back in his office he pulls it all together for Mo Cheol Thú

TODAY TONIGHT

A 1982 photograph of Today Tonight *reporter Carolyn Fisher Sorry, Carolyn, you were on your holidays when we went looking for your 1989 look!*

Ann O'Donnell talked to Carolyn Fisher about highlighting the horror of some people's lives

(Opposite) The photographer Amelia Steen found the Today Tonight *team amazingly awake when she took this picture during the marathon-like general election in June — (left to right, front ground) Sheila Ahearn, John Masterson, Deirdre Younge, Paddy Brady, Olivia O'Leary, Fintan Cronin, Deirdre Holacher, Rhona O'Byrne, Vincent Scally Tony McDonnell;(left to right, up stairs) Eugene Murray, Liz White, Feargus Ó Raghallaigh, John Blackman*

Carolyn Fisher is a reporter on *Today Tonight*. She is probably best known for her sensitive and probing examination of difficult social issues, such as drug abuse, sexual abuse and male prostitution. Making programmes about human distress or social injustice can be emotionally draining: 'As an individual I put a lot of myself into those programmes and I do find the nature of the stories to be very upsetting.'

Some programmes were particularly harrowing to make. 'The one on child sexual abuse really stands out in my mind,' says Carolyn, 'because I never realised how widespread it is or how horrific are the stories of people's lives.' Carolyn met many victims in Dublin hotels, where they told her of their abused childhoods and poured out their hearts—often they would finish by saying that they could never tell their

story on TV. Carolyn finds herself responding to these people on three levels. 'Firstly, I have an individual human response of sympathy, empathy and listening. Secondly, I am operating as a researcher, mentally picking out bits of their story which might be used on *Today Tonight*. Thirdly, I am like a watchdog over my own shoulder, evaluating where I must draw the line between sensationalism and making a good programme.'

She is quite clear that her job is to act as a professional broadcaster and make the best possible programme on the issue. *Today Tonight* can highlight the problems for others, but she expects the social services or other agencies to carry on where *Today Tonight* leaves off. However, she is often amazed and concerned at the lack of services available, especially to families bereaved by suicide or to those addicted to tranquillisers.

Carolyn feels a deep concern for homeless young people. In London she found that many of these young people were very willing to talk, provided they were paid to do so. She thought about this situation and, when preparing for a *Today Tonight* programme in London, decided that she would not pay them, as she wanted honesty, not just the story they thought she might like to buy. It was Christmastime when she visited London and there were TV crews and newspaper journalists from France, Germany, Ireland and Britain making programmes and writing stories about these homeless kids. All the companies were paying the youngsters for their stories. She returned after Christmas when the hype had died down. She feels that she could have paid the kids but that it would have been exploitation. 'I had to reach into their lives and really communicate with them to encourage them to talk about their stories. I shared cigarettes with them.'

The public perception of TV interviewers is that many of them have no scruples. Carolyn accepts that there are interviewers who believe that the end justifies the means and who do manipulate interviewees. She is conscious of sensationalist or voyeuristic possibilities in making such programmes: 'If I had two people with relatively similar stories to tell, but one had a weak or fragile personality, I would pick the stronger of the two to be interviewed.' She believes that it could be wrong to expose certain people to the TV camera. People often get cold feet at the last minute and will not do an interview. It would be very easy for her to put pressure on them or to make promises that she couldn't keep in order to convince them to co-operate. 'I wouldn't do that,' she says, 'as if I did I wouldn't be able to sleep in peace.'

Her job has changed her perception in many ways. She finds that she no longer sees situations in vivid black and white: 'Some of the sex abusers I spoke to had been horrifically sexually abused themselves as children, so I could not see them as totally bad.' She frequently sees two sides to stories —she might be very concerned about a homeless kid but knows that the kid has recently mugged an old woman. 'I never knew about the extent of teenage male prostitution until we were making the programme on that subject,' she says.

MASSIVE SOCIAL INJUSTICE

To Carolyn, making these programmes is a continual learning process. She considers herself and all the *Today Tonight* team lucky and privileged to be able, for instance, to be in a travellers' caravan at 3.00 pm and at a reception in the Department of Foreign Affairs at 5.00 pm. She feels that very few people have such diverse opportunities in human experiences. She thinks that the contrast between the travellers' caravan and the lavish reception does show up the massive social injustice that exists but at the same time she believes that it's not just society that's unequal: 'It's me also. I often go to a concert or a gig and I spend the evening listening to good music and discussing it with my friends, and a few hours before I left behind a homeless kid sleeping in a doorway.' She may be sitting in a fast-food joint with a young male prostitute, knowing that her mates are eating a good meal in a restaurant nearby: 'Not everyone who scoffs smoked salmon is bad,' she says. What does disturb Carolyn are the smoked salmon scoffers who don't believe these problems exist and who don't know what she's talking about.

Carolyn wouldn't consider herself to be very ambitious but she is delighted to be a reporter who is in a position to highlight issues which she would have been concerned about as an individual. 'We dip into people's lives to a frightening degree,' she says, 'and I cannot forget these people.' She has kept in touch with several of the people she interviewed and often thinks of others. There was one homeless boy called Josh whom she really got to know because she hung around with him so much while making a programme. She used to meet him regularly for up to a year and a half afterwards and then he suddenly disappeared. There's another kid she often thinks about who sleeps under the embankment in London.

Opposite:
RTE Guide team: *(left to right, seated front) Mary Finn, John Walsh, Lucille Redmond; (left to right, standing rear) Michael Fitzpatrick, Ursula Curry, Ultan Macken, Patrick Quilligan, Frank Spears, Tom Cooney, Eve Holmes, Alan Corsini.*

John Walsh, its editor is modest about

THE RTE GUIDE

Peter Somerville-Large, in the course of a trek across Ireland which he wrote about in *From Bantry Bay to Leitrim*, hit a bad patch. It was, if I remember right, on a wet January Sunday afternoon in Limerick. He sheltered in a doorway on a deserted street and stared into a shop window. It contained some dead flies and—yellowed and ancient—a copy of the *RTE Guide*.

I must admit I winced at first sight of what may well be the only reference in literature to our little magazine. Later I came to look on the bright side. The traveller, I reasoned, was recording one of the archetypal images of our land in the last quarter-century or so.

There it lay, dog-eared but enduring, along with the 'Guinness is Good for You' signs and the voice of Micheál Ó Hehir and the face of Charles Mitchel and the big black bike outside the pub. Part of what we are.

That copy in the shop window would have been one of the old stagers. Remember them? Big, tabloid-size, black-and-white covers, maybe even saying RTV instead of RTE. We marvel at them now, and chuckle a bit, when we have occasion to thumb through the old files. All those faces which only turn out to be well-known when you allow for their being ridiculously young, long-haired, got up in fashions the

younger crowd among us don't even remember. Sometimes we plan to publish a few of them for badness.

Because, of course, we in the *Guide* suffer greatly at the hands of the others around the station. Get quite a nose on, they do, if we don't say the nicest things about themselves and their programmes. Trouble is, we have to live with the people we write about. Not to mention the public. When they're not giving out about our being staid they're giving out about smut in a family magazine. Not to mention the critics who blame us for programmes that get changed after we've gone to press. Not to mention the com-

(cont. on page 50)

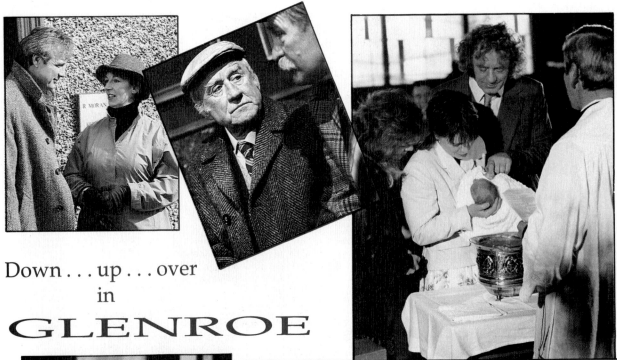

Down . . . up . . . over
in
GLENROE

(cont. from page 137)
Eroica String Trio (ent)
Richie Ryan (pg)
Michael Farrell (pg)
Mary McAleese (pg)
Donal Donnelly (pg)

28 January 1984
Fr Gabriel Daly (pg)
Eamonn McCann (med)
Prof Des Corrigan (pg)
McStay family (pg)
Pulling Faces (ent)
Peter Mack (ent)
Patricia Barden (ent)
Alison Young (pg)
Seán Doherty (pg)

4 February 1984
Colin Turner (wr)
Francoise Letellier (pg)
Ronnie Turner (pg)
Dr John Fleetwood (pg)
Dr Liam Lacey (pg)
Caroline Buchanan (pg)
Sandra Sedgebeer (pg)
The Dixies/Buddy Holly (ent)
St Louis Musical (ent)
Jimmy Witherspoon (ent)
College of Music (ent)
Veronica Dunne (pg)

11 February 1984
Andrea Dworkin (wr)
Rosalind Miles (wr)
John J May (pg)
Martin Merriman (pg)
Leif Reck (ent)
'Air Stream' (ent)

18 February 1984
Giant Haystack (ent)
Brenda Crowe (pg)
Maurice Seddon (pg)
Patsy Lalor (pol)
Seán Flanagan (pol)
Seán Fitzpatrick (pol)
Stephen Rabbette (pg)
Seán Calleary (ent)
John Woods (ent)
Martin Finn (pg)
Poitín (ent)
Enda Murray (pg)

25 February 1984
Nolan Sisters (ent)
Anna Raeburn (med)
Peggy Thomas (pg)
Feargal Quinn (pg)
Fintan O'Toole (med)
Gerry Scully (pg)
Seán Barrett (pg)
Niall Andrews (pol)
Myra Barry (pg)
Bertie Aherne (pol)
Paul Darragh (pg)
Frank Fahy (pol)
Eileen Lemass (pol)
Nora Owen (pol)
George Birmingham (pol)
Ivan Yates (pol)
Twink (ent)
Yvonne Dolan (pg)

3 March 1984
Special on Divorce

10 March 1984
Sweets Eddison Quartet (ent)
Paul Eddington (pg)
T R Dallas (ent)
Denis O'Neill (ent)
Billy Magra (ent)
Michael Redmond (ent)
Gerry Lavelle (ent)
Ian McPhearson (ent)

Bards (ent)
Fr Francis (pg)

17 March 1984
Special from Galway

24 March 1984
Dublin Concert Band (ent)
Geraldine Doyle (ent)
Richard Clayderman (ent)
Aileen Pringle (ent)
Vidal Sassoon (pg)
Sheeba (ent)
Sheila Graham (ent)
Charlie Pride (ent)

31 March 1984
No Show

7 April 1984
Colin McStay film
'3-Degrees' (ent)
Stan Tracey Quartet (ent)
Chieftains (ent)
Tony Stevens (ent)
Brian Hayes (pg)
Dr Julian Leff (pg)
Hector Laing (pg)

14 April 1984
Dale Hayes (ent)
The Crankies (ent)
Alan Price (ent)
Stuntmen, Peter and Pat
Brendan Grace (ent)
The Brass Ensemble (ent)
Frank and Deborah Spungen (wr)

21 April 1984
Mr Gay and the City Gents (ent)
Frank Carson (ent)
Fr Dara Molloy (pg)
Eamonn O'Brien (pg)
Declan Kibird (med)
Joan Kelley (pg)
Aisling and Anne Heneghan (ent)
Bunratty Singers (ent)
Rosaleen Linehan (ent)
Frank McNamara (ent)

28 April 1984
Lynda Martin (ent)
Dick Spring (pol)
Philomena Begley (ent)
The Clancy Brothers and Tommy Makem (ent)

5 May 1984
No Show

12 May 1984
Les Enfants (ent)
David Shaw-Smith (pg)
Maíreád O'Gorman (pg)
Paddy Murphy (pg)
Tony Marshal (pg)
The Shannons (ent)
Maureen O'Donnell (pg)
Gary O'Brien (pg)
Ned Gavin (pg)
John Healy (med)
Pádraig Flynn (pol)
Monica Barnes (pol)
Eamonn McCann (pol)

19 May 1984
Zero One (ent)
John B Keane (wr)
Una Hunt (ent)
The Dubliners (ent)
Tom O'Neill (pg)
Trafford Tanzi (pg)
Fr Joseph Martin (pg)

26 May 1984
Gotham City Swingers (ent)
David Norris (pol)
Frank McNamara (ent)
Debbie Kempton Smith (pg)
Fr Laurence Cassidy, SJ (pg)
Breda Kelly (pg)
Maura Phelan (pg)
Marie Doran (pg)
Brian Marlborough (pg)
Nella Clingenberg (pg)
Gerald Davis (pg)
Brian Doyle (pg)
David Heffernan (med)

8 September 1984
Lyall Watson (sp)
John Treacy (sp)
James Last (ent)
Clogs Gallagher (ent)
Red Hurley (ent)

Long John Jump Band (ent)
Sylvia Sydney (ent)

15 September 1984
Alex Higgins (sp)
Jimmy White (sp)
Tony Knowles (sp)
Peter Deighan (pg)
Nicky Kelly (pg)
Elike Brookes (ent)
Phil Lynott & Clan Eadair (ent)
The Kaye Twins (ent)
Frederick Forsythe (wr)

22 September 1984
Special on GAA Centenary

29 September 1984
Fashion Awards Special

6 October 1984
Ranier Brüenhans German Jazz (ent)
Seán Kinsella (pg)
Vince Hill (ent)
Bonnie Langford (pg)
Jimmy Boyle (pg)
Tom Paxton (ent)
Fr Andrew Greeley (wr)
Marie Barrett (pg)
Fr Pat Buckley (pg)
Joe Foyle (pg)
Fr Denis Callaghan (pg)
Jackie Healy Ray (pg)

13 October 1984
Flamenco Jazz (ent)
Freddie Starr (ent)
Paul Melba (ent)
Ronan Tynan (ent)
Peter Thompson (pg)
Noelle Campbell-Sharpe (med)
Gloria Hunniford (med)

20 October 1984
Butch Moore-Capitol (ent)
Malibu Disco Dancers (ent)
Meatloaf (ent)
Marion Fossett (ent)

Sandie Kelly (Duskey) (ent)
Jonathan Miller (wr)
Laurie Hearts (ent)
Fr Tom Leigh (pg)
Eleanor McFadden (pg)
Jim Dolan (pg)

27 October 1984
Joanna and Tequila Sunrise (ent)
Anita Ruddick (pg)
David Essex (ent)
Ethiopia Appeal & VTR
Gerry Corrigan (in audience)
Joey Maher GAA Handballer (pg)
Charles Mitchel (med)

3 November 1984
Phil Coulter (ent)
Dr Dan Kiely (wr)
Clog Dance (ent)
Elaine Crowley (wr)

Paddy Madigan (pg)
Paul & Aine Sexton (pg)

10 November 1984
Kevin Keegan (sp)
Veronica McSwiney (ent)
Smock Alley—Shakespeare (ent)
Jimmy Bartley, etc (ent)
Larry Adler (ent)
Fergal Tobin (wr)
Nell McCafferty (med)
Austin Flannery, OFM (pg)
Des Fennell (med)

17 November 1984
Gerry Carr (ent)
Brendan Kennelly (wr)
Jan Leaming (med)
Patrick O'Byrne (ent)
Love Bug (ent)
Éamon de Buitléar (pg)
John Cashmore (ent)
James Wilson (ent)
Robin Hanbury-Tenison (wr)

24 November 1984
Josef Locke Special

1 December 1984
Eddie Grant (ent)
Donnacha Ó Dúlaing (pg)
Elaine Paige (ent)
Frank Bough (wr)
Paul Ashford (ent)
Siobhán Cuffe (pg)
Emer O'Sullivan (pg)
Jonathan Bardon (wr)
Stephen Conlin (pg)
Peter Jennings (wr)

8 December 1984
Toy Show

15 December 1984
Johnny McEvoy (ent)
Stephen Roche (sp)
Seán Kelly (sp)
Susan McCann (ent)
Lenny Henry (ent)

Oba Seagrave (pg)
Rabbi Rosen (pg)
Ita & Des Fitzsimons (pg)

22 December 1984
Glen Abbey Legs:
Fr Brian D'Arcy
Charlie McGreevy
Grace O'Shaughnessy
Mick Lally
Brendan Grace & Kids (ent)
Eileen Reid (ent)
Aisling Henehan (ent)
Palestrina Choir (ent)
Gerald Gillen (ent)
Ita O'Donovan (ent)
Eddie Lenihan (pg)
Micháel Ó Súilleabhain (pg)
Frank Kelly (ent)
Des Keogh (ent)

29 December 1984
No Show

1985

5 January 1985
No Show

12 January 1985
Dublin City Ramblers (ent)
Ciaran Gavin (pg)
Dave Finney (pg)
John McNally (ent)
Eamonn Dunphy (med)
Patricia Bardon and Alison Young (ent)
Bishop Edward Daly (pg)
Freddie White (ent)

19 January 1985
State of the Nation—Special

26 January 1985
The Mimmiks (ent)
Barry Norman (pg)
Helena Moloney (ent)
Shirley Eskapa (wr)
9 out of 10 Cats (ent)
Linda Scotson (wr)
Frances Biggs (pg)
Melanie White (pg)

2 February 1985
Anna McGoldrick (ent)
Dickie Rock (ent)
Marisa Robles (ent)
Christine Piff (wr)
Gillespie Sisters (ent)
Pauline Bewick (pg)
James Burke (wr)

9 February 1985
Brendan Shine (ent)
Sal Solo & Mt Argus Children's Choir (ent)
Brendan Kennelly (wr)
Fr Peter Hughes (pg)
Rev Kenneth Todd (pg)
Barbara Dixon (ent)
Roly Daniels (ent)

16 February 1985
Nervous Animals (ent)
Ulick O'Connor (wr)
Juliette Kavanagh (ent)
Rory Grealish (pg)
Barry Thrower (pg)
Alan Bates (pg)
Alex Clarke Quartet (ent)
P J O'Connor—Superstars (ent)
Polly Devlin (wr)
Fay Weldon (wr)

23 February 1985
Paul Daniels Special (ent)

Rosaleen Linehan (ent)
Des Keogh (ent)
Two's Company (ent)
The Fureys (ent)
Brian Inglis (wr)

2 March 1985
Ground Zero Group (ent)
Stocktons Wing (ent)
Alex Bird (wr)
Fascinating Aida (ent)
Mark Ella (sp)
Kieran Fitzgerald (sp)
Serge Blanco (sp)
Concern VTR
George Best (sp)

9 March 1985
Val Doonican (ent)
Lesly Kenton (wr)
Pasadena Roof Band (ent)
Derek Daly (sp)
R D Laing (wr)
Patrick Collins (ent)

16 March 1985
Special on Co. Derry

23 March 1985
Princess Tiny Meat (ent)
Anthony Cronin (wr)
Ray Lynam (ent)
John Hurt (pg)
Brian O'Reilly (ent)
Break-Dance Group (ent)
Arthur Wilson (wr)
Capt Tighe (wr)
Barbara Taylor Bradford (wr)

30 March 1985
Tír na nÓg (ent)
Michael O'Halloran (pol)
Doris Keogh's Group (ent)
Rita and Seán Kinneally (pg)
Prof Thornes (pg)
Harvey and the Wallbangers
  (ent)
Niall O'Donoghue (sp)
Julian Lloyd Webber (ent)

6 April 1985
Special Show on Travellers

13 April 1985
Screen Test Winner (pg)
Henry Kelly (med)
Dickie Rock (ent)
Ellen Kuzwayo (pg)
Mary Hegarty (ent)
Stephan Pearce (pg)
Seán Flynn (wr)
Padraig Yeates (wr)
Tony Gregory (pol)

20 April 1985
Georgian State Dancers (ent)
David Norris (pol)
Margaret Thatcher (pg)
Quentin Crisp (wr)
Tony Kenny (ent)
Faith Browne (ent)

Philomena Begley (ent)
Arthur Scargill (pol)

27 April 1985
Marcalla Band (ent)
Alistair McGuckian (pg)
ICA Dancers (ent)
Colombiani Brothers (ent)
Billy Connolly (ent)
Maria Christian (ent)
Mary Duffy (pg)
Maggie McFadden (pg)

4 May 1985
No Show

11 May 1985
That Crowd (ent)
Tony Scott Jazz Band (ent)
Bishop Comiskey (pg)
Gerty (ent)
Na Casadaigh (ent)
Pete Townsend (pg)
Patricia Bardon (ent)
Anne-Marie Smith (ent)
Kieran Fitzgerald (sp)
David Yallop (wr)

18 May 1985
Stephen Duffy (ent)
Ruairí Quinn (pol)
Niall Greene (pg)
That Crowd (ent)
De Danann (ent)
Mary Black (ent)
Alexis Sayle (ent)
Peter Bowles (ent)

25 May 1985
Clipper Carlton (ent)
Brian Coyle (pg)
Wolfe Tones (ent)
Michael Connolly (ent)
Cormack Breathnach (ent)
Cian O'Sullivan (ent)
That Crowd (ent)
Shay Healy (ent)
Maureen Potter & Thelma
  Ramsey (ent)
Burke Family (pg)
Aine Hoffman (pg)
Anya Massey (ent)
Mary O'Lehan (pg)
Thomas Duffy (pg)
Noel Tobin (pg)
Patsy Wickham (pg)

13 September 1985
Blue In Heaven (ent)
Dr Kurt and Mrs Kathy
  Wagner (pols)
Danny Doyle (ent)
Ian Meldon (ent)
Brian Ruddin (ent)
Eileen and Dermot Corcoran
  (pg)
Pat Moran (pg)
Mr and Mrs John Miller (pg)
Rosemary Curf (pg)
Nancy Managhan (pg)

Sister Maura (pg)
Fr Raphael Gallagher (pg)

20 September 1985
Bob Geldof (ent)
The Pogues (ent)
Denis Allen (ent)
Betty Tootell (pg)
Capt Eric Moody (pg)
Barley Corn (ent)
Sandra McGuigan (pg)
Mrs Pat McGuigan (pg)
Gus Martin (pg)
Dr Peter Heseltine (pg)

27 September 1985
Fashion Show Special

4 October 1985
Liz Myers (pg)
Anne Shultz (pg)
Les Enfants (ent)
John McNally (ent)
Thompson Twins (ent)
Spike Milligan (ent)
Mary Clifford (ent)
Peter Doyle (pg)
The Kristoffs (ent)
Mrs Victorier Gillick (pg)
Christine Donaghy (pg)

11 October 1985
Special on Law and Order

18 October 1985
Gina, Dale Hayes and
  Champions (ent)
John Boorman (pg)
Dickie Rock (ent)
Des Keogh (ent)
Anna Managhan (ent)
Donal Kearney (ent)
Joanne Hayes (pg)
John Barrett (wr)
Barry O'Halloran (wr)
Nell McCafferty (wr)
Michael O'Regan (wr)
Gerard Colleran (pg)
Don Buckley (pg)
Joe Joyce (pg)

25 October 1985
Special from Co. Cork

1 November 1985
Bagatelle (ent)
John Gore Grimes (sp)
Tom Lawlor (sp)
Mary Sheridan (pg)
Peter McBrian (pg)
John Mortimer (wr)
Eric Segal (wr)
Rebecca Storm (ent)
Grace O'Sullivan (ent)
Phil Coulter (ent)

8 November 1985
Stocktons Wing (ent)
Maureen Johnston (wr)
Fascinating Aida (ent)
Denis Taylor (sp)
Scullion (ent)
Eamonn Kelly (ent)
Maura O'Sullivan (ent)
Fr John Emerson (pg)
Fr Seán Collins (pg)
Seán Mac Réamoinn (pg)
David Yallop (wr)

15 November 1985
Anne-Marie Gannon (pg)
Frank McNamara (ent)
Fr Pat Lawton Group (ent)
Rathmines & Rathgar
  Musical Society (ent)
Mike Yarwood (ent)
Mark Moran (ent)

Orla Mulvaney (ent)
Dermot Magennis (ent)
Aideen Mulligan (ent)
Pat Quinn (pg)

21 November 1985
The Flying Pigotts (ent)
Russell Grant (wr)
The Poor Scholar Group (ent)
Gabriel Byrne (pg)
Éamon de Buitléar (pg)
Mairead McCrane (ent)
Frank Clarke (ent)
The Patchells Couple and
  John (pg)

29 November 1985
The Incomparable Benzini
  Bros (ent)
Nancy Roberts (wr)
Keith Floyd (wr)
Melli Sande (ent)
Feargal Quinn (pg)

6 December 1985
Toy Show
Billie Barry's Group (ent)
Phoebe O'Donoghue School
  of Dancing (ent)
Rosalyn O'Dowd Group (ent)
David Halpin (ent)
St Colmcille's Boys School
  and John Fahy (ent)
Fran Dempsey (ent)
Alma Carroll (ent)
Richard Crowley (ent)
Susan McCann (ent)
Barry Desmond (ent)
Barry McGuigan (sp)

13 December 1985
Rick Walsh and Helen (ent)
Siobhán Cuffe (pg)
Kevin Flynn (ent)
Mary O'Hara (ent)
Aled Jones (ent)
Joan Fitzgerald (pg)/
Garret Fitzgerald (pol)

20 December 1985
Frank Kelly (ent)
Helen Morrissey (ent)
Rose Tynan (ent)
Éamon de Buitléar (pg)
Gerry Van Sust (ent)
Mairéad McCrane (ent)
Chris Rea (ent)
Marie Pyne (pg)
Rita Fagan (pg)

1986
No records for early part of
  1986

14 February 1986
Special Valentine's Day
  Show

19 September 1986
Noelle Campbell-Sharpe
  (med)

Feargal Quinn (pg)
Brush Shiels (med)
David Hanly (med)
Siobhán Cleary (med)
Bob Hoskins (pg)
Anthony Summers (pg)
Charlie McGettigan (ent)
Linda Martin (ent)
Stephen Scotti (ent)

26 September 1986
Peter Cox (wr)
Alan Gillis (pg)
Noel Molloy (pg)
Patrick Moore (pg)
James Kenny (pg)
Ellen Kenny (pg)
Tony Kenny (ent)
Mrs Eva Sheridan (pg)
John B Keane (wr)
Galleon (ent)
The Morrisseys (ent)
Steel Moon (ent)
Mick Lally (pg)
Joan Brosnan-Walsh (ent)

3 October 1986
Greg Le Mond (sp)
Fr Michael Cleary (pg)
Hugh O'Connor (pg)
David Marcus (wr)
Gordon Thomas (wr)
Stocktons Wing (ent)
Geoffries First Affair (ent)
Jonathan Lambert (ent)
Mary Sheridan de Bruin (ent)
Louis Browne (ent)
Peter McBrien (ent)
Jimmy Vaughan (ent)

10 October 1986
Fashion Awards Special

17 October 1986
Dr David Bellamy (wr)
Chris Mullin (wr)
Norris McWhirter (wr)

Dr Conor Cruise O'Brien (pg)
Patrick Cruise O'Brien (pg)
Dr Kader Asmal (pg)
Howard Jones (ent)
Alexander Brothers (ent)

24 October 1986
Jazz Coasters (ent)
Liam Ó Murchú (wr)
Courtney Kenny (ent)
Teresa Lowe (ent)
Tom McArdle (pg)
John McArdle (pg)
Cathal Dunne (ent)
Veronica Lawlor (pg)
Germaine Greer (wr)

31 October 1986
Ann Breen (ent)
Kevin Sharkey (med)
John Glenn and the
  Wranglers (ent)

Martin Dempsey (ent)
F McNamara (ent)
Bernie Harold (sp)
Barry McGuigan (sp)
Everything But the Girl (ent)
Dungan Goodhew (sp)

7 November 1986
Prelude Brass (ent)
Noel Pearson (ent)
Mario Malagnini (ent)
Niall McDonagh (pg)
Mary Coughlan (ent)
Fashion (Male Fashion/Alias
    Tom) (ent)
Barry Norman (med)

14 November 1986
The Drifters (ent)
Sonny Knowles (ent)
Eumju Chae (ent)
David Bond (ent)
Jim Aiken (pg)
Dr Noel Brown (pg)

21 November 1986
Wiltschinsky Duo (ent)
Pierce Brosnan (pg)
David Essex (ent)
Carolann Lowe (ent)
Maura O'Connell (ent)
Peter Ustinov (pg)
Sydney Biddle Barrows (pg)

28 November 1986
Gems (ent)
David Frost (pg)
Kiki Dee (ent)
Dublin Grand Opera Society:
    Liu Yue (ent)
Fr Joe Dunne (pg)
Minor Detail (ent)
Kathleen Kennedy
    Townsend (pol)
Michael O'Leary TD (pol)

5 December 1986
Toy Show
Anne Doyle (pg)
David Norris (pol)
Carolyn Fischer (pg)
Joe Lynch (pg)
Little People (ent)
Mini-Pops (ent)
Gertrude Walsh School of
    Irish Dancing (ent)
Freda Bannon Group (ent)
The Stauntons (ent)
Gareth Costello (ent)
Bugsy Malone Group (ent)
The McGinleys (ent)
Billy Barry Group (ent)
Liberties Music and Drama
    Group (ent)
Mt Sion Silver Band (ent)
Pam Collins (pg)

12 December 1986
Jennie Stanley (ent)
Siobhán Cuffe (pg)
Christina Kelly (pg)
Gina (ent)
Spyder Sympson (ent)
Gerry Lavelle (pg)
Barbara Dixon (ent)
Tom McGinty (pg)
Wesley Burrows (pg)
Peig Sayers: The Motion
    Picture Comedy Group
    (ent)

19 December 1986
Dave Maher and the Rockets
    (ent)
Morris Major and Morris

Minor (ent)
Cecil Nash (ent)
Seán Mooney (ent)
Daniel Rovai (pg)
Len McCarthy Jazz Group
    (ent)
Roland Purcell (ent)
The Black Family (ent)
Eamon Kelly (pg)
Aelish de Barra (pg)
Rita Clarke (pg)
Anne Gahan (pg)

26 December 1986
25th Anniversary Show

1987

16 January 1987
Joe Boland (pg)
Tony Boland (pg)
Vincent Finn (pg)
Vincent Browne (med)
Ivan Yates (pol)
Seamus Brennan (pol)
Mary Harney (pol)
Ruairi Quinn (pol)

23 January 1987
High Energy (ent)
Dr Muriel Gahan (pg)
An Post Group (pg)
Veronica McSwiney (ent)
Austin Gaffney and daughter
    (pg)
Hotfoot (ent)
Bill Cullen (pg)

30 January 1987
Zoom (ent)
Patrick O'Hagan (ent)
Johnny Logan (ent)
Peig Sayers: The Motion
    Picture Show (ent)
Peter St John (ent)
Dublin City Ramblers (ent)
Vincent Smith and Pete St
    John (ent)
Margaret Brennan (ent)

6 February 1987
Smokie (ent)
Kieran & Michael Lawlor (pg)
Colette Conlon (Coyne) (ent)
Jim Doherty (ent)
Na Casaidaigh (ent)
Pat Cullen (wr)
Catríona Ní Dhomhnaill (ent)
Niall Toibín (ent)
Donal Farmer (ent)
Brendan Conroy (ent)
John Olohan (ent)
Richard Boyle (pg)

13 February 1987
The Chieftains (ent)
Lilian Young (wr)
Chris de Burgh (ent)
Uri Geller (pg)
Suzi Quatro (ent)
Lisa Sliwa (wr)

20 February 1987
Ghost of an American
    Airman (ent)
Tamzara (ent)
Niall O'Dowd (pg)
The Wolfe Tones (ent)
Daniel O'Donnell (Ent)
Stevie Starr (ent)
Enya Ní Bhraonáin (ent)
Pat Conroy (pg)

27 February 1987
Dara Ó Lochlainn's Jazz
    News (ent)

Pat Crowley (pg)
The McCalmans (ent)
Jan Alexander (pg)
Mick Hanly & Rusty Old
    Halo (ent)
Cry Before Dawn (ent)
Peter Ustinov (pg)

6 March 1987
Dubliners' Special 25th
    Anniversary Show

13 March 1987
In Tua Nua (ent)
Prof Augustine Martin (pg)
Larry Gogan (med)
Irish String Trio (ent)
Ann Bushnell (ent)
Good Morning America (ent)
Geoff Read (pg)
Micro Disney (ent)
Ian Botham (sp)

20 March 1987
The St Laurence O'Toole
    Pipe Band (ent)
Batt Purns (pg)
The Brooks Academy Set
    Dancers & Volunteers
    from audience (ent)

Celtic Fusion (ent)
Frank O'Meara (sp)
Paul Donovan (sp)
Marese Heavin (ent)
Peter Howick (pg)
Maria Simmonds Gooding
    (pg)
Patrick Wally (pg)
Con Power (pg)
Brendan Solan (pg)

27 March 1987
Susan McCann (ent)
Ronan Collins (ent)
Flex and the Fastweather
    (ent)
Nell McCafferty (med)
Honor Heffernan (ent)
Paul Brady (ent)
Frank Feely (pg)
Carol Stephenson (pg)
Ken Cummins (pg)

3 April 1987
Eileen Reid and the Cadets
    (ent)
National Lottery Draw
Tina Morahan and son James
    (pg)
Pulling Faces (ent)
Nuala Lawler (pg)
Barry Warner & Band (ent)
The Allen Brothers (ent)
Shane Kenny (med)
Fergal Keane (med)
Fr Bernard Lynch (pg)

10 April 1987
I Giovani Solisti (ent)
Hidden Fears (ent)

Bill Scott (pg)
Bob Whelan (ent)
Marilyn and Harvey
    Diamond (wr)
Dublin Grand Opera Society
    (ent)
Joanna Shapland (pg)
Derek Nally (pg)

17 April 1987
Carysfort Jazz Speech Choir
Tim Severin (wr)
Margo (ent)
Kathleen Tynan (ent)
Finbar Furey (ent)
Pádraig Ó Flannabhra (wr)
Ladysmith Black Mambazo
    Group (ent)
Elmer Bernstein (pg)
Raymond Crotty (pg)
The Lindsay Singers (ent)

24 April 1987
MACNAS Drama Group
    (ent)
Philip Greene (sp)
Link to National Concert Hall
    for Ó Riada concert

Lombard & Ulster Music
    Competition
Billy Connolly (ent)

1 May 1987
Joe Dolan (ent)
Anne Kidman (pg)
John McNally (ent)
Johnny Logan (ent)
Don Stoltz (pg)
Marshall Stoltz (pg)
Peter Skellern (ent)
Mari O'Leary and Alex
    Fraser (pg)
Seán Kent (pg)
Hal Roach (ent)
Excerpt from Jurys Cabaret
    (ent)

8 May 1987
Gung Ho (ent)
Brendan Balfe (med)
The Thompson Twins (ent)
The Murtaghs (pg)
Extract from Abbey play *Say
    Cheese* (ent)
John Waters (pg)

15 May 1987
The Don Dorsey Big Band
    (ent)
Emelyn Heaps (pg)
This Is This (ent)
John Harris (pg)
Dr Bryan Alton (pg)
Hothouse Flowers (ent)
Dr Derek Freedman (pg)
Fr Paul Lavelle (pg)
Dr Harry Crawley (pg)
Anne-Marie Hourihane (pg)

22 May 1987
De Danann (ent)
Lenny Henry (ent)
Danny Doyle (ent)
Labhrás Ó Murchú (pg)
Comhaltas Ceoltóirí Éireann
    (ent)
Bagatelle (ent)
Mr and Mrs Patchell (pg)
Fr Finbarr Wright (pg)
Frank Carroll (pg)
Whitley Strieber (wr)

29 May 1987
Christy Moore (ent)
Mike Harding (pg)
Chris Meehan & The
    Rednecks (ent)
Phil Coulter (ent)
The Amazing Orchante (ent)
Patrick Street Band (ent)
Maureen Potter (ent)
Josef Locke (ent)
Philip Kampff (pg)

18 September 1987
Boney M (ent)
Maxi (ent)
Hamish Imlach (ent)
Seán McKeown and Cheetah
    Cubs from FOTA Wildlife
    Park (pg)
Chris de Burgh (ent)
Frank McNamara (ent)
Chris O'Donoghue (ent)
Sorcha Cusack (pg)
Francis Canning (pg)
Ken Livingstone (pol)

25 September 1987
Touchdown (ent)
Richard Crowley (med)
Suzie Kennedy (ent)
The Croft Ensemble (ent)
Ted Kennedy Jr (pg)
Tim McDonnell (pg)
Victoria Wood (ent)
Cardinal Tomás Ó Fiaich (pg)
John Hume (pol)
Jim Aitken (pg)
Mons Michael Ledwith (pg)
Ray McAnally (pg)
Mary O'Rourke (pg)

2 October 1987
Dorchadas (ent)
Jonathan Philbin Bowman
    (med)
The Dixies (ent)
Ladies Football Finalists (pg)
Roddy Doyle (wr)
Ra Ra Zoo (ent)
Donny Osmond (ent)
June Levine (med)

9 October 1987
Hue & Cry (ent)
Martin Sheehan (pg)
Deirdre Crowley (ent)
Phil Cool (ent)
David Norris (pol)
Vicki Crowley (pg)
Eartha Kitt (ent)

16 October 1987
Fashion Awards Special

23 October 1987
Bob Darch (ent)
Spike Milligan (ent)
Cynthia Clarey and Jake
    Gardner (ent)
Maeve Binchy (wr)
Michael Sheehan (pg)
(cont. on page 154)

To be soothed, relaxed, pampered, admired, fixed up generally . . . go to

MAKE-UP

by Deirdre Purcell

How many people would you think might pass through RTE's make-up department every year?

After all, RTE is a little Irish station and isn't everyone always complaining about all the pre-packaged, imported 'rubbish' on our screens? So go on … How many? 5000 people? 6000? 10,000? Wrong! The actual figure is close to 20,000.

Make-up is one of those departments which bears immediately the brunt of any expansion in home production. And this, in the last number of years, particularly since the advent of Network 2, has been dramatic. The women (and one man, John Havelin) in the department have made a smooth transition since the old days when

they were incarcerated in a completely inadequate little room with two washbasins, which was swamped if a big programme like the *Late Late Show* decided to feature, for instance, a number of bands. There would be jostling for mirror space, and even queues. The decibel level would be intense.

Now, when they are not on the studio floor or attached to outside broadcast units—like the one for *Glenroe* or the one for sports or for 'outside' concerts—the staff work in a custom-designed area, well-lit and well-appointed with its own hairdressing room attached. The very first aspect of this area which strikes a newcomer is its tranquillity. There can be bedlam everywhere else in the station, but in the hushed make-up room, even the most hyperactive of customers is soothed. Take the day of the *People in Need Telethon*. In the main reception area, in the corridors and even outside on the lawn, there was a great mill of celebrity guests and children in their party frocks, pom poms, sailor suits and Spanish costumes, technicians trailing cables and excited members of audiences clutching tickets. But in make-up, here was Gay, sitting calmly in the make-up chair having his handsome face done, conversing quietly in tones barely above a relaxed whisper, with John, who was doing the make-up.

This department, of all departments in RTE, is uniquely placed to have an overview of the home output of the station. On that same day of the Telethon, the pro-

duction assistants moved efficiently in and out of the room with their running orders, alerting the make-up staff as to when Enya and Lynsey de Paul and the three stars from *Dynasty* and Captain Furillo from *Hill Street Blues* would be in. The head of TV sales, Peadar Pierce, was having a clown's make-up applied in order to do his bit for the people in need. But Thelma and Derek still had to be made up for *Live At Three*; Vere Wynne Jones came in to wash his hair before News; Theresa Mannion came in for *Newsline*; Pádraig Ó Gaora was on duty for *Nuacht*; Evelyn Cusack came in before predicting the weather—and of course there was *Cúrsaí*. And that was all within an hour or so.

The head of make-up is Stella Bowen, and the longest serving member of staff in the department is Eveleen Lunny, who has been making people up (and at the same time, calming them down) since 1971. By and large, she says, people are terrific—and the bigger the star, the more terrific they are.

'Fortunately you don't often get difficult people. And anyway, in the long run, you tend to forget about the nasty ones. They are normally people who are starting off, not the real professionals. Quite honestly, I can't remember any stars, any real stars, being rude to me.'

With the increasing awareness of the importance of the communications media, people are now very conscious of how they look. 'TDs and people in the public eye are far more aware of their appearance over the last six or seven years than ever before' and even 'ordinary' folk appreciate the transformation which occurs in this room. 'Most people want to look a little different—maybe a bit thinner here, a bit of shader there...' And with all the new products on the market the task is a lot easier.

But one programme contributor, a lady who was about seventy years old and obviously the possessor of a wonderful sense of humour, had her own views of what was needed in her case. She took a critical look at herself in the bright mirror. Then she turned to Eveleen: 'Heavy on the miracle...!'

(left to right) Eveleen Lunny, Margaret Curran, Stella Bowen, Dorothy McEvoy

QUIZTIME
FOLK MUSIC QUIZ
set by Fíach Ó Broin

The RTE Guide
(cont. from page 143)

mercial element who want us to make even more money for RTE. Not to mention the ones who say we're always grumbling.

That aside, it's not a bad little outfit to work with. In all honesty, we find very little of the prima donna among the big names who must often be sick and tired of the demands we make on them. Most of them, indeed, have written for us in their day. You'll find Gay Byrne on music, Terry Wogan sounding remarkably like he does today, Frank Hall, Pat Kenny, Donncha Ó Dúlaing, David Hanly for many years, along with such as Peadar O'Donnell, Benedict Kiely, Patrick Kavanagh... Some of them, very likely, featured in the *Guide* in that Limerick window.

I'm afraid we on the shop floor derive our greatest pride from the little clangers—after the event. I look back with affection on a picture which was described as showing a crowd with arms upraised hailing the take-off of an airship. There was no affection evident in the reader who pointed out that the upraised arms were in fact holding on to the guy-ropes. Others will remember that we billed *News for the Deaf* as *News for the Dead*. There's more where that came from. Quite recently, indeed, the hard of hearing had their revenge when our billing of a war-time movie had a French freighter rescuing 'a motley bunch of half-deaf escapees from Devil's Island'. It's all, as the ads say, in the *RTE Guide*.

1. Who recorded the *a cappella* (voices only, no words) version of Carolan's Concerto?

2. Who wrote *Fields of Athenry*?

3. Who wrote *Planxty Irwin*?

4. What was the name of Clannad's first record?

5. Who wrote *The Patriot Game*?

6. Frankie Gavin of De Danann plays the flute. True or false?

7. James Joyce named *Finnegans Wake* after the ballad of the same name. True or false?

8. Is balladeer Franke Harte an architect or a doctor?

9. Who was the main vocalist with Planxty?

10. In what year was the first Fleadh Cheoil held?

11. Who wrote *The Boys of Wexford*?

12. *The Red Flag* was written by Meath-man John O'Connell. To what air?

13. Paddy Moloney of the Chieftains was in the same class in school as John Sheahan of the Dubliners. True or false?

14. What is the term used to describe songs, eg *The Palatine's Daughter*, which are partly in Irish, partly in English?

15. A fifteenth-century Italian folksong called *Piva Piva*, used by Tchaikovsky in his Pathétique Symphony, became *Story of a Starry Night* in the 1950s. It returned to the folk idiom with words by Bill Caddick and was recorded by Mick Moloney, Christy Moore and the Furey Brothers. What is the modern folk title?

16. *Lament for Staker Wallace* commemorates a hero of which Irish historical event?

17. *The Dingle Regatta* was the signature tune of which man and which group?

18. Bagpipes are played in Greece, Italy, Galicia and Romania. True or false?

19. Brendan Grace was a folk-singer before he became a comedian. True or false?

20. The first recording of Irish traditional music was of a céilí band in 1899 on an Edison Records wax cylinder. True or false?

21. *Cailín ó cois tSiúire mé*, is misspelled in Shakespeare's *Henry IV* as 'Kaleno custurame'. What song is normally sung to the air nowadays?

22. What folk number by an Irish group reached the British and Irish top tens and was banned on RTE?

23. *The Long Note* programme took its name from a jammed chanter on Seamus Ennis' pipes at the first recording? True or false?

24. How many strings on a traditional fiddle?

25. Ronnie Drew was a boy soprano. True or false?
(Answers on page 159)

OBSERVATIONS OF A LISTENER—BRUSH SHIELS

as heard from him by Deirdre Purcell

'What I've felt in the last few years about Radio 2, for instance, would be that the jockeys used to get embarrassed when they met me because they knew they were too old to be playing the records they were playing! The station badly needed to change to something more middle of the road rather than the Kylie Minogue/Samantha Fox kind of thing. We all got the impression that nobody in RTE ever went any further than Moore Street to find out what was happening. And they found that all the shops in Moore Street were playing Q102, and then you inform them that all the taxi-drivers were playing Treble TR! If they were looking for the taxi-driver market they were in big trouble! If they were looking for the boutiques, they'd be sure to find that there was a security guard in every single boutique that would be sure to tell them that Q102 was bleedin' driving them around the twist...

So I thought it was wrong that the national radio station was chasing the pirates around, they should have been leading the way. They've been at it so long, surely they would have realised that the Dubliner—I'm not talking about the Gay Byrne Dubliner, but the young punter—would have followed if they thought there was anything anti-establishment. In my opinion, all they had to do, if they wanted to be one up on the pirates, was to be slightly more off the wall.

But the other thing I found in the past, is that in the business—if you go around the ballrooms, it's a great barometer for what's happening—the biggest draws are

the ones that aren't getting played. Smokey, possibly for reasons that no-one in FM2 or Radio 1 could understand, would be the biggest draw in Ireland. And this would be because the average Irish person would still have a cowboy in his soul. They're all into country music so long as you don't say that it is country music. I play country music, but I don't say it's country music and consequently I make a very good living out of it. It's the word that turns people off. But if you play it and say nothing, they might think you're Doctor Hook or something like that, or Rod Stewart, who played country music, or Bob Dylan, who never told anybody about it... or Ray Charles.

So I find that FM2 now, have loosened up a bit and they're getting into what I think the Irish people prefer, which is a song, whether it's a ballad with a message, but a song with a start and a finish. But as far as the charts are concerned, it's age four to six for a certain type. Heavy metal is ten to fourteen. It's all very strange. The real middle of the market is really the ordinary song. It's really strange when Chris de Burgh can do six nights in the RDS and Bon Jovi can only do one. Which basically speaks in volumes, when you think how big Bon Jovi would be world-wide...

Radio 1, it is going to be their biggest year ever. FM2, I think it's going to be their biggest year ever. I think the new stations will mean that there will be more people listening than ever before. The element of competition appeals to the person at home as much as to anybody else. It's a topic of conversation: ''have you listened to the old station or the new station, and what do you think?'' I think the more stations that are on that are official, it's going to be the better for the Irish band business. That's not to say that the Irish records are world-class but the great thing about the Kylie Minogues and the Jason Donovans and all these other people from Stock Aitken and Waterman is they actually make a lot of the Irish bands sound very talented! which is a thing that wouldn't have happened in the Sixties... The great thing about pop music being so bad now, is it actually sounds like there's human beings on the Irish records, and consequently the English and American charts are responsible for a bit of resurgence around the Irish ballrooms. I think Radio 1 and FM2 are beginning to sense that there's more to what they do than they did in the past—but I don't think Gay can ever fail, I think that Pat Kenny is doing very well, and on television I think that Bibi Baskin is starting to come into her own...'

ÉAMON DE BUITLÉAR

The independent film-maker

National television had not arrived here when I closed the pet shop door for the last time. When my nature series *Amuigh Faoin Spéir* began about four years later, it was a studio programme and the birds and mammals I needed were borrowed from my old customers in that famous shop in Dublin's Parnell Street.

There were just two of us involved in the making of that original series. A Dutch friend and illustrator, Gerrit van Gelderen, sketched the animals and plants and the commentary and presentation were my responsibility. As all those early programmes were in Irish, the scripts had to be carefully marked for Gerrit's benefit so that the drawings would coincide with what I was saying. Somebody must have been praying for us in those times because there were never any mishaps in any of the sketching sequences.

That is not to say that everything went smoothly with *Amuigh Faoin Spéir*. Indeed there were times when the situation in studio was absolutely chaotic and if it were possible to have a re-showing of some of the programmes today, we would surely be in the running for top ratings in comedy!

Some producers simply did not understand animals and had no feelings for them. There was one in particular who couldn't be persuaded that the squirrel's cage should not be opened to obtain that extra camera angle. We were recording a programme about woodland animals at the time. Nutkin needed no second invitation when he saw that the way was clear. With a leap he shot out of the cage, streaked across the floor and headed straight for the more expansive habitat of heavy draped curtains surrounding the walls. The squirrel didn't stop until he reached the top and sat on his lofty perch, eyeing all of us with what seemed to be utter contempt.

As the programme had already begun and time was running short, everybody did the best they could. Shooting scripts were thrown aside as cameramen flew around the studio in their attempts to capture any kind of picture of that little chattering red menace. The squirrel obviously felt it safer to be well above all this chaos and as the operators pushed and pulled their heavy equipment, missing one another at times only by inches, the cameras took on the appearance of a team of demon dodgems in some crazy amusement arcade!

It was this incident and others like it which reinforced the fact that the title *Amuigh Faoin Spéir* (out under the sky) never really suited an indoor programme, and it was a newly arrived American producer, Don Lennox, who decided that a change was necessary. We would have to have some film footage of real wildlife in its natural habitat if the series was to develop. There were no natural history cameramen or women in Ireland in those days and the solution to the problem as we saw it was to fall back on our own resources. This immediately created a situation we had not at all expected. The taking of pictures by outsiders who were regarded by some of the RTE staff as pure amateurs was not looked upon too kindly and our plan was objected to in no uncertain terms, especially by one news cameraman.

The film sequence which we required was of house sparrows, as we wanted to include them in a programme on birds of the city. We suggested that the objecting gentleman might like to obtain the sequence for us himself and that we would like to have it within two days. It is generally agreed that the first essential for any wildlife film-maker is to be a good naturalist. That this newsman had no knowledge whatsoever of our kind of wildlife was to be a distinct disadvantage when he would go on that particular safari. We will never know how many hours he spent over those few days, throwing breadcrumbs at the sparrows as he crawled on his tummy under the park seats in St Stephen's Green, but we were to hear graphic descriptions from onlookers for months afterwards. We never got our pictures from him but there were no further objections as we began to take our first steps in becoming real wildlife film-makers.

Leaving a pensionable job to work on a short-term contract was not at all fashionable in the sixties. As far as I was concerned it was a definite risk and there were no guarantees beyond the programmes ordered by RTE for that particular year. Nevertheless, there has never been a year since those adventurous days with the animals in studio, that I have not had films to make.

Any film-maker today who wishes to survive financially must give a great deal of attention to the business end of the organisation; the standard and price of equipment has risen dramatically in recent years. Money is difficult to find and costs are now extremely high. Competition is much greater now, not alone here but abroad as well. All this demands that budgets be carefully worked out and filming days require thoughtful planning.

The experience gained from producing so much material for RTE down through the years has been most enjoyable. It is probably some kind of record that there has never been any form of disagreement in all these years between RTE and myself.

The list of completed films is a very long one, with programmes in Irish, in English and many with a bilingual commentary. The subjects have been quite diverse and include series such as *Island Wildlife*, shown in the USA and in Europe, and once-off films such as *Hy-Brasil, Séamus Ennis* (piper and folk collector) and *The Conamara Boatmen*. The present series *Exploring the Landscape* has been very successful and that series will hopefully make many more people aware of the beautiful country in which we live.

The knowledge gained from working with film-makers outside of Ireland has been of tremendous benefit. The resulting improvement in the standard of films I have made since then for RTE could be regarded in a way as a fair exchange for the experience enjoyed in those pioneering days of the sixties!

Éamon exploring the landscape with John Feehan

(cont. from page 147)
Colm Toibín (pg)
Angel and the Clowns (ent)
Hugo Meenan (pg)

30 October 1987
Aslan (ent)
Kate McIlhenny (pg)
Icon Trail (ent)
Gyles Brandreth (pg)
Stocktons Wing (ent)
Danny La Rue (ent)

6 November 1987
The Pogues (ent)
Eamon Dunphy (med)
Louden Wainwright III (ent)
John O'Conor (ent)
Demis Roussos (ent)
Tribute to Eamon Andrews
Mary O'Sullivan (pg)
Paul McGettigan (pg)
Donncha O'Donoghue (pg)

13 November 1987
We Free Kings (ent)
Mary Mooney (pol)
The Bhundu Boys (ent)
Suzanne Murphy (ent)
Earl Okin (ent)
Joyce O'Connor (pg)
Jonathan Philbin Bowman
(pg)
Dr John Harris (pg)

20 November 1987
Lord Mayor Carmencita
Hederman (pol)
Ben Elton (ent)
Christy Moore (ent)
Bree Harris (ent)
Alan Pease (pg)
Jimmy Sheehan (pg)
Dr Paddy Leahy (pg)
Tom Ryan (pg)

27 November 1987
Barbara Dickson (ent)
Virgina Kerr (ent)
D Cooling-Nolan (ent)
Peter McBrien (ent)
Ingus Peterson (ent)
Martin Collins (pg)
Muiris Mac Conghail (wr)
Philip Childs (pg)
Peadar Ó Riada & Cóir
Cuilaodha (ent)

4 December 1987
Toy Show

11 December 1987
De Danann (ent)
Frankie Gavin (ent)
Mary Coughlan (ent)
Gerry Lundberg (pg)
Dermot O'Connell (pg)
Ray Barry (pg)
Zita Rehill (pg)
Phil Coulter & Dublin Boys
Choir (ent)
Jim Maher (ent)

Jack Charlton (sp)

18 December 1987
Drogheda Brass Band (ent)
Micheál Ó Suilleabháin Band
(ent)
John Concannon (pg)
Maura O'Connell (ent)
Rolf Harris (ent)
Don Baker & Band (ent)
Peter Caviston (pg)
Charlie McCreevey (pg)
Mary Harney (pg)
Ted Nealon (pg)
Una Claffey (pg)
Chris Glennon (pg)
E McEldowney (pg)
Dickie Rock (ent)
Ruth Kelly and Pat Ingoldsby
(pg)

31 December 1987
New Year's Eve Special

1988

15 January 1988
Glen Miller Legacy (ent)
Stephen and Lydia Roche
(sp)
Feargal Sharkey (ent)
Johanna Saar (pg)
Michael D'Arcy (ent)
Do-O-Douglas (Courtneys
Circus Act) (ent)
Brush Shiels (ent)
Richard Attenborough (pg)
Donald Woods (pg)
Wendy Woods (pg)

22 January 1988
Christopher Nolan and his
mother (pg)
Joe Foyle (pg)
Seán Barrett (pg)
Liam Ó Cuinneagáin (pg)
The Fireflys (ent)
Catherine Coates (ent)
Peter Wilson with Lion Cub
(pg)
Clodagh Corcoran (pg)
Constance Nightingale (wr)
Rosemary Troy (ent)
The Ash String Trio (ent)

29 January 1988
Bros (ent)
Alan Wicker (wr)
Mike Murphy (pg)
Jermaine Stewart (ent)
Terry Willers (pg)
Tom Robinson (ent)
Nanci Griffith (ent)
Ed Harpur (pg)
Gillian Bowler (pg)

5 February 1988
Tommy Makem & Liam
Clancy (ent)
Sonny Knowles (ent)
Dr Paul Carson (pg)
John Stalker (wr)

Michael Heney (pg)
Flo (ent)
John Kavanagh (ent)
Terry Neeson (ent)
Enda Oates (ent)

12 February 1988
Rory Gallagher (ent)
Eddie Dunne (ent)
Dr Jonathan Miller (wr)
Colm Wilkinson (ent)
Tony Byrne (pg)
Peter Mangan (pg)
Mona Hannon (pg)
Caroline Mitchell (pg)
Emma Jordan (pg)
Julie Hanna (pg)

19 February 1988
Michelle Rocca (pg)
Pat Kenny (pg)
The Stargazers (ent)
Capriol Consort (ent)
Alaistair Logan (pg)
Ted Hawkins (ent)
Maggie Noonan (ent)
Michael Fields (pg)
Jack Powell (pg)
Rosemary McCarthy (pg)
John Leader (pg)

26 February 1988
Sinéad O'Connor (ent)
The Proclaimers (ent)
Jump the Gun (ent)
Ellsworth Chytka (pg)
Clannad (ent)
Comhaltas Ceoltóirí Éireann
(ent)
Niall Toibín (ent)

4 March 1988
Special Chieftains Show

11 March 1988
Moonshine (ent)
Willie De Ville (ent)
Alan Stanford (pg)
Hugh Tinney (ent)
Elizabeth Caffrey (pg)
Yasha Malhotray (ent)
Des O'Connor (ent)

18 March 1988
Pastimes (ent)
O'Brien Family (dance) (pg)
Feargal Quinn (pg)
The Fleadh Cowboys (ent)
Cathy Durkin (ent)
Peter Wilson (pg)
The Ryan Family (ent)
Brendan Harvey (pg)
Jack McNiece (pg)

25 March 1988
Nuala Lawlor (pg)
Colin McStay (pg)
James Morahan (pg)
Louise Morrissey & Band
(ent)
Betty Mahmoody (wr)
Comic Soufflé (ent)
Dublin Grand Opera Society
(ent)
Sr Kilian (pg)
Sr Columba Horgan (pg)
Kronos (ent)
Jimmy Greely (pg)
Mary Fitzgerald (pg)
Eileen Dunne (pg)
Fr Brian Darcy (pg)
Fran Dempsey (pg)
Elaine Murphy (pg)
Miss Tyrell (pg)
Miss Rainer (pg)

1 April 1988
Jazz Coasters (ent)
Vincent Dowling (pg)
Peanuts Hucko & Jazz
Coasters (ent)
Foster & Allen (ent)
Everything But the Girl (ent)
John Howard Taylor (pg)
Joan Lombard (pg)
Bishop Brendan Commiskey
(pg)
Eamon Toland (pg)
Listowel Singers (pg)
John B and Conor Keane (pg)
Jim and Derek Hand (pg)
Brush and Matthew Shiels
(pg)

8 April 1988
Donna Grucci (pg)
Rio Trio (ent)
Congressman Joe Kennedy
(pol)
Rachel Quinn (ent)
Gerard McChrystal (ent)
Edel Loftus (ent)
Michael D'Arch (ent)
Marika Murnahan (pg)

15 April 1988
Prefab Sprout (ent)
Donal McCann (med)
Seán Maguire (ent)
Patsy McCabe (ent)
Margaret Kent (pg)
Rosemary Henderson (ent)
Sarah Jane Scaife (ent)
Cliona Mulloy (ent)
Paddy Cole (ent)
Liam O'Flynn (ent)
Gráinne Cronin (pg)
Nanci Griffith (ent)
Gabriel Byrne (pg)
Tribute to Kenneth Williams

22 April 1988
Hale & Pace (ent)
Cry Before Dawn (ent)
Ferdia MacAnna (med)
Kathryn Holmquist (pg)
Johnny McEvoy (ent)
Michael Colgan (pg)
Arthur Murphy (ent)
Eamon Campbell (ent)
Peter Mantle (pg)
Fr Michael Kean (pg)

29 April 1988
Eraseur (ent)
Ian McKellan (pg)
Ewan MacColl (ent)
Peggy Seeger (ent)
Julie Forsythe (ent)
Bruce Forsythe (ent)
Jump the Gun (ent)
Myles Tierney (pg)
Pat McCartan (pg)
James Simmons (ent)
Brendan Kennelly (wr)
Mary Coughlan (ent)

6 May 1988
Hothouse Flowers (ent)
Peter Wilson (pg)
Brendan Shine (ent)
Anneka Rice (med)
Kieran Halpin & The Guest
List Band (ent)
Tom O'Neill (pg)
Nigel Williams (ent)
Gerry Fitt (pol)

13 May 1988
Sr Simwa and 3 nuns from
Kenya in audience (ent)

Comic Soufflé (ent)
Luka Bloom (ent)
Eilish Moore (ent)
Edward Kelly (pg)
Daniel O'Donnell (ent)
Frankie Laine (ent)
Gillian Bowler (pg)
Martin Dully (pg)

20 May 1988
Irish Soccer Squad (sp)
Fountainhead (ent)
Rose Brennan (ent)
Dublin Contemporary Dance
(ent)
Douglas Fairbanks Jr (pg)
Derek Bell (pg)
Vanbrugh Quartet (ent)
Selina Scott (pg)
Sybil Connolly (pg)
Robert Lawrence (wr)

27 May 1988
Michelle Rocca (med)
John McHugh (pg)
In Tua Nua (ent)
Mike Walsh (pg)
Lonnie Donnegan (ent)
Fascinating Aida (ent)
Sue Pollard (pg)
Candy Devine (ent)
Eileen Reid (ent)

16 September 1988
Zig and Zag (ent)
Brendan Bowyer & Band
(ent)
Conor Mullen (pg)
Christopher Nolan (wr)
Mrs Nolan (pg)
T'Pau (ent)
Bibi Baskin (med)
Frances Duff (med)
John Hogan (ent)
Jonathan Irwin (pg)
Michael Holroyd (wr)

23 September 1988
Tanita Tickaram (ent)
Sukeroko Taiko Drum Group
(ent)
Enya Ní Bhraonáin (ent)
The Vicious Boys (ent)
David Kelly (pg)
Nana Mouskouri (ent)
The Dubliners (ent)
Seán Crowley (sp)
Lenny Henry (ent)
Dame Edna Everage (ent)
Paddy Monaghan (pg)
Peter de Rosa (pg)
Kevin Rockett (pg)

30 September 1988
Julia Fordham (ent)
Seán Duignan (med)
Joan Collins Fan Club (pg)
Audrey Hepburn (pg)
Suzi Kennedy accompanied
by John Dunne (ent)
Amanpondo (ent)
Trouble & Strife Theatre Co
(ent)
Bernadette McAlliskey (pol)
Ken Maginnis (pol)

7 October 1988
The Big Noise (ent)
Penny Junor (wr)
The Drifters (ent)
John Cleese (pg)
Chris de Burgh (ent)
Peter Wilson and Vickie
Kuder (and 2 Koalas from
Zoo) (pg)

Dr Edward Walsh (pg)
Anastacia Crickley (pg)

14 October 1988
A House (ent)
Joseph Heller (wr)
Phil Collins (ent)
Linda Martin (ent)
Barbara Nugent (med)
VTR with Joan Collins (pg)
Sylvia Meyers (pg)

21 October 1988
The O'Malleys (ent)
Roald Dahl (wr)
Dolores Keane (ent)
Robert Meyers (pg)
Stephen Pile (wr)
Alice Taylor (wr)

28 October 1988
John Twomey (sp)
George Melley & Band (ent)
Joan McGinley (pg)
Nanci Griffith (ent)
James Galway (ent)
Daniel O'Donnell (ent)
Sir Terence Conran (pg)
Donny Osmond (ent)
Melvyn Bragg (wr)

4 November 1988
Derek Dunne (wr)
Sen John A Murphy (pol)
Jim Dougal (pg)
Liam Clancy (ent)
Something Happens (ent)
Michael Bentine (wr)

11 November 1988
Archer's Peach County Big
  Band (ent)
Dickie Rock (ent)
Jack Campbell (pg)
Johnny Cash (link from
  Olympia) (ent)
Enya Ní Bhraonáin (ent)
Jim O'Brien (sp)
Máire Ní Chathasaigh (ent)
Chris Newman (ent)
IDJ Dancers (ent)
Miss Asia contestants &
  Filipino dance (ent)
Deirdre Purcell (wr)
Bishop Eamon Duffy (pg)

18 November 1988
Boston Cheerleaders (sp)
Mark Murphy (sp)
Jim Kwitchoff (sp)
Missing Link (ent)
Gina, Dale Hayes & The
  Champions (ent)
Victor Kiam (pg)
Claude Rael (pg)
Brenda Fricker (pg)
West Point Choir (ent)
Boston College Band (ent)

25 November 1988
The Real Sounds of Africa
  (ent)
Nuala Ó Faoláin (pg)
Mary Black (ent)
Bruce Kent (pg)
Gerry Kelly (med)
Derek Davis (med)
Cathal McCabe (med)
The Adventures (ent)
Simon Group (ent)

2 December 1988
Fairground Attraction (ent)

Sybil Connolly (pg)
Micheál Ó Súilleabháin (ent)
Derek Jameson (med)
London Chamber Orchestra
  (ent)
Paddy Doyle (wr)
Paddy McGrory (pg)

9 December 1988
Toy Show

16 December 1988
Care Bears (ent)
Sonny Knowles (ent)
Tony Kenny (ent)
Terry Kelly (pg)
Elaine Paige (ent)
Brian Duffy (pg)
Matt Dowling (pg)
U2 (ent)

Caption for this photograph on inside back cover

Mary McEvoy (ent)
Bibi (ent)
Marguerite McCurtin (pg)
Micheline McCormick (pg)
Sharon Bacon (pg)
Nell McCafferty (pg)
Michelle Rocca (pg)
Donal Byrne (pg)
Pat Ingoldsby (pg)

23 December 1988
Archer's Peach County Big
  Band (ent)
Jeffrey Archer (wr)
Peter Wilson and Keeper
  Michael Clarke with 2
  chimps from Zoo (pgs)
Enya (ent)
Ray Treacy (sp)
Angela Reegan (pg)
The Beatless & Drummer Boy
  (ent)
Phil Anderson (ent)
Philip Peris (ent)
Gruesome Twosome (ent)
David Herlihy (pg)
Pauline McGlinn (pg)
McKenna Family (pg)
Listowel Singers (ent)

30 December 1988
Peter O'Toole (pg)
Bernadette Masterson (pg)
Frances Duane (pg)
John O'Boyle (pg)
Tony Malone (ent)
Peter McBrien (pg)
Noel V Ginnity (ent)
Anne-Marie McCormack &
  Band (ent)

Gillian Bowler (pg)
Frank Whelan (pg)

1989

20 January 1989
Jimmy Magee Special
  Birthday Tribute

27 January 1989
Brendan O'Brien (med)
Dr John O'Connell (pg)
Allies (ent)
Peggy Connolly (pg)
John Concannon (pg)
Kevin Sharkey (pg)
Dr John O'Connell (pg)
Gay Fitzgerald (pg)
Kieran Fitzgerald (pg)

3 February 1989
De Danann (ent)

Vicki Charlton (pg)
Peter Brightman (pg)
Mike Berry (ent)
Sinéad O'Connor (ent)
Kenny Everett (ent)
John O'Conor (ent)
Philip Martin (ent)
Tim Morrissey (pg)
Peter Sutherland (pg)

10 February 1989
Simply Red (ent)
Ted Walsh (sp)
Mary O'Rourke (pol)
Tánaiste Brian Linehan (pol)
Leo Sayer (ent)
Julie McGeever (pg)
Matt O'Donoghue (pg)
Pat Crowley (pg)
Jerry Hall (pg)

17 February 1989
Foster & Allen (ent)
Hallelujah Freedom (ent)
Dr Seán O'Loughlin (pg)
Rebecca Storm (ent)
Kevin Coniffe (ent)
Gay and John Walsh (pg)
Isabella Leitner (pg)

24 February 1989
No Show

3 March 1989
Davy Spillane & Band (ent)
National Lottery: 5
  Participants (pg)
Teresa Lawlor (ent)
Daniel Day Lewis (pg)
Christy Dignam (ent)
Winifred Blight (pg)

Maureen Carinduff (pg)
Ronan Smith (pg)
Rosaleen Linehan (ent)

10 March 1989
Don Baker & Band (ent)
Tom King MP (pol)
Darina Allen (med)
Excerpt from Muiris Mac
  Conghail's film on Aran
  Islands (ent)
Yvonne Brennan (pg)
Richard Lyndon (pg)

17 March 1989
Carmel Quinn (ent)
Noel Hill (ent)
Charlie Lennon (ent)
Siobhán and Joe Donovan
  accompanied by Máire
  Donovan (pg)

Kieran & Musicians (link
  from Galway) (ent)
Denise Parker (pg)
Hugh Leonard (wr)
Comhaltas Ceoltóirí Éireann
  Group (ent)
Macro Micro Cousins (ent)
Cantairí Óga Átha Cliath
  (ent)

24 March 1989
Brendan Daly (pol)
Martin McEnrow (pg)
Barry Flynn (pg)
Al Cunningham (pg)
Jim Denby (pg)
Hot City Orchestra (ent)
Ben Elton (ent)
Stanley Woods (pg)
Joe Eliott (Def Leppard) (ent)
Carl Chase & The Hank
  Williams Band (ent)
Elizabeth Shannon (wr)

31 March 1989
Neil Cooney (ent)
Anne O'Byrne (ent)
Aubrey Murphy (ent)
Richard McCready (ent)
Sulamita Aranowsky (pg)
Kenneth Woolam (pg)
Clarence Myerscough (pg)
Philippa Davies (pg)
Kevin Roche (pg)
Ruby Wax (ent)
Brother Barry Butler (pg)
Miriam Sheridan (pg)
Kieran Kenny (pg)
Paul Newman (pg)
Tom Tighe (pg)

7 April 1989
Peach County Big Band (ent)
Tracy Piggott (sp)
Red Hurley (ent)
Dr Ken McAll (wr)
The Values (ent)
Cathy Nugent (ent)
Jennie Stanley (ent)
Min Seamus Brennan (pol)
Prof Joe Lee (ent)
Chris O'Malley (pg)
Raymond Crotty (pg)
Bruce Mullan (pg)

14 April 1989
Link-up with Mary
  O'Sullivan in Cork:
Driver Jimmy Nyhan
Organiser Denis Horgan

Mike Harding (ent)
Dr Seán Barrett (pg)
Michael Bishop (pg)
Cathal Mullan (pg)
P J McGoldrick (pg)
Up With People (ent)
Billy Connolly (ent)
Diane Trowbridge (pg)
Kyriakos Markou (pg)

21 April 1989
No Show

28 April 1989
Seán Norman Céilí Band
  (ent)
Gerry Ryan (med)
'Terence' John Creedon (ent)
Kiev Connolly & Band (ent)
Barry Warner (ent)
Lord Henry Mountcharles
  (pg)
The Leningrad Choir (ent)
Sylvia Fraser (wr)

5 May 1989
Special on Islands

12 May 1989
The Rocking Chairs (ent)
John Walsh (wr)
Colm C T Wilkinson (ent)
Joe Rea (pg)
Snow White & the Seven
  Dwarfs (ent)
Zig and Zag (wr)
Dagmar O'Connor (wr)

19 May 1989
Apex Jazz Band (ent)
Marie Helvin (pg)
David Agnew/Frank
  McNamara and Orchestra
  (ent)
Dr Deepak Chopra (wr)
Yorke Family (pg)
Shakin' Stevens (ent)
Maureen O'Hara (pg)
Terry and Madeleine Keane
  (pg)
Grace O'Shaughnessy and
  Emma Kane (pg)
Eileen Reid and Pamela Day
  (pg)

26 May 1989
The Valentines (ent)
Freda Hayes (pg)
Kelleher Family (pg)
Susan McCann (ent)
Josiah Thompson (wr)
No Sweat (ent)
Paul Malone (ent)
Tom Kavanagh (pg)
Michael O'Reilly (pg)

For an extremely practical, down-to-earth person (when he's not parachuting) myth and magic and fairy-tales have played a big part in the life of

AONGHUS McANALLY

Playing Oisín in panto in the Peacock, Christmas '77, he met his wife Billie Morton, who has since become a well-known actress and mother of Aonghus Óg and Andrew. Now they live happily, not in Tír na nÓg, but in Port Mearnóg. Some time later he was in a musical called *Aladdin* written by Carolyn Swift and Fran Dempsey. The musical didn't do very well and sometimes no audience turned up. On one such day, when there was actually no audience at all, the cast clowned around, the actors played music and the musicians acted. Carolyn Swift saw Aonghus the musician acting and was impressed. At that time she was writing *Wanderly Wagon* and she asked him to play Fergus, the magic postman (that ole magic again!). He took up her offer and for two years he delighted young viewers before moving on to present *Anything Goes* in 1980. This was a revolutionary, new, three and a half hour Saturday morning TV programme that was such a huge success it ran for six years. He worked on the programme with Mary Fitzgerald, Kathy Parke and Dave Heffernan.

The experience and reputation he had built up led to shows such as *Blockbuster*, *Breakaway*, the Youth International Knockout programmes, *Box Camera*, *Borderline*, snooker commentaries, and culminated in his big 'adult' programme *Evening Extra*, where he co-hosted with such luminaries of the screen as Bibi Baskin, Shay Healy and Siobhán Cleary. But

how did snooker sneak in there? Well, one has to admit that in this area (as in so many others) his credentials are impeccable. He was Irish Boys Billiards Champion in 1971 and represented Ireland in Birmingham where he got to the semi-final. In 1971 only one boy entered the Irish Boys Billiards competition: Aonghus Brendan Aloysius McAnally. He didn't even have to hit a ball to qualify —witchcraft and magic again.

Then he started to take over the airways. First he worked for the wise old wizard, Merlin, sorry, I mean Gay Byrne! Do you remember himself and Philip Kampf on their aircell phones calling in from snow-locked Balbriggan in the winter of '86 (another fairytale there!)? He became a regular contributor to the *Gay Byrne Show* from around the country, singing in Ennis, talking in Skibbereen, doing treasure hunts on the *Ronan Collins Show* and taking over the show when Ronan was sick.

'BOTH SIDES NOW'

In 1988 it became obvious to the powers that be in RTE that the Irish abroad were calling this youth to walk among them and talk to them, so he was put on a new show, *Both Sides Now*. Then his serious and sensitive side began to appear. He took to the new show like Goldilocks to her

porridge and the listeners took to him, so that it became one of RTE's night-time star programmes. It's seen as a very important programme, serving as a link with home for emigrants, reflecting their success stories, pointing out the pitfalls, mixing information with chat and music. The programme regularly broadcasts from London, Cardiff, Leeds, Manchester and Birmingham.

Such was his individual success on this programme that in late spring of this year he was asked to take over *The Leisure Centre*, a high profile magazine-type programme that runs for two hours on Saturday mornings; it includes Gerry Daly's *Ask About Gardening*, *Sports Line Up* and *Brehon's Law*. As the name implies, *The Leisure Centre* deals with all kinds of pastimes (active and passive), sporting activities, genealogy, DIY, collectors and collections, health matters, out and about reports on what's going on around the country in the area of leisure pursuits, talking to various personalities in their own surroundings, and everything and anything to do with switching off and relaxing. It's proving extremely popular and people are continually phoning in queries, tips, information and their own unusual hobbies and collections.

On the musical side he plays guitar, banjo and tin whistle. As a youth he took some lessons from Louis Stewart, which were far more to his liking than the violin lessons he was packed off to for two hated years. Even before he left school he had been playing guitar in a rock band called Mushroom for some time. They broke up in '75, then followed a summer stint in Butlin's playing guitar, acting as compère and singing; nine months then in the orchestra of the Burlington hotel; a good time as musical director, singer, guitarist and compère with Joe Cuddy; professional acclaim as resident guitar player in the Chariot Inn in Ranelagh, where he played for the Platters, Sandie Shaw, Jimmy Tarbuck, the Drifters (the American ones!) and Vince Hill, who since then has always asked for Aonghus to accompany him when he plays in Dublin. Off on the road then with Sheba, the Starband, Crackers and finally Maxband. (It's the baby-faced look that deceives people—this lad has packed a lot into a short time!) Now he plays solo guitar and does his own show in venues around the country.

On the less-often-seen 'serious' side he has written music for two shows, *Lón Rinn an Chairn*, which was the Peacock's Festival show in 1985, and *Parliament Chlann Thomáis* which was staged in the Damer.

RADIO OR TV?

So it looks like this fairytale character should broadcast happily ever after. But will it be on radio or television? Aonghus himself finds radio and TV very different. He loves the intimate feel of radio and the small team. He's a great believer in the idea of the programme only being as strong as its weakest link, and in the teamwork of producer, presenter, researcher and sound operator. He feels he is more responsible for his own programme on radio and that it has given him a permanent sub-editing role in his head. In television, however, there are so many areas to be considered: the sound or the weather or the colour of clothes.

Aonghus McAnally on cue

But there is no conflict for him. He enjoys TV work immensely. He likes the light entertainment side of TV—it appeals to the vaudevillian in him. Ideally he would like to continue working in both media. He's not really interested in the current affairs, investigative side of TV, but he would like his own show and he has drafted proposals for a music, chat and entertainment show with the provisional title of *McAnally's Playhouse*.

He has no great pretensions to serious acting but wouldn't mind taking part in revue-type shows. (He played Dick Whittington in the Gaiety with Maureen Potter in 1985.)

What about family and hobbies? Can there be time left for them? Most definitely! His family are extremely important to him. Having grown up with freelance working parents, the late Ray McAnally and actress Ronnie Masterson, he is used to an environment where both parents may work erratic hours outside the home. So when Billie's workload occupies a great deal of her time, Aonghus isn't left standing in the kitchen wondering how the washing machine works. This year, among other things, Billie has been busy filming *The Real Charlotte* and their schedules can mean they are passing each other by in the doorway, but they cope very well. Aonghus

is into equality in the home (he positively enjoys cooking) and he feels his sons should benefit from this as they grow up.

Practical, not high-flying! Well, he has a D-licence to parachute, when he gets a chance. He also has a provisional pilot's licence and hopes to qualify for a full pilot's licence at some stage. Can't you just see him hosting a chat-show in the cockpit or conducting interviews from a parachute?

Should everything else fail him he could survive as a successful magician. His interest in magic started as a review of Paul Daniel's book for *Anything Goes*. He enjoyed it so much and became so fascinated that he went to Tony Thirsby, a Dublin magician, who taught him some tricks. Now he has built up a reasonable collection of props, hankies, books, coins, card-tricks and the like.

Is there no end to this man's talents? It would seem he's got it all—TV and radio star, showman and entertainer. Sometimes people have difficulty with his name. One Scottish man at Goffs kept referring to him as 'Angus'. He must have been thinking about Aberdeen, but there's no bull about young McAnally! It's easy, really, to pronounce Aonghus, and easier still to spell it. It begins with a V for versatile!

COUNTRY MUSIC

1. Nashville, Tennessee
2. Kentucky, the bluegrass state
3. Johnny Cash
4. Philip Donnelly
5. A parody song composed by Johnny Moynihan—*Mamma, don't let your babies grow into fleadh cowboys*
6. Hank Williams
7. George Jones
8. Albert Lee
9. *Has anybody seen Hank?* by The Waterboys
10. Jesse and the James Boys
11. *Blue eyes cryin' in the rain* composed by Fred Rose
12. The Dukes
13. Buck Owens
14. The 'Trio' album
15. John Prine
16. The Ryman Auditorium
17. Johnny Cash
18. Ray Lynam and Philomena Begley
19. Banjo, mandolin, fiddle or Dobro guitar
20. *Duelling banjos* and/or *Foggy mountain breakdown*
21. Billie Jo Spears
22. Nashville skyline
23. *Country honk* became *Honkytonk woman*

OPERA

1. The Latin word means 'works' (of art) and early opera was seen as a combination of the arts—music, drama (spectacle/literature) and dance
2. Italy
3. During the Italian Risorgimento the letters of the composer's name were used in the slogan 'Vittore Emmanuele, Re d'Italia' (Victor Emmanuel, King of Italy)
4. Jester to the Duke of Mantua
5. Giacomo
6. *Pelleas and Melisande*
7. Air
8. The libretto
9. Mary Garden (1877-1967)
10. Madrid (21 January 1941)
11. Margaret Burke Sheridan (1889-1958) (She sang at La Scala and Covent Garden)
12. *Maritana* (Vincent Wallace, 1812-1865)

The Bohemian Girl (Michael Balfe, 1808-1870)
The Lily of Killarney (Julius Benedict, 1804-1885)

13. 1951
14. Dr Tom Walshe
15. Opera Theatre Company
16. Susanne Murphy
17. Dublin
18. James Wilson (whose opera *Grinning at the Devil*, based on the life of Karen Blixen, was staged this spring)
19. *Riders to the Sea* (Synge, set by Vaughan-Williams) or *The Colleen Bawn* (Boucicault, set by Benedict as *The Lily of Killarney*)
20. Yes. (For the DGOS in the 1963 and '64 seasons. He sang *Duke of Mantua* in *Rigoletto* in '63 and *Alfredo/La Traviata* and *Rudolfo/La Boheme* in '64)
21. Three (*Macbeth, Othello, Falstaff*)
22. Catania, Sicily
23. Michael Kelly (tenor, 1762-1826)
24. Mozart
25. Richard
26. Bayreuth, Bavaria

FARMING

1. 20p
2. Teagasc
3. Landmark
4. Michael O'Kennedy
5. Rynchosporium
6. Buachalán
7. 9 per cent
8. Potato blight
9. Deer
10. April
11. Fully fleeced sheep
12. Newborn pig
13. T J Maher
14. Hind
15. Belgium, France, W. Germany, Italy, Luxembourg, The Netherlands
16. Sugar
17. Foot and mouth
18. Safety cabs or roll-bars
19. Hereford
20. Bovine disease eradication
21. Alan Dukes
22. Silage effluent
23. Agricultural Institute
24. Poor Law Valuation (PLV) system for farmland
25. Earlsfort Terrace, Dublin
26. Beef
27. Fifty-seven acres
28. Thirty-eight acres
29. Nineteen acres
30. Irish Creamery Milk Suppliers Association
31. Limerick
32. Joe O'Brien
33. Larry Goodman's Food Industries plc
34. 1961
35. Donegal
36. Deer

POP MUSIC

1. Gloria, ninety weeks with *One Day at a Time*
2. *Wuthering Heights*
3. *Out of Control*
4. Tom Allen
5. *People*
6. Robert Zimmerman
7. Peggy Sue Gerrow, who married Jerry Allison, Holly's drummer
8. Vincent Van Gogh
9. Don McLean
10. Elvis Costello
11. Bono
12. Gilbert O'Sullivan
13. Declan McManus
14. Ringo Starr—thirteen films to date
15. Debbie Harry
16. The Velvet Underground
17. Boris Pickett and The Crypt Kickers
18. 1962
19. Cliff Richard
20. The Sweet
21. Madonna Louise Veronica Ciccione
22. Gordon Sumner
23. Stewart Copeland and Andy Summers
24. New Jersey
25. Jim Kerr
26. *Boy, October, War, Under a Blood Red Sky, The Unforgettable Fire, The Joshua Tree, Rattle and Hum*
27. Brian Eno
28. 1983
29. Brian May
30. John Lydon
31. Aaron
32. Graceland
33. Something Happens!
34. New Order's *Blue Monday*.
35. Paul McCartney
36. Paul McGuinness
37. M.
38. Philip Chevron and Terry Woods
39. Prince Rogers Nelson
40. Phil Joanou
41. George, Paul, Finbarr and Eddie
42. *The Wonder of You*
43. Matt Goss, Luke Goss and Craig Logan
44. The Fleadh Cowboys
45. *Moonwalker*
46. Eamon Dunphy
47. Ringo Starr
48. Albert Goldman
49. Andrew Ridgely
50. Frank Sinatra's *My Way*
51. Bill Wyman
52. Sid Vicious
53. DA Pennebaker
54. George Gershwin
55. James Dean
56. The The's *Mind Bomb*
57. Stock, Aitken and Waterman
58. Anton Corbijn
59. Peter Rowen
60. They both sang on *Stay Awake*, a Walt Disney compilation album
61. Iggy Pop
62. Liza Minnelli and Sammy Davis Jnr
63. The Beatles, in 1962
64. Madonna's *Like a Prayer*
65. James Brown
66. Stevie Wonder
67. The CIA
68. Tipp-Ex
69. Frank Zappa
70. Peter Gabriel
71. Keith Richards
72. Alex Higgins
73. Ross
74. Dandelion
75. Neil Tennant and Chris Lowe
76. The Jam and The Style Council

CURRENT AFFAIRS

1. Raglan House
2. Dessie O'Hare
3. John O'Grady
4. Dan Quayle and Lloyd Bentsen
5. Piper Alpha
6. John McMichael
7. For having their phones tapped
8. Services Industrial and Professional Trade Union
9. South West African Peoples Organisation
10. *The Joy of Sex*
11. The Turin shroud

QUIZ ANSWERS

12. The holiday plans of Nicholas Fenn, British Ambassador, whose plans to holiday in the south-west of Ireland fell into the hands of the IRA
13. Pernod Ricard
14. Jean Marie le Pen, leader of the French National Front
15. Mairéad Farrell, Danny McCann and Seán Savage
16. Senator David Norris, when the European Court of Human Rights called on the Irish government to decriminalise homosexual activity between consenting adults.
17. Market Research Bureau of Ireland
18. They brought a constitutional challenge to the Anglo-Irish Agreement, which they later appealed to the Supreme Court, where it was rejected
19. Lord Killanin
20. John Donnellan was expelled from the Fine Gael parliamentary party for saying that if it was raining soup, Alan Dukes would try to catch it with a fork
21. *Karin B* was a ship loaded with toxic waste which could not find a port to dock in. It finally landed its cargo in Italy
22. Patrick Cooney (Fine Gael, Leinster)
23. Samora Machel
24. The Kowloon Bridge
25. Conor Cruise O'Brien
26. Grotesque Unprecedented Bizarre and Unbelievable
27. Kevin MacDonald
28. Peter Wright
29. Matthias Rust landed his light aircraft in Red Square
30. Hungerford
31. Stompie Moeketsi
32. Father Patrick Ryan who was deported by the Belgian authorities; was not extradited to Britain and failed to get elected to the European Parliament.

33. Abdullah, Crown Prince of Saudi Arabia
34. Vice-admiral John Poindexter
35. *The Herald of Free Enterprise*
36. a) Raymond Keaveney, b) Pat Donlon, c) Pat Wallace
37. John Boland, who held the health portfolio briefly after the Labour ministers resigned from the 1982-87 coalition government
38. Séamus Brennan (Fianna Fáil) who received 13,927 votes in Dublin South
39. Benazzir Bhutto, when she was elected president of Pakistan
40. Daniel Ortega, president of Nicaragua
41. Agriculture and rural development
42. The Knesset
43. Neil Blaney (Independent Fianna Fáil, Donegal North-East) who was first elected in 1957
44. Michael Moynihan (Labour, Kerry South) who was 72 when elected
45. John McGee, Bishop of Cloyne
46. Jim Kemmy TD, leader of the Democratic Socialist Party
47. Seven
48. The Labour Party, founded in Clonmel in 1912
49. John Cushnahan, former leader of the Alliance Party won a seat for Fine Gael in Munster
50. Organisation for Economic and Cultural Development

KNOW YOUR SPORT
1. Jackie Carey, Manchester United, 1948; Danny Blanchflower, Tottenham Hotspur, 1961 and 1962; Noel Cantwell, Manchester United, 1963; Pat Rice, Arsenal, 1978
2. James; Lansdowne Road, 1975, against France
3. Klaus Richtzenhain, East Germany, silver; John Landy, Australia, bronze
4. Mick McCarthy; Dublin, Czechoslovakia, April 1981
5. Brisbane, Australia; rugby
6. Scottish Premier Division club, St Mirren
7. Zürich, Switzerland

RTE QUIZ
1. 2 RN
2. Ronan Collins
3. 1964 Tokyo Olympic Games
4. The Nolans
5. 8.00 am in summer, 7.30 am in winter
6. Degrassi
7. Mike Murphy
8. Marie Keane
9. Bunny Carr
10. Tyne Daly and Sharon Gless
11. John Bowman
12. Tico's Tune
13. Australia
14. Minnie Brennan
15. Michael Lyster
16. The 1971 Eurovision Song Contest
17. Three times, 1970, 1980 and 1987
18. Jock Ewing
19. Leo Maguire
20. John-Boy
21. Eamonn Andrews
22. Zig and Zag
23. Victoria Principle
24. 1979
25. Brenda Costigan
26. Roseanne Barr
27. George Hamilton
28. The Rover's Return
29. Richard Deane Anderson
30. The Phoenix Foundation
31. Anne Doyle, Eileen Dunne, Emer O'Kelly and Anna Chisnell
32. Denise
33. Crockett and Tubbs
34. c) 15 hours
35. Darina Allen
36. Terence
37. Twink
38. Jim Fahy
39. Donal Farmer
40. Evening Extra
41. Ciana Campbell and Siobhán Cleary

42. Joan Collins
43. Rugby—South Africa and Australia
44. David Bellamy
45. The Rose of Tralee and The Housewife of the Year.
46. Pat Kenny and Michelle Rocca
47. Switzerland

FOLK MUSIC
1. Emmet Spiceland
2. Pete St John
3. Carolan
4. Clannad
5. Dominic Behan
6. True. He also plays the fiddle, or course.
7. True
8. An architect
9. Christy Moore
10. 1951
11. P J McCall
12. *The Dashing White Sergeant*, or *Mo Ghile Mear*. It was a couple of decades before the Austrian air *Tannenbaum* was used
13. True. Liam Rowsome was in the same class also, as was fiddler Liam O'Reilly
14. Macaronic
15. *John O'Dreams*
16. *The Siege of Limerick*
17. Séan Ó Riada and Ceoltóirí Cualann
18. True
19. True
20. False. James C MacAuliffe, uileann piper, was the man. Everything else is correct.
21. *The Croppy Boy*
22. *Seven Drunken Nights* by the Dubliners
23. False. It's the title of a tune
24. All fiddles or violins have four strings. The bass-fiddle does have a fifth string but is not played in folk music in Western Europe. Three-and five-string fiddles did exist in the Middle Ages
25. True

BIBI BASKIN

by Deirdre Purcell

ibi never arrives into a room. She gusts. By her own admission, her boredom threshold is 'extremely low' and her energy level extremely high—'I have bundles of energy. I know I can pack more into one day, and frequently do, than most people I know. I think it's a terrific thing.' All of this, coupled with the speed of her normal speech, means that an encounter with Bibi is, to put it mildly, a stimulating experience.

She never planned a career—for a very good reason: 'I have nobody to support me, not that I particularly feel that anybody should—male or mother, but I have always recognised that I'll have to work at least until I'm sixty. For that reason I have always been guided by one particular factor, which is, because you have to work for so many hours and so many years, you should, for God's sake, get a job that you enjoy! If you look back over the pattern of my life, I chopped and changed until I got a job that I enjoyed. Broadcasting is that job...'

The job, on the other hand, is not the most important thing in her life. 'Health—I really value my excellent health...' And attitude—no negative waves: 'I try very hard in life not to get hassled about things that cannot be. There are people who are driving along and get a puncture and there's nobody around to help them. They get into a huge panic...' Not Bibi. When something like that happens, out of Bibi's control, that's just the way things are. 'I try to adopt more of a "So what!" attitude.'

Now don't get the wrong impression, it is not that she does not care. 'I like to let people know if I'm going to be late, well in advance, so they can make alternative plans. I'm very fussy about time because I think it's a huge arrogance to think that you can waste other people's time...' And even Bibi cannot altogether escape stress. 'Of course I get stressed! Especially on live TV, there's a huge amount of stress!' She simply tries to minimise the stress by 'working like a beaver' to control the factors she can and passes over those she cannot.

One of the most attractive factors in Bibi's make-up is her honesty. She has no prima donna illusions about her role in her show. *The Bibi Show* has two producers, Niall Mathews and Justin Nelson 'and I suppose if a brief existed for our particular roles, mine would be that I am the puppet that asks the questions. That's what being a TV presenter really means!' She exaggerates... she exaggerates but not, she insists, all that much... 'I could never be terribly happy in a job where I really was just that puppet. The producers do give me

great scope, but the amount of the so-called influence that I have varies according to a number of different factors.' (One is, she says, that she works in the same office as Niall Mathews, but since Justin Nelson is actually in a different building she overhears Niall's side of the telephone conversations between the two. 'I can say, "Hey, listen, we don't want to do *that*!" ')

There are drawbacks to being suddenly famous, the main drawback being the loss of privacy. She mourns this loss, 'but I keep reminding myself that if people didn't recognise me, it would be because they weren't watching the programme; if they weren't watching, there wouldn't be the success; if there was no success I mightn't have that job; if I didn't have that job I mightn't be an independent lady and we're back to what I started talking about.'

Bibi was born and brought up in Ardara, County Donegal, of good Protestant business stock. She regards her upbringing as a great advantage: 'I would hate to have been brought up a Catholic. I feel that the sort of Catholicism that was flying around Ireland when I was growing up was extremely intolerant. Catholics in those days couldn't go into a Protestant church—and the *ne temere* decree was used so tightly it was a very very sad and sorrowful thing for a lot of Protestants. There was respect between Roman Catholics and Protestants, but you had these very right-wing elderly Catholic priests who came for these missions every year, pumping the fuel of the fire back into the gangs. "We're the only true religion"—that's a very offensive thing to be told.'

One of the greatest advantages of all was individual education. Bibi went to her local school, which never had more than twelve children, spread over eight classes. 'I never had a classmate!'

Independence learned early...